NORBERT ELIAS
AND MODERN
SOCIAL THEORY

Theory, Culture & Society

Theory, Culture & Society caters for the resurgence of interest in culture within contemporary social science and the humanities. Building on the heritage of classical social theory, the book series examines ways in which this tradition has been reshaped by a new generation of theorists. It also publishes theoretically informed analyses of everyday life, popular culture, and new intellectual movements.

EDITOR: Mike Featherstone, *Nottingham Trent University*

SERIES EDITORIAL BOARD
Roy Boyne, *University of Durham*
Mike Hepworth, *University of Aberdeen*
Scott Lash, *Goldsmiths College, University of London*
Roland Robertson, *University of Pittsburgh*
Bryan S. Turner, *University of Cambridge*

THE TCS CENTRE
The Theory, Culture & Society book series, the journals *Theory, Culture & Society* and *Body & Society*, and related conference, seminar and postgraduate programmes operate from the TCS Centre at Nottingham Trent University. For further details of the TCS Centre's activities please contact:

Centre Administrator
The TCS Centre, Room 175
Faculty of Humanities
Nottingham Trent University
Clifton Lane, Nottingham, NG11 8NS, UK
e-mail: tcs@ntu.ac.uk
web: http://tcs@ntu.ac.uk

Recent volumes include:

Feminist Imagination
Genealogies in Feminist Theory
Vikki Bell

Michel de Certeau
Cultural Theorist
Ian Buchanan

The Cultural Economy of Cities
Allen J. Scott

Body Modification
edited by Mike Featherstone

Paul Virilio
From Modernism to Hypermodernism
edited by John Armitage

Subject, Society and Culture
Roy Boyne

NORBERT ELIAS AND MODERN SOCIAL THEORY

DENNIS SMITH

SAGE Publications
London • Thousand Oaks • New Delhi

First published 2001

 SAGE Publications Ltd
6 Bonhill Street
London EC2A 4PU

SAGE Publications Inc
2455 Teller Road
Thousand Oaks, California 91320

SAGE Publications India Pvt Ltd
32, M-Block Market
Greater Kailash – I
New Delhi 110 048

Published in association with *Theory, Culture & Society*, Nottingham Trent University

British Library Cataloguing in Publication data

A catalogue record for this book is available from the British Library

ISBN 0-7619-6107-0
ISBN 0-7619-6108-9 (pbk)

Library of Congress catalog record available

Typeset by Mayhew Typesetting, Rhayader, Powys
Printed in Great Britain by The Cromwell Press Ltd, Trowbridge, Wiltshire

CONTENTS

PREFACE

Intellectual exploration is a 'serious game'. A game is most exciting when there is something at stake. What should be at stake is 'getting things right' which is different from 'making other people see the world as you do'. The game of intellectual exploration is most productive when the personal honour of the players is not tied to the particular model of reality they bring to the game. When honour is tied to defending a particular model, then learning new things is very difficult. Some may win and others lose but the game itself will be intrinsically worthless.

We should all be prepared to revise any aspect of our thinking at any time if this is demanded by new evidence or new ways of seeing existing evidence. That means keeping our minds receptive and the 'game' open. Thinking about the world should be an adventure, a continuing search for clues about how things work and what can be done to make them better or at least more bearable.

In this game the ultimate enemy is any obstacle to clear thought that exists inside oneself. The part played by a thinker's distinctive 'vision' is important. A vision can impel a writer in a particular direction, possibly leading him or her to look in new areas and have original thoughts. But if the thinker loses detachment from the vision, becomes the servant of the vision, then this vision becomes a form of blindness. At worst, it may become an obstacle to clear thought. In practice, this possibility is even more likely to arise among the followers or disciples of a thinker, be they Parsonians, Marxians, Durkheimians, Freudians, Eliasians or whatever.

Norbert Elias was a very creative player in the serious game of intellectual exploration. He was engaged in it for a very long time. He was gripped by a very strong vision of how the world worked from an early stage in a career that endured for most of the last century. For Elias, I believe, this vision was, in part, a way of restoring unity to his fractured experience as a German Jew. At its best – in *The Court Society* (Elias 1983), *The Civilizing Process* (Elias 1994a) and *The Germans* (Elias 1996) – Elias's writing has an excitement that comes, in large part, from his struggle to cope with the tension between his Jewish identity and his German identity.

Elias is the most Jewish of names, inherited by the son of a textile manufacturer in Breslau (now Wroclaw in Poland). By contrast, Norbert is a name that is strongly associated with the propagation of the Catholic faith among the Poles in the twelfth century. The most famous Norbert in the German branch of Christendom is St Norbert. He was originally from an aristocratic family in North Germany. St Norbert became Archbishop of Magdeburg, a major headquarters for stamping out heresy among the Slavs.

Elias – Jewish, German, European and global – devoted a lot of time and energy to exploring the connections between two things: our complex sense of identity and broader social processes. Those social processes shape that identity and they are, in turn, influenced by the ways we act out that identity. The key word is 'exploring.' Elias was an explorer. It is the sense of it being an unfinished search that is the most attractive aspect of Elias's work. It gives it an openness, a feeling that it is part of a larger adventure that others can join in on equal terms.

This book is not just about Elias. It is also about Talcott Parsons, Michel Foucault, Zygmunt Bauman and Hannah Arendt. All of these writers are most interesting when they are in 'search mode,' when they are becoming gripped by a strong sense of what matters in the world or how the world 'is', but have not resolved matters to their own satisfaction or become the agents for a formula. In truth, it is usually some of their followers who make this last move rather than the thinkers themselves.

Foucault was searching all his life, constantly reinventing himself. That makes him fascinating. The same is true for Zygmunt Bauman whose metamorphoses continue. Parsons never again wrote a book as exciting as *The Structure of Social Action* which ends with his 'discovery' of the voluntary theory of action. After that he was busy assaying his treasure and the excitement goes out of the project. Hannah Arendt's book *The Origins of Totalitarianism* has a wonderful 'unfinished' character. In it she is still reaching towards the more polished philosophy of *The Human Condition*.

Perhaps it is time to rescue some of these writers from some of their followers. There is a perpetual danger that 'social theory' may become an accumulation of closed 'approaches' – Parsonian, Foucauldian, Eliasian and so on – whose disciples talk past each other. What I have tried to do here is to open up these approaches so that they may, so to speak, spill into each other.

I have not attempted to integrate the results into a 'big theory'. It was, briefly, a temptation and, indeed, there is nothing intrinsically wrong with big theories, especially when they are grounded in real-world research and lead back towards it. Big theories are good to have around, especially when no single theory dominates in an unchallenged way. It is also important to have a strong culture of open-minded empirical enquiry that is always ready to doubt received wisdom.

However, I decided to resist the temptation to 'tidy up' the outcomes of the four comparative chapters in this book that juxtapose Elias with, in turn, Arendt, Parsons, Foucault and Bauman. To use a metaphor from the game of pool or snooker, I have left the balls on the green baize table where they came to rest after my shots had been played. There is a certain pattern in the way they lie which I sketch out in the final chapter but that is not an attempt to 'integrate' my 'findings'. Instead, I have drawn on the insights produced to explore two questions: what is the sociological significance of the European movement? And what is the nature of humiliation and shame?

These questions and these comparisons feed into a larger enquiry which is to investigate the character of the developing global society. This agenda can only be stated here, and then only in a very preliminary way, in the opening and closing chapters of the book. It will be taken further in other work.

I am grateful to many colleagues who have commented on various aspects of the argument. I do not think of myself as an 'Eliasian.' However, I have benefited from the warmth and friendliness of 'Eliasians' including Johan Goudsblom, Richard Kilminster, Cas Wouters, Stephen Mennell, Willem Mastenbroek, and Ad van Iterson. Elizabeth Foulkes was kind enough to share her memories of Elias with me.

My thinking has been helped by the astute comments of Tim Newton, Marja Gastelaars, Teresa Whitaker, Sue Wright and Tanya Smith. In this and other work, my approach has been greatly influenced by the insights of Evelin Lindner. Finally, I would like to thank my colleagues at the Department of Social Sciences of Loughborough University.

PART 1

MODERNITY AND ELIAS

1

THE SOUND OF CANON-FIRE

Modernity and Elias

Norbert Elias, the sociologist of the civilizing process, is worth reading because he is one of the important resources available to us in trying to make sense of our human condition in late modernity: not the only resource by any means but an important part of the repertoire of key ideas produced by scholars during the twentieth century.

Elias has a powerful vision of how human beings and societies inter-connect and develop. At the centre of this vision are these ideas:

- human beings live and exist together as part of complex networks (Elias called them '*figurations*') linking people, groups and institutions;
- these figurations are shaped by social *processes*: long-term, and largely unplanned, processes which have a pattern, structure and direction that can be discovered by patient scholarly investigation looking at empirical data and interpreting them carefully;
- figurations and processes have a powerful shaping effect upon the psychological make-up [or '*habitus*'] of individuals and groups and upon their capacity to exercise *control*: control over themselves, control over others, and control over nature;
- sociologists can help people increase their capacity to exercise control in a rational and reasonable way by providing them with *knowledge* about the social processes and figurations that shape their social existence; and
- a central characteristic of European social development during the last millennium has been a tendency towards increasingly dense and complex figurations with relatively *stable power monopolies* associated with increasingly high levels of control in all respects. These are key features of *the civilizing process* that has occurred, interwoven with significant *de-civilizing* tendencies.

Elias haunts this book on every page. However, this study is not just about Elias and his ideas. At the heart of the book are a series of systematic comparisons between Elias and, in turn, Michel Foucault, Talcott Parsons, Hannah Arendt and Zygmunt Bauman.

However, the book is not just a critique of Elias and four other social theorists.[1] It is also about the Western experience of modernity in the twentieth century. The theorists are important because they give us grappling irons to seize hold of a runaway world, conceptually at least. This is an important step towards the understanding we need for more effective practical interventions. These theorists help us understand the past that shaped our present: for example, the decline of Europe's empires, the rise and fall of fascism and communism, and the changing balance of power between Europe and the United States. They also help us come to terms with the global society coming into existence which seems likely to bring intensified consumerism, sharper polarization between rich and poor, increased fear and uncertainty and the extension on all sides of surveillance-based management techniques.

Elias's work is an important resource. It can be used to confront the challenge of making sense of modernity. Contrasting Elias with Foucault, Parsons, Arendt and Bauman helps to identify Elias's strengths and weakness. It also throws light on the strengths and weaknesses of the four others. Are their strengths complementary and do they compensate for the weaknesses that they all, inevitably, bring to the table? My answer is yes.

Elias's ideas will make an important contribution to the future of modern social theory. However, they will not do this by displacing all rivals. Elias has very valuable insights but these are accompanied by blind spots such as his lack of attention to large-scale business corporations or the particular dynamics of post-Schumpeterian capitalism.[2] In fact, Elias's work is useful for two reasons.

One reason is that Elias confronts the nature of Western modernity in a way that makes strong links between large-scale social processes and transformations in our psychological make-up and ways of seeing, thinking and feeling.[3] The second reason is, quite simply, that Elias was born in 1897 and died in 1990. In other words, because Elias lived so long and kept working, he has been part of the intellectual life of two successive generations. Parsons (born 1902) and Arendt (born 1906) come from the same generation as Elias (born 1987). Bauman (born 1925) and Foucault (born 1926) come from the generation that followed.

Creative interplay between Elias's ideas and those of two generations of contemporaries can help us move towards a focused understanding of the structure and significance of the processes that have shaped Western modernity. This will contribute to a larger task, which is to discover what can be salvaged from the recent experience of *Western* modernity to help us survive and, perhaps, civilize *global* modernity in the new millennium.

America and Europe

Western modernity is a transatlantic phenomenon[4] and two of the five writers discussed (Parsons and Arendt) were American citizens. The saga of American modernity was the big story of the twentieth century. The world watched as Americans survived the Great Depression of the 1930s, re-ignited the engine of capitalism through the New Deal and war production, and then grew fat on a diet of abundance and anxiety. The biggest story of all, a story not yet over, is race.

Gunnar Myrdal's words from the early 1940s still ring true, even though some of his terminology is now 'politically incorrect': 'To the great majority of white Americans the Negro problem has distinctly negative connotations. It suggests something difficult to settle and equally difficult to leave alone. It is embarrassing. It makes for moral uneasiness . . . To many . . . [it] takes on the proportion of a menace – biological, economic, social, cultural, and, at times, political. This anxiety may be mingled with a feeling of individual and collective guilt. A few may see the problem as a challenge to statesmanship. To all it is a trouble' (Myrdal 1962, lxxvii).

Who knows what the next instalment of the American story will be? Meanwhile, there is an equally gripping European story still to be told. While Americans struggle with the issue of race, Europeans are smarting from the psychic pain caused by the loss of their position of imperial pre-eminence throughout the world.

This has been difficult to speak about directly, a delicate subject in a democratic age. After all, European global dominance was based upon domination over subject peoples who were denied rights and often exploited and victimized. However, European reactions to imperial decline are complex. The most complex emotions, eclipsing the others, are shame and humiliation. Europeans have hardly begun to confront these emotions and the social mechanisms associated with them, despite their importance in national identity and national politics. The social and psychological processes that shape the experience of humiliation and shame, collective and individual, in the modern epoch need to be studied and understood.

The decline of empire is intimately related to the rise of the European Union. A notable fact about the EU is that its leading members consist of the old 'headquarter societies' of the European empires, now almost completely shorn of their colonies. The European Union has provided a new home, a new political centre, for the political establishments of Paris, London, Bonn (and, more recently, Berlin), Vienna, Brussels, the Hague, Madrid and Lisbon.[5] All the old imperial capitals of Europe are represented there – except for Moscow.

The case of the European Union is a fascinating one because it apparently offers a potential model for the development of supranational polities elsewhere in the world. Is it a possible prototype for other regional organizations and, perhaps, a guide to future developments at the global level?

A critical examination of the work of Elias can contribute to our under-standing of the themes just mentioned: the loss of empire, the postwar European movement, and the role of humiliation and shame in modern European (and, more broadly, Western) society. However, before approach-ing those themes, Elias's work needs to be located within the broader context of the on-going debate about the nature of modernity.

The Organization of this Book

The book is organized in three parts. The first part, entitled 'Modernity and Elias', examines the issues raised by Elias's entry into the canon (Chapter 1). It goes on to discuss the biographical origins of Elias's particular intel-lectual concerns and his decision to explore them by developing a distinc-tive approach to sociology and modernity (Chapter 2).

The second part of the book, entitled 'The wider debate', compares Elias's approach with those taken by Arendt (Chapter 3), Parsons (Chapter 4), Foucault (Chapter 5) and Bauman (Chapter 6). This part of the book covers a number of related aspects of the shaping of modernity including the causes and character of the Holocaust, the nature of German society, the dynamics of intellectual change, the development of sexuality and the implications of the decline of the European empires. The analyses in these chapters indicate a number of points of convergence and complementary emphases between the five scholars as well as some obvious points where they diverge.

The third part of the book is called 'Towards global modernity'. Elias, Parsons and Arendt are drawn upon to explain the sociogenesis of the European Union and identify the issues at stake in its further development (Chapter 7). In the next chapter, the ideas of Bauman, Foucault and Elias contribute to an investigation of the part played by humiliation and shame in modern social, political and organizational life (Chapter 8). Finally, the theoretical findings of Part 2 and the empirical explorations in Part 3 are drawn together in an argument about the need for social theory to orient itself to the issue of global modernity (Chapter 9).

Elias, Foucault, Arendt, Parsons, Bauman

Bauman and Foucault are among Elias's admirers[6] and their interests overlap to a high degree. For their part, Parsons and Arendt, like Elias, were greatly influenced in their youth by the intellectual conflicts raging within the German universities; indeed, all three spent time at Heidelberg University in the 1920s. On the face of it, the basis for a fruitful intellectual interchange exists – and indeed it does.

This fact has been obscured by a number of factors: the hostility of Foucault towards 'the discourse on modern sexual repression' (Foucault

1978, 5) which seems to include Elias as well as Marcuse; Bauman's criticism of Elias in *Modernity and the Holocaust* (Bauman 1989);[7] Elias's dismissal of Arendt's work; and, finally, Elias's repeated direct attacks upon Parsons. For their part, Arendt and Parsons paid no attention to Elias, in print at least.[8] However, all this evidence of hostility, *froideur* or indifference should not disguise the fundamental sympathies between these writers.

Why should we pay any attention to what Elias, Foucault or the others say? What effect do their formulations have upon how most ordinary people behave or how they feel, think and judge things? How important are intellectuals in shaping our intellects and imaginations compared with the slow, anonymous processing of shared experience in the household, at work, in battle, and so on?

There are strict limits to the influence of intellectuals, either as individuals or collectively. Professional thinkers only make a real difference at the level of everyday life when their formulations are backed by power and the capacity to transmit ideas effectively through time and across space. It may be true, for example, that the medieval concept of the soul owed much to Augustine just as Freud shaped the twentieth century's view of the mind and body. However, Augustinian theology was vigorously enforced by the medieval Church. Freudian theory was energetically promoted by a well-organised and dominant branch of the psychiatry profession. To take a more recent example, Mao-Tse-Tung's thoughts did not become current throughout China in the 1960s because of their intellectual power and poetic expression. It was because Mao's 'little red book' was carried by all members of a violent mass movement which crushed all opposition.

The subjects of this book could not, and would not, claim to be *makers* of modernity in the sense just described. However, they are all thoroughly expert and highly persuasive *witnesses* to modernity. Their authority flows from the success of the appeals they make to our reason and imagination. There is no need to assume any one of them has the final and definitive 'answer' to the question 'what is modernity?' However, taken together, their writings and experience make up an important body of evidence with respect to that issue. This is because each writer has been picking up signals, so to speak, from different parts or aspects of modernity. The spread is both geographical and historical. They come from two successive generations and four different national societies (Germany, France, Poland and the United States) all deeply involved in this century's battle over modernity's nature and direction.

In the first half of the century Germany played the key role in this struggle, both politically and in the world of ideas. German philosophy – Hegel, Marx, Nietzsche, Husserl, Heidegger and so on – made a deep impact throughout Europe, especially in France. However, during and after the Cold War, three things happened. Firstly, French and German ideas permeated intellectual life in Britain and the United States. Secondly, Europeans paid more attention to American life and ideas. Thirdly, as the barriers between East and West grew weaker there was increased understanding of

how the Soviet Union and Central Europe had undergone the experience
of modernity.

Artists and Surveyors

Elias and the four other writers being discussed have all operated primarily
within a transatlantic context although all have intellectual, moral or
professional interests in the wider world.[9] Four of the five were born in
Europe although one of these (Arendt) became resident in the United
States. Only one of the five is female. Three out of the five are of Jewish
origin. All five are white.

  This limited spread or, to put it another way, this high degree of overlap,
has both disadvantages and advantages. The disadvantage is that none of
the writers can report directly on the experience of being a non-white and/
or non-European victim (or, indeed, beneficiary) of European and
American modernity. Nor are the experiences of major civilizations now
emerging as competitors to Europe and the United States, such as China
and Japan, represented here. Indian, African, Arabic and Latin American
perspectives are not in evidence either. We have to bear these facts in mind
when our writers make generalizations about the human condition. This is
a very important issue and I hope to return to it in other work.

  However, the other side of the coin is that the relative homogeneity of
our witnesses, combined with their dispersion across transatlantic space and
time, gives us the advantages of triangulation. In other words, we get
sightings of the same or closely related phenomena taken from a range of
positions. They are, in a sense, like a team of surveyors.

  Another image also springs to mind, one which recognizes the different
preoccupations of our witnesses, the differences not in what they are
looking *at* but in what they are looking *for*. Imagine that Cézanne were
joined in the South of France by Renoir, Picasso, Magritte and Edward
Munch and they all set about painting Cézanne's beloved Mont St-Victoire.
At the end of the day you would get five distinctive and highly individual
pictures of the same mountain.

  The evidence provided by our key witnesses lies somewhere between the
surveyors' notebooks and the artists' pictures, each one expressing a specific
'vision'. The challenge is to find a way of interpreting the dense and detailed
'reading' of modernity which their work provides. That involves, among
other things, taking account of each writer's particular vision.

Visions of Modernity

In this context, a writer's vision is the expression of his or her capacity to
intuit in a creative and original way how the world fits together socially and
morally, how human beings fit into it, and what scope there is for acting
within and upon that world.[10] By 'intuition' is meant a strong sense of or

feeling about the nature of existence which is not initially derived from either logical deduction or empirical research. Intuition may be regarded as insightful when it draws attention to previously unconsidered or rarely considered possibilities.

Schumpeter wrote that

> the strongest achievements in science proceed not from observation or experimentation and orderly logic-chopping but from something that is best called vision and is akin to artistic creation . . . In every scientific venture, the thing that comes first is Vision. That is to say, before embarking upon analytic work of any kind we must first single out the set of phenomena we wish to investigate, and acquire 'intuitively' a preliminary notion of how they hang together or, in other words, of what appear from our standpoint to be their fundamental properties . . . [This] preanalytical cognitive act . . . supplies the raw material for the analytic effort. (Schumpeter 1986, 41, 113–4, 561–2; emphasis in original)

To exercise the capacity for vision an author does not have to feel the earth move. They just have to be receptive to hunches, including small ones, about 'the way things work' in the area they are interested in. Vision is stimulated by challenging experiences under conditions in which the person involved is receptive to new ways of thinking and feeling.[11] The real-life challenges posed by modernity for individuals produce a range of reactions from fear and anguish to boredom and frustration. Whatever their particular form, involving and meaningful experiences may produce intuitions which are usually 'wrapped up', so to speak, in emotion. Vision works upon these intuitions and organizes them within the imagination. As a result the person concerned may come to 'see' certain aspects of the world as being particularly significant. Things may seem to fall into a specific pattern that had not been noticed before.

These processes do not happen to authors only. They are part of the accidents of life that occur to many people. Human beings react to these events in the imagination in many ways. They may, for example, take up painting, join a resistance movement, compose poetry, give all their wealth to the poor or commit suicide. It so happens that in the cases we are examining the people concerned eventually wrote books to be read by other intellectuals.

This is not all they did. Elias helped to found the group analysis movement.[12] Arendt campaigned for a Jewish army.[13] Foucault fought the police and struggled on behalf of prisoners.[14] Parsons tried to influence the attitudes of the US government towards the use of propaganda and the reconstruction of Germany after World War II.[15] Bauman served with the Red Army and later rose to be a high-ranking military officer in the Polish Army before turning himself into a sociologist during the 1950s.[16] All these writers were, to a significant degree, moved by a sense of special insight and fired by a determination to elaborate and communicate the contents of their vision.

Even Talcott Parsons, who has rightly acquired a reputation for writing impenetrable texts, strongly conveys through his prose in *The Structure of Social Action* (Parsons 1968), his greatest work, the sense of having been inspired to penetrate further and deeper than others into the nature of things. He could barely disguise his delight at having seen that sociology was, as he put it, 'a special analytical science on the same level as economic theory', a view that 'runs counter to the bulk of methodological tradition on the matter' (772).

Parsons felt he was building on the 'sound insight' of Simmel. However, the arrival of 'an analytical sociological theory' had been forced to 'wait upon a relatively full development of the generalized theory of action' (773–4). To do this it had been necessary to 'dig deep enough' and get beyond 'the more superficial levels'. Parsons had been the man with the imagination and intellect to do this, so the text implies. His pride beats like a mighty drum beneath the words, barely restrained by the modesty and good manners that were, it may be surmised, second nature to this son of a Congregationalist minister from Ohio.

Parsons claims that his investigation had revealed 'a great deep stream of the movement of scientific thought' (774–5). This visionary phrase occurs on the very last page of Parsons's last chapter. It is reminiscent of the verse that begins the last chapter of *Revelation*, the last book of the Bible: 'And he shewed me a pure river of water of life, clear as crystal, proceeding out of the throne of God and of the Lamb' (Revelation 22, v1). Parsons's father, the Congregationalist minister, checked the whole book for its prose style. He may well have picked up the Biblical connection.[17]

To return to the main argument, and put the matter slightly more formally, all five writers set the intellect to work on the intuitions organized by vision, and produced texts containing substantive accounts of various aspects of modernity.[18]

To anticipate the argument, the writings of Elias, Arendt and Bauman, the later work of Foucault (especially *The History of Sexuality*) and the early work of Parsons (including *The Structure of Social Action*)[19] all share three characteristics.

- They all incorporate a powerful sense of long-term processes, extending over generations and even centuries.
- They all focus upon the tension between forces engendering conflict and tendencies towards order.
- They all express approval for polities which permit an orderly if passionate dialogue between competing approaches to life.[20]

These themes will be taken up in more detail in the course of the following chapters. In the meantime, back to Norbert Elias.

Scenes from the Life of a Sociologist[21]

SCENE ONE: a park or garden on a sunny day in 1906 or thereabouts. A boy about nine years old, dressed in a sailor suit, lies on his side, supported on one elbow. The young lad smiles up at the camera, shielding his eyes against the sun. He is grasping a tennis racket. Behind him stand two women: his mother, hair in a bun, and his nanny. The youngster is Norbert Elias. The photograph was probably taken near his home in Breslau, now Wroclaw in Poland, or on holiday, perhaps at Ostend or Scheveningen.[22]

SCENE TWO: near Peronne, in Northern France, 1915. Norbert Elias is speaking, remembering: 'Because we had the heavy rolls of wire, the heavy Morse apparatus and a lot of equipment, we were taken close to the front on a vehicle . . . Someone was singing. And then far away we saw flashes of light. It was *Trommelfeuer*, a barrage, from a battle to the west . . . We were a telegraph group, a corporal and eight men, all specialists, who could be attached here and there. And as I drove with my comrades through the night, towards the incessant flashes and the *Trommelfeuer*, someone next to me was playing the mouth-organ – it probably was a horsedrawn wagon we were riding on. Then we arrived just behind the front, where there were lots of dead horses lying around. And dead people. The whole scene, the bodies, the gunfire, the flashes of light, the sentimental songs, the nostalgic sound of the mouth-organ – that picture is very vivid in my mind'.[23]

SCENE THREE: Frankfurt during the early 1930s. Ilse Seglow recalls: 'I heard that Mannheim and Elias had come to . . . my home town and given the University Department . . . a "facelift." . . . I was increasingly drawn into its "inner circle" where there was little formality . . . In our case we had the coffee-house, mixed company, University staff and students sitting and talking together on an equal footing, whereas the traditional departments had the *Gasthaus*, male company of students (apart from excursions to women of another class) and staff and students joining socially only on formal occasions . . . I remember once Paul Tillich, at one o'clock in the morning, finishing a discussion with the sociologists in their favourite coffee-house, the Cafe Laumer, with the words: "Now you can go to your structure, I go to bed"'.[24]

SCENE FOUR: an alien internment camp in Huyton, near Liverpool, 1940. An ex-inmate remembers: 'The camp was located in an unfinished housing project, taken over for the occasion. The half-built houses, only partially fitted with windows and doors, were supplemented with army tents; the gentle English rain quickly turned the tenting area and unpaved roadways into mudflats and rivulets. Food was scanty, consisting mostly of a watery soup in which swam an occasional disintegrating piece of fish or meat. For a 17-year-old it was all great fun; for most other inmates it was a disaster. Most of them were Jewish refugees from the Continent; the camp commander was quoted as saying that he never knew so many Jews were Nazis . . . Many lapsed into despair; a few took their lives . . . In this context, a choir practice or soccer game acquired life-giving qualities. Some groups . . . gathered to listen to lectures . . . When the sun was out, the

listeners sat "outside," drawn up in a semi-circle around the lecturer . . .
One day, a Prof. Elias, drawing lines and crosses on a dirty piece of paper
which served as a blackboard, spoke of how a person is born into the world
not as a pristine and isolated individual, but as a nexus in a social network.
It was a simple idea, but it changed my way of thinking about social
phenomena'.[25]

SCENE FIVE: Ghana in the early 1960s. A balding Norbert Elias, Professor
of Sociology at the University of Ghana, is standing before the latticed
windows of his dwelling flanked by his cook and his chauffeur. Elias,
dressed in white shirt and tie and wearing heavy glasses, is beaming with
pleasure. The picture is strangely reminiscent of the photograph, taken half
a century before, of young Norbert in his sailor suit attended by his mother
and nanny. It conveys the same sense of happy security.

SCENE SIX: Leicester University in the late 1960s or early 1970s. Norbert
Elias is walking across Victoria Park towards the Sociology Department.
Members of staff on the right side of the Attenborough Building can see
him making his steady progress across the park, just like yesterday, just like
tomorrow. He always appears at about the same time, head leaning slightly
to one side, always with the same regular, shuffling pace, almost always
briefcase in hand.

SCENE SEVEN: A lecture room in a German university during the early
1980s. Elias, now a spritely eighty-five, is in full flight, making a telling
point. One arm is pointing towards the ceiling, the other holds a piece of
chalk. Elias is wearing a fisherman's sweater and his jacket is lying crumpled
on a nearby bench.[26] He is in his element.

These are glimpses of Elias captured at odd moments during a long life. We
see him observing the world around him: a world in which he was
thoroughly, sometimes dangerously, involved; a world from which he was
also remarkably detached. We see him restlessly exploring and expounding
his vision in good times and bad.

   I was one of the lecturers who used to glance out of the window in the
morning and see Norbert Elias making his way across Victoria Park. Like
the neighbours of Immanuel Kant in Königsberg, we could set our watches
by the footfall of Elias. I am not sure that Elias would have appreciated this
comparison.

   I only knew him very slightly. However, that was enough to convince me
that he had a considerable intellect and a strong belief in the importance of
his own ideas. The Leicester department was very large and was, for a
while, the most important training ground for sociologists in Britain.
Within the department Elias had a circle of admirers and a small number of
disciples. To me at least, at the time, his message was not very clear. His

major works, such as *The Civilizing Process* (Elias 1994a) and *The Court Society* (Elias 1983) were not yet translated into English.

I watched Elias lecture on a few occasions, attended a couple of seminars he gave, and sat in on the fringe of some fairly lively coffee-break discussions. I never tried to become a close member of Elias's circle but I do not remember being deliberately excluded either. I can recall two occasions when I had extended conversations with Elias directly. He was kind and helpful to a beginner. Others also found him helpful. I remember that a colleague of mine, appointed at the same time, once said that listening to Elias was like 'warming yourself at a fire'.

Gradually, over the years, Elias's appearances at Leicester became less frequent. This was not due to infirmity. It was because in his seventies he became a celebrity in continental Europe, gave public lectures, received awards, and was interviewed by journalists. He left Leicester in 1975 to live in Germany, then Holland. When he died in 1990 aged ninety-three Elias was widely recognized as a great sociologist.

A Survivor's Vision

Elias had a strong sense of personal destiny. He believed he was part of 'a chain of generations' and was contributing to 'the task of elaborating a comprehensive theory of human society, or, more exactly, a theory of the development of humanity' (Elias 1994b, 131–2).

That last quotation sounds a little Wagnerian. However, while there may be a little bit of Siegfried's sense of destiny in Elias there is also something of Charlie Chaplin's determination to survive against the odds. Elias and Chaplin were born within two years of each other, in 1897 and 1899, respectively. Elias, like Chaplin's 'little man with the bowler hat', sometimes sailed close to the wind. He suffered many setbacks, knew what it was like to be short of funds, and often stumbled into minor conflicts. At times he was laughed at and scorned, usually behind his back. But after every difficulty Elias, like Charlie, carried on along his chosen course.

Elias looked like a middle manager in a metal goods factory. In fact, for a while, in his twenties, he was exactly that. After he completed his doctorate in philosophy at Breslau university he had to earn money to help his family survive the postwar inflation. He helped a local industrialist build up his export order book. As he later recalled, 'My view of capitalism was greatly influenced by that factory owner, a very nice person' (Elias 1994a, 32). Later, in his thirties, Elias opened a small toy factory with two partners. Elias was the marketing man in this operation. He did the rounds of the stores, getting to know the buyers, trying to persuade them to take orders for elephants on wheels and jumping jacks.

It was no ordinary toy business. All three partners were German. One of them, Elias, was a philosopher-turned-sociologist and the other two were a writer and a sculptor, both communists. The enterprise folded after nine months. The time and place – Paris in the early 1930s – were against it. The would-be toy manufacturers were strangers in town, exiles steering clear of the Nazi regime. Their hearts were not in it. Their minds were elsewhere. Elias, for example, was busy writing essays for publication. One of these was about the expulsion of the Huguenots from France.[27] As a Jew forced to emigrate from Germany he had some feeling for this topic.

Some of the escapades in Elias's life between the wars could have come straight out of Chaplin's film, *The Great Dictator*. Before leaving Germany, Elias lived in Frankfurt, working in the sociology department at the university. When Hitler came to that city in order to address a Nazi rally. Elias decided to go and hear Hitler speak. Here is how Elias told the story half a century later:

> A big speech by Hitler was announced and I was burning with curiosity to see him in the flesh. But that was dangerous, because I was recognizable as a Jew. On the other hand, with a suitable disguise my features could pass as aristocratic. If I took off my spectacles, wedged a monocle in my eye, put on a little hunter's hat and different clothes, I was a different person. And so, accompanied by two towering, very Aryan-looking students, I walked between the rows of SS. (Elias 1994a, 46)

At about the same time, in 1933, Elias had another encounter with the SS. When the Nazis came to power he realized that it would be sensible to make sure that there were no compromising papers left lying around in the sociology department. As the keyholder of the building he was able to do this. Again, we can hear the story in Elias's own words:

> When the SS came for me some days later so that I could hand over the department to them, I was very impertinent, as I knew they would not find anything. They came to my rooms to fetch me, and then, I, Norbert Elias, was driven through Frankfurt in an open jeep, a Nazi flag beside me . . . I can still see the scene before me. An SS lieutenant looked at the shelves of books and pulled out Marx: 'Aha, Marx – of course! These filthy Communists.' When I asked him, 'What are you actually looking for?', he replied, 'That's none of your damned business'. (48)

A few weeks after his drive in the SS jeep Elias was out of Germany. After Paris he went to London.

Elias spent nearly four decades in Britain. They were a time of almost complete obscurity. For Elias, unlike Chaplin, the limelight came late. After he published his two-volume classic, *The Civilizing Process*, in 1939 he had a very long period during which he published hardly anything. Over the next quarter of a century he did not manage to get more than a few thousand words into print. Nor did he obtain a full-time, tenured academic post until appointed to a lecturing position at Leicester in 1954 at the age of fifty-seven.

Elias remained an outsider in the transatlantic academic world at least until 1977, when he received the Adorno prize. Only in the late 1970s and 1980s, twenty years after his 'official' retirement from university teaching, did he enjoy a degree of international fame.

The Canonization of Elias

Elias finally became fashionable during the 1990s. Unfortunately for him, he missed this experience. This was because he died in 1990. In fact, Elias's death gave his ideas more publicity than they received in the ninety-three years of his life.

According to the *Social Sciences Citation Index* (SSCI), the number of publications which take Elias's work as a central theme has been on a steady upward trajectory since the early 1980s. If we take each of the four-year periods beginning in 1981, then the number of SSCI-recorded publications of this kind is as follows:

- 1981–4   23
- 1985–8   26
- 1989–92   39
- 1993–6   69

During the following two years (1997 and 1998), the figure was thirty-nine publications; in other words, the upward trajectory of interest in Elias's work became even steeper. This does not match the kind of attention attracted by Anthony Giddens, whose work was a major theme in fifty-four publications during 1997 and 1998, nor by Pierre Bourdieu, who achieved a score of eighty-six. However, according to this measure, Elias attracted more attention than, say, Talcott Parsons, whose work was a major theme in twenty-three publications recorded by the SSCI for those two years, and Zygmunt Bauman, who scored twenty-six such citations.

If we spread the net wider and take into account all the SSCI-indexed publications that cite Elias's work in their bibliographies, whether or not this work is mentioned in the title or abstract, this exercise confirms and strengthens the impression of a steady increase of interest in Elias (see Figure 1.1).

1981	32	1985	70	1989	87	1993	86
1982	31	1986	73	1990	99	1994	95
1983	50	1987	73	1991	96	1995	115
1984	55	1988	81	1992	101	1996	149

Figure 1.1[28]   *Number of SSCI-indexed publications citing Norbert Elias. Source: Social Sciences Citation Index*

After the sustained campaign by his supporters during the last few years, which included several centenary conferences in 1997, a number of introductory texts and two collections of extracts from his work, there is absolutely no danger that the writings of Elias will be forgotten. He has 'arrived'. He has been presented at the gates of the Hall of Fame and admitted. Elias is established. His work is part of the canon.

Elias's theory is a valuable resource. This present book is not concerned with trying either to prove it or to disprove it. Elias's work is present in every chapter but it is there as a means, not an end. The main object is to put his important ideas into fruitful interchange with some other major contributions to understanding the modern human condition. This is done without making an *a priori* assumption that Elias's theory is in all, or in most respects, 'the best'.

Almost the worst treatment for Elias, and for his exciting books, would be to wall him up in a temple to be tended only by the faithful. That is the way to drive away the curious, shooing them off with the feeling that they are not 'good enough' to be true Eliasians. This is not what Elias needs at this posthumous phase of his career.

Releasing Elias into the Wild

Now that Elias has been canonized, his works are likely to receive treatment that is less deferential than before. They can take it. Only the toughest make it to the top. Sociology's classics are resilient. They have to be. The ideas of Weber, Durkheim and Marx, for example, have been pushed, pulled, stretched, twisted and squeezed into all kinds of shapes. In different hands, these approaches to understanding human societies have been dissected almost out of existence, interpreted from a dozen different perspectives, and rendered down into convenient bite-sized bars. Again and again, they re-emerge from these assaults, full of sap, spring and bounce.

The classics can survive the most trying circumstances. As long as the original texts are available, preferably in print and well-translated, no lasting harm is done. It is always possible to return to the words themselves, rediscover the context in which they were written, and reconsider their significance.

Interest in Durkheim's work continued to flourish despite the collapse of the Third French Republic for which he was 'a semiofficial ideologist' [Bellah 1973, xvii]. Marxian analysis regained its nerve after the collapse of communism and the accompanying vilification. Weberian studies recovered from the fact that Max Weber's work was introduced to the English-speaking world through the very particular viewpoint of Talcott Parsons, the dominant American sociologist of the first few postwar decades.

This last example is worth pursuing. As is well known, Parsons interwove aspects of Weber, Durkheim and other theorists, as he understood them, in *The Structure of Social Action* (Parsons 1968) which first appeared in 1937. When the social sciences rapidly expanded in the United States after World War II, Parsons's work was available to supply the demand for a theory that could be taught to the thousands of new students flocking into American classrooms. As a result, Weber and Durkheim became familiar names to later generations of sociology graduates, some of whom have returned to the original texts and discovered their 'own' versions of these writers.[29]

Parsons is now widely reckoned to have misunderstood Weber, and to have imposed meanings on his work that were not present.[30] However, on balance, the Parsonian episode has been good for Weberians. Once Parsons with his stockbreeder's eye had 'bred' Weber into his theory, this meant that the Weberian influence was able to make the transition from local to international: from a Heidelberg speciality to a major influence on sociologists both sides of the Atlantic

There are two separate points. The first is that being one element within a hybrid that travels far and is widely discussed may be better for a theorist's long-term influence than being exclusively cultivated by a school that it primarily concerned with protecting the purity of the founder's vision. Best of all, perhaps, is to have the 'purists' (not too powerful) and the 'hybridizers' (not too brash) side by side and in vigorous but friendly communication.

The second point is that hybridization is not an aberration. Nor is it a retreat from a standard of 'purity' maintained by the 'best'. The canon is full of creative *bricoleurs* or improvisers with highly original minds full of the most profound insights who have not shied away from using the most useful materials to hand when constructing their schemes. Marx, Durkheim and Weber all borrowed from others and they have all in turn been pillaged to good effect.

It is almost a cliché to state that Marx fused in his work elements from the French physiocrats, the British political economists and the German philosophers. Durkheim drew inspiration from Comte, Rousseau, and many others. For his part, Weber has been persuasively characterized as 'primarily a reconceptualizer of material that had been worked up by others' (Turner and Factor 1994, 8).

These writers all engaged in synthesis; in other words, very high-level *bricolage*, the inventive combination of elements seized from diverse structures. It is an important aspect of intellectual creativity.[31] It would be a pity if Elias were to be excluded from these processes. In his lifetime he resisted acknowledging the influence of others upon him, and some of his supporters have been vigorous in coming to his aid on this front.[32] However, scholars are likely to take what they need from Elias and combine it with ideas and approaches taken from other sources.

Maps of Modernity

The object of this book is to trace, juxtapose and compare five different pathways through the dense forest of modernity. Each scholar studied has his or her own 'map', focusing upon certain aspects of the psycho-socio-historical terrain while neglecting others.

The information contained in these maps or readings of modernity will be approached in two ways. First, consideration will be given to the location in time and space, in history and in culture, of each map's author. This kind of information combined with the author's own statements helps towards working out how the aspects of modernity emphasized by the author are related to that author's projects. To put it another way, when you evaluate a map, it is helpful to know who drew it and what their chief preoccupations were. For example, someone who is prospecting for oil may highlight different features in a terrain from someone who is trying to establish a guerrilla base.[33]

A second task is to examine the assumptions and arguments embedded in these readings and search for patterns of similarities and difference among them. This is done in the chapters comparing Elias with, in turn, Foucault, Bauman, Parsons and Arendt. Some elements of a potential composite map of modernity begin to take shape. A more detailed mapping is attempted of two specific regions of modernity: the postwar shift towards supranational organization in Europe and the part played by humiliation and shame in political and organizational life.

In a final chapter some of the main conclusions are drawn together and elaborated, examining their possible implications for further development of social theory focused on the attempt to understand modernity.

Sociology and Philosophy

As has been seen, the main object of this book is to consider what Elias's theory contributes to our understanding of modernity and whether it is possible to combine his insights with those of other major sociologists and philosophers. Elias would have been rather unsympathetic to this project for two reasons. One reason is that he paid very little attention to other approaches within sociology apart from his own. The other reason is that he was not prepared to accept that philosophers could make a significant contribution to our knowledge and understanding of society, since philosophy, unlike sociology, was not a science.[34]

The following statement, which does not come from Elias, offers a view of the relationship between science and philosophy which seems more reasonable than Elias's:

> The distinction of science from all the philosophical disciplines is vital . . . But this is *not* to be taken to mean that the two kinds of discipline are without significant mutual interrelations and that each can afford to ignore the other . . . [Philosophy] is the attempt to achieve a rational cognitive understanding by methods other than those of empirical science. That there are important mutual relations of philosophy and science, once the distinction between them is established, is a simple deduction from the most general nature of reason itself. The tendency of theoretical systems in science to become logically closed is a special case. The general principle is that it is in the nature of reason to strive for a rationally consistent account of all experience which comes within its range at all . . . It . . . follows that there are no logically watertight compartments in human experience. Rational knowledge is a single organic whole.

The writer adds that science and philosophy 'stand in a relation of mutually corrective criticism'. On the one hand, evidence from scientific sources and from the observation of fact could provide 'valid ground for criticism of philosophical views'. On the other hand, 'every system of scientific theory involves philosophical assumptions'. For example, 'questions of the grounds of empirical validity of scientific propositions, the kinds of procedures which may on general grounds be expected to yield valid knowledge, etc., impinge directly on the philosophical fields of logic and epistemology'.

These words come from Talcott Parsons, writing in *The Structure of Social Action* (Parsons 1968, 22–30). Parsons adds that supporters of one particular approach to scientific methodology 'deny the legitimacy of theoretical abstraction' of the kind carried out by philosophers. This approach is empiricism. The main characteristic of this approach is 'the *identification* of the meanings of the concrete specific propositions of a given science, theoretical or empirical, with the scientifically knowable totality of the external reality to which they refer. They maintain, that is, that there is an immediate correspondence between *concrete* experienceable reality and scientific propositions, and only in so far as this exists can there be scientific knowledge' (23; emphasis in original).

The methodology just described is intended to produce what Elias describes as 'object-adequate' knowledge.[35] Elias's position has been described by Derek Layder as '"sophisticated" empiricism' (Layder 1986, 380). Elias assumes that there is a long-term tendency for human perceptions of the world to move in the direction of increased object adequacy, in other words, to become increasingly complete and accurate. This assumption allows him to treat as irrelevant 'philosophical' questions about the *criteria* by which you can tell just *how* 'adequate' our knowledge of the objective world is at any one point in time.

There are other reasons also for Elias's dismissal of philosophy, as will be seen in the next chapter. However, his hostility to philosophers does not mean that his work cannot be compared with theirs. In fact, all four of the writers discussed, as well as Elias himself, make philosophical assumptions that can be disputed in the course of rational argument and make statements about social processes that can be tested empirically. Although Arendt and Foucault are conventionally aligned with philosophy while Parsons and Bauman were employed in sociology departments, they could all, including Elias, be described as 'philosophers' in some respects and 'sociologists' in other respects.[36]

My next task is to provide a brief introduction to the biography, 'vision' and intellectual output of Elias, a scholar whose reputation has grown so quickly over the past few years that there must be many people who have heard the name but who have little idea what it stands for.

Notes

1 Elias's arguments have often been discussed before. There have been empirical works inspired by Elias's theory as well as attempts to extend the theory. (See, for example, Swaan 1988; Elias and Dunning 1986; Goudsblom 1992; Mastenbroek 1993; Mennell 1985; Spierenberg 1984; Wouters 1986; Wouters 1992. This list is not comprehensive.) They have

been analysed by committed friends. (See, for example, van Benthem van den Bergh 1971; Bogner 1986; Bogner 1992; Fletcher 1997; Goudsblom 1987; Kilminster 1998; van Krieken 1998; Kuzmics 1987; Mennell 1989. As before, this list is not comprehensive.) Elias has also been discussed by friendly critics (e.g. Bauman 1979 and Rojek 1986) and less friendly critics (see Coser 1980; Lasch 1985; Layder 1986; see also Breuer 1991). Comparing Elias with other writers is not a new activity either. Adorno, Simmel, Mannheim, Goffman, Foucault, Cassirer and Parsons have all had full-dress treatments and there have also been shorter discussions of Wallerstein, Habermas, Sennett, Bourdieu and Arendt. See, for example, Arnason 1987; Bauman 1979; Bogner 1987; Breuer 1991; Chartier 1988a; Déchaux 1995; Eyerman 1995; Goudsblom 1987; Goudsblom 1995; Kilminster 1993; Kilminster and Wouters 1995; van Krieken 1990; Kuzmics 1988; Kuzmics 1991; Maso 1995a; Maso 1995b; Mongardini 1995; Mouzelis 1993; Newton 1999; Robertson 1992a.

2 Elias tends to treat capitalism in a pre-Schumpterian way, as a field of competition among small or medium-sized enterprises (see Elias 1994b, 32–3). Barrington Moore, also from a pre-World War I generation, has a blind spot of a similar kind although the two cases are not the same (see Smith 1983, 145). It is, perhaps, understandable in some ways that Elias should have this blind spot. *The Civilizing Process* was written before Schumpter and his intellectual heir, Galbraith, had produced their best-known work – although Elias was familiar with Veblen whose writings inspired both. For references to Veblen, see Elias 1983, 38, 62, 67.

3 Elias is obviously not the only person to have made such connections. They were, for example, a central preoccupation of the Frankfurt School. The sociology department to which Elias was attached while working in Frankfurt during the early 1930s shared a building with the Frankfurt School, although this title was only given later. On the Frankfurt School see Elias 1994b, 48; Jay 1996; Wiggershaus 1994.

4 Although the geographical boundaries of the 'West' are often stretched to include Australasia.

5 Even Ankara, heir to the Ottoman empire, is represented in Nato, an organization which has moved closer to the EU in recent years during the Balkan crisis.

6 'Elias is indeed a great sociologist. Even if he does not provide answers to all past and future questions of sociology, as some of the most ardent of his disciples seem to suggest he is much, much greater than the collective blindness to his work would imply' (Bauman 1979, 123). Research by Arpad Szakolczai shows that in the last few years of his life Foucault became acquainted with Elias's work. In his last months, Foucault translated Elias's *The Loneliness of the Dying* for his own private use. See Szakolczai 1998; Elias 1985a.

7 See Bauman 1989, 12–13.

8 For Elias on Parsons, see Elias 1994a, 181–215; Elias 1972. According to Richard Kilminster, who knew Elias well, he once commented that Hannah Arendt was a nice person but working on completely the wrong lines (conversation with Richard Kilminster).

9 See next part of this chapter.

10 The word 'vision' may mean either 'the content of a vision' or 'the capacity to have intuitions'. The context will make it clear in each case which meaning is intended.

11 At this point in my argument, I am touching on areas that have been investigated in depth by Arpad Szakolczai. I have not tried to take his analysis into account at this point, partly because his book on 'reflexive historical sociology' is not yet available.

12 See, for example, Foulkes 1990, 145; Foulkes and Steward Prince 1969.

13 See Young-Bruehl 1982, 170–1, 173–81.

14 Eribon 1991, 209, 224.

15 Buxton 1985, 97–104.

16 See Smith 1999b.

17 See Parsons 1968, xxiii–xxiv.

18 At least part of the excitement in the texts produced by our social theorists comes from the interplay, and sometimes the struggle, between vision and intellect. Does vision point the way, insisting that the intellect should reach a pre-determined goal, or does the intellect simply take some initial pointers from vision, returning with its findings to correct the original 'take'? One variable may be the intensity of the experience from which vision flows and hence the

depth of the emotions in which the writer's initial insights are embedded. Arguably, the stronger the experience and, perhaps, the more deeply it is repressed, the more determined will the writer be to understand, elaborate and communicate the contents revealed in the original act of vision. Where the experience of modernity's challenges is less intense, it is more likely that intellect, not vision, will take the lead. This account is, in fact, vastly oversimplified since the discovery or recognition of unexpected connections depends partly upon intuitive acts of imagination and partly upon realizing the logical implications of those connections, once made. Intellect and vision are densely intertwined.

19 Also, Parsons's work during the early 1940s on German society. See Parsons 1942a; Parsons 1942b; Parsons 1945.

20 Commitment to this final point is strongest in the case of Arendt, Elias and Bauman. Foucault tends to 'drift' in the direction of creative anarchy while Parsons has an occasional bias in the other direction. For example, in a wartime memorandum for the Council for Democracy, an organization directed by Carl Friedrich, Parsons maintained that in Germany the most urgent matter was to strengthen rational-legal authority rather than democracy: 'some modification of traditional conceptions of civil liberties . . . seem to be needed [for] they have often been formulated in such a way as to suggest absolute inalienability regardless of the ethical quality of action under their protection' (quoted in Buxton 1985, 103). This should not be misinterpreted. Parsons was anti-fascist rather than anti-democratic. See Nielsen 1991.

21 Cf Elias 1994a, 168–78; Dunning 1987.

22 For the photograph and background details see Elias 1994b, 9, 15.

23 See Elias 1994b, 24.

24 Ilse Seglow in Gleichmann et al. 1977, 16–17.

25 Eric Wolf in Gleichmann et al. 1977, 29–30. Wolf became a renowned social anthropologist.

26 This picture may be found on the back cover of Stephen Mennell's introduction to Elias and his work, originally published by Blackwell in 1989. For the latest edition see Mennell 1998.

27 See Elias 1935; reprinted in English in Goudsblom and Mennell 1998, 18–25.

28 These figures exclude publications by Elias himself. They include publications in refereed academic journals mentioned in the *Social Science Citation Index* that mention Elias or his work in the title or the abstract. Such publications include articles, reviews, editorials, letters, and memorials. SSCI indexes publications in the major European languages, so these figures are not restricted to English-language publications.

29 For example, Charles Camic, Jeffrey Alexander, Lawrence Scaff and, in the UK, Anthony Giddens. This list could be considerably extended.

30 See, for example, Giddens 1971, 106; Mestrovic 1993, 46, 60; Scaff 1989, x; Turner and Factor 1994, 175; Tenbruck 1987, 262–3.

31 On this point, see Koestler's *Act of Creation* (Koestler 1964).

32 See, for example, Goudsblom 1995; Kilminster and Wouters 1995; Maso 1995a; Maso 1995b.

33 This point was very familiar to Parsons who, in his early work, repeatedly stressed the importance of 'the definition of the situation', following W.I. Thomas. Parsons writes, for example, that 'A tract of land . . . represents an aspect of the physical environment which would be quite differently "defined" by a geological survey of the topology of a region, by a farmer whose produce is grown on it, and a military officer interested in making it secure against an enemy attack' (Parsons 1942a, 553).

34 See, for example, Elias 1978, chapter one.

35 The concept of 'object adequacy' is discussed by Elias in Elias 1971.

36 It may or may not be significant that when I was looking for the works of Elias recently in the bookshop at Warwick University, I found *The Civilizing Process* shelved under 'philosophy'.

2

CULTURE AND CIVILIZATION

A Science for Survival

Norbert Elias wanted sociology to deliver to his fellow human beings the knowledge they need to survive modernity and, if possible, enjoy the experience. As a German Jew Elias also knew about the difficulties of trying to survive. He suffered greatly in the 1930s and 1940s. After World War II he confronted three challenges: to recover from this experience; to clarify what he had learned from it; and to pass on these lessons to others through his work.

In Elias's view, the sociologists' task is 'to find connections between particular social events' and discover 'how their sequence can actually be explained'. Once this knowledge is obtained it can be put to use in 'explaining and determining the trend of social problems' and 'last but not least, in providing practical solutions to them' (Elias 1978, 153).

Elias believes that the science of sociology, if developed successfully, will be able to explain how people's lives interconnect in a structured way within societies and through history. It will become a science of human figurations and long-term social processes. Sociology will produce knowledge that, if disseminated effectively, will erode the fear and illusion endemic to relations between individuals, groups and nations. Such knowledge should be 'a destroyer of myths' (50).

According to Elias, sociology must develop as a 'relatively autonomous science' (111) with its own standards. Sociology should be a self-regulating scientific activity. It should be autonomous, not heteronomous (i.e. not controlled from outside or above). If a sociologist's 'attitudes and scientific criteria are to any extent shaped by heteronomous, extra-scientific considerations, whether political, religious or national – his efforts may all amount to a waste of time' (61).

Sociology needs to protect its standards and defend its capacity for independent thought. It is a special kind of science, not like the physical sciences. It needs 'new ways of speaking and thinking' (111). For example, sociologists should think in terms of networks of relationships (or figurations) that have a 'processual nature' (115); in other words, these figurations are caught up in long-term processes that have a distinctive structure. Power and identity (the sense of having a self and belonging to a group) are both deeply embedded within human relationships. Power is not a 'substance', nor is identity a 'thing' (112). They are both relational.[1]

Elias's sociology is a science for survival, which he hopes will provide knowledge to help us understand and even partially control the processes shaping our lives – or, at least, to avoid some of their bad effects. This idea of sociology is rooted deep in Elias's intuitive sense of how things fit together in the world.[2]

Interconnectedness and Separation

Elias has a very strong feeling for interconnectedness and growth, for processes of integration and expansion and, also, for the intertwining processes of disarticulation and fragmentation that always accompany them. However, he can also empathize with those who stand apart, feel sequestered, and look at life through glass.

Elias understands the appeal of an apparently well-defended and protected existence: for example, within a royal court, within a bourgeois household, within a university college,[3] within an academic department, or within the self. In a sheltered environment you are able to think, reflect and imagine, play games, develop your taste. However, Elias also understands the peril of such an existence. The walls of your shelter may conceal evidence of the broader social processes occurring beyond them.

These broader social processes may destroy the apparently safe cocoon, as happened in the case of the French court in 1789, to take a dramatic example.[4] Elias's own childhood and youth in provincial Germany were spent in one such cocoon, occupied by the assimilating Jewish bourgeoisie. That apparently secure form of existence was destroyed in 1914. During the 1950s and 1960s Elias found another bolt-hole in provincial England.

Elias's 'way of looking' expresses a powerful vision, a guiding model in the imagination. This vision contains a central tension: between merging and separation, between jumping in and holding back, between involvement and detachment, between inhibition and expression, between being 'part of' and being 'apart from'. Both these aspects of his vision come through strongly in Elias's most important work, *The Civilizing Process* (Elias 1994a), first published in 1939.

The Civilizing Process

In this study Elias traces what he believes is a long-term process (not without reversals) of increasing pacification and self-control within Europe since the early Middle Ages. This civilizing process has a paradoxical effect. It increases human interconnectedness but at the same time increases people's feelings of being isolated from each other. The civilizing process gives modern men and women the capacity to have a detached attitude towards themselves and their relationships with others. It also tends to make them very inhibited. Men and women are liable to hold back their

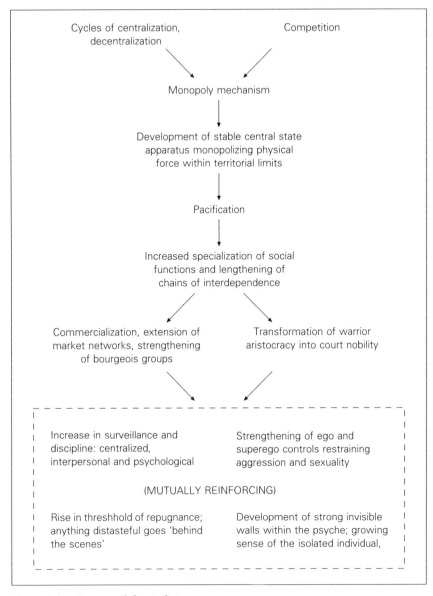

Figure 2.1 *Aspects of the civilizing process*

emotions to an unhealthy degree. At the same time, however, the civilizing process joins people together, intertwining their fates. Human beings are drawn into ever-denser relations of mutual interdependence.

It is worth briefly summarizing the central argument of *The Civilizing Process*, although in a highly simplified form (see Figure 2.1). In this book, Elias looks at how 'the done thing' has changed through the ages. As every civilized person knows, there are rules about when, where and how you should blow your nose, spit, sneeze, scratch yourself, enjoy sex, throw a punch, break wind, urinate and defecate. Elias shows that over the centuries these rules have changed. Standards have become more 'delicate', do's and don't's have become more detailed, and behaviour has become more tightly regulated.

Elias argues that this long-term tendency is related to changes in the way societies are governed. In early times, feudal life was a bloody round of violent struggles for survival or local supremacy. Aggression and fear were vital triggers, priming human beings to fight or flee at a moment's notice. When top-down authority was loose or fragmented, there was no consistent external pressure upon subjects (imposed by a lord or a king) to curtail these violent emotions and drives. Restraints upon human urges were intermittent, irregular and unstable, whether those restraints were imposed by other people or exercised within the self.

Eventually, a few castle-based dynasties succeeded in dominating all the others. They built up more stable centralized regimes. Bureaucrats were recruited. Merchants and peasants started to be taxed on a regular basis. These new lords pacified their realms and turned armed opponents into obedient subjects. It became expedient to curb those violent emotions that led to uproar and disorder. Tighter, more centralized external controls produced greater self-control within the subordinate population.

The civilized habitus was calculating and controlled, devious and detached. It first took root in the court, later spread to the bourgeoisie and, still later, found expression in the lives of ordinary people throughout society. It was a central aspect of the civilizing process, closely related to the development of stable power monopolies, especially the bureaucratic state, and the growth of a complex urban-industrial occupational structure and market.

Elias wrote *The Civilizing Process* on the eve of World War II. His initial research project had been on nineteenth-century French liberalism. However, he became interested in the occurrence and significance of 'attitudes and words like *courtoisie, civilité* and civilisation which led [him] . . . to reflect on the process of civilization' (Fontaine 1978, 252). His work was also a response to, as he put it, 'the experiences in whose shadows we all live' (Elias 1994a, xvi): in other words, the collapse of socio-political stability in Germany during the 1920s, the rise of the Nazi party and the increasing fear of war in Europe.

Elias hated war and oppression but he 'loved Germany very much' (Elias 1994b, 18). Both considerations underlie *The Civilizing Process*, as they do *The Germans* (Elias 1996; see Table 2.1). But why should the troubles of modern Germany send Elias back to warring knights in the feudal forest? One reason might be that a German interested in the origins (or 'sociogenesis') of his country's collapse into barbarism would find it both natural and congenial to begin in the eighth century AD, which is, indeed, where Elias's analysis of the 'dynamics of feudalism' begins (Elias 1994a, 275).

Table 2.1 *Key works by Norbert Elias*

Title	Date of composition	Publication in German	Publication in English
The Court Society	1933	1969	1983
The Civilizing Process (2 vols)	mid/late 1930s	1939 1968/69	1978/82
The Society of Individuals (3 essays)	1939 1940s/1950s 1987	1987	1991
The Germans (5 essays)	1960s–1980s	1989	1996

This was the epoch of Charlemagne, ruler of the Holy Roman or 'German Empire' (Elias 1994a, 282). As Elias later wrote in *The Germans*, for his compatriots in the 1920s and 1930s 'The medieval German empire and particularly some of the more notable medieval emperors long served as symbols of a Greater Germany that had been lost' (Elias 1996, 4). For Elias's compatriots, a central feature of Germany's history was the German people's failure to live up to its early promise.

As Elias argues, after the eighth century Germany experienced a very long period of decline. In his view, a major factor was the strength of centrifugal forces splitting up the German empire. As a result of these pressures, 'the actual power of the central authority of the German Empire (remained) low for many centuries, while the power and independence of the territorial rulers increased – the inverse of what happened in France' (Elias 1994a, 279).

The failure of Germany coincided with the success of France, which became the leading centralized absolutist state in Europe during the seventeenth and eighteenth centuries. German intellectuals during the nineteenth and early twentieth centuries developed a contempt for French claims to be highly 'civilized'. In German eyes, the word 'civilization' indicated a superficial concern with manners and a preoccupation with the material advantages brought by industrial technology and commerce.[5]

It was not uncommon for educated Germans to be rather proud of being 'uncivilized' in the sense of not being superficial. German intellectuals did not concentrate upon developing the 'civilized' skills of building up political influence or engaging in trade and industry. Instead, they placed emphasis upon *Kultur*, or self-cultivation. They sought deep understanding of nature and themselves. This was the tradition in which Elias himself was educated.

It is against this background that Elias wrote *The Civilizing Process*. Although he does not make this point explicitly, the book is grounded in a puzzle: if *Kultur* was so manifestly superior to civilization, why was Germany brought so low during the 1920s and 1930s? The puzzle is linked to a challenge: what lay 'behind' or 'beneath' the apparent superficiality of 'civilization'? Was there something in the process leading to civilization that helped other societies avoid Germany's fate?

The Court Society

Elias's inquiry into the 'sociogenesis' of the 'civilized habitus' was already underway by the early 1930s, although he had not yet adopted this terminology and was probably not fully aware of the direction in which he was travelling. Elias looked at the French absolutist court in *The Court Society*, published six years before *The Civilizing Process* appeared. The two books are closely related.

In *The Court Society*, Elias explored the aftermath of the pacification of the warlike French nobility following the dynastic conflicts of the sixteenth century and intermittent revolts in the early seventeenth. By the 1640s monarchic authority had been successfully imposed over most of France. The king's 'overmighty subjects' were disarmed. Men whose fathers had been feudal warriors had to put away their swords and learn to dance and charm if they wanted to come to the royal court.

To put it starkly, aristocrats had to give up their headstrong ways – or give up their heads. At court they bowed, scraped and played by the rules of etiquette. These rules decreed who should defer to whom, how, and when. Life at court involved rigid self-control, calculated use of resources, and careful pursuit of self-interest. At court everyone watched everyone else. It was rather like a poker game. The emotional cost of self-restraint was high, especially for those low in the pecking order. As Elias shows, minor nobles wrote minor novels full of carefree shepherd folk. They mourned their own lost freedom.

During the eighteenth century the balance of class power shifted. Upstart bourgeois financiers held the purse strings and kept some of the best salons at Versailles and in Paris. They competed with established nobles, adopting their habits of *civilité*. Behind their *politesse*, the aristocrats and their bourgeois imitators were in a struggle for power like 'boxers in a clinch' (274). For a long time the monarchy was able to play one class against the other. However, all the participants in this struggle for influence ignored the wider society 'outside'. Finally, the people swept the royal court away in the French Revolution.

After 1789 the bourgeoisie became the dominant national class. Bourgeois families acquired the civilized *habitus* of the aristocracy and made it their own. Their tendency to behave in a calculating, careful and controlled way was reinforced by the competitive pressures of the capitalist market place. As the figurations of urban-industrial society became increasingly dense and extensive, an increasingly high proportion of the population were affected by the civilizing process and acquired a civilized habitus.

Seeing, Believing and Knowing

Elias wove a whole 'sociology' from the densely tangled skein of insight and intuition contained in these two books. One of its themes is the way 'civilized' men and women perceive themselves and the world of which they are a part.

Elias believes that the civilizing process has the desirable effect of lowering the level of interpersonal violence in everyday life. However, the very mechanisms within the psyche that impose restraint upon human drives such as aggression also have the undesirable effect of distorting our understanding. The pressures 'holding us back', so to speak, act like a surrounding wall confining us within ourselves and giving us a false sense of our own nature.

Modern men and women have come to believe 'that their actual "selves" somehow exist "inside" them . . . [while] an invisible barrier separates their "inside" from everything "outside" – the so-called "outside" world' (Elias 1978, 119). People feel that the self 'inside' the invisible world is a knowable reality whereas the 'outside' world is perceived, quite wrongly, as unreal, unknowable, or both.

Elias gives this 'closed' self-image a name: 'homo clausus'. It is a false and harmful perception that distorts our understanding of reality. Elias stresses repeatedly that, whatever they imagine, human beings are actually thoroughly embedded in the social world around them. They are, as he put it, 'homines aperti', open to the influence of others and influencing them in turn. Homo clausus is a myth.

There is another sense in which the civilizing process has produced both advantages and disadvantages. The strong self-control of civilized human beings enables them to be relatively 'detached' in their responses to what they observe about them. They can look at the world in a 'cold' and systematic way, so to speak, keeping their emotions under control. People have learned to keep their hopes and fears under wraps, to be less 'involved'. This detached approach has been institutionalized in the procedures of modern science.

Detached investigation in the pursuit of organized knowledge has become the preserve of the specialized scientific professions. Modern science has increased the human capacity to control certain aspects of nature and society, which is a potential advantage. However, science now intervenes between human beings and the world. We have become dependent upon professional instruction about the nature of reality. Unfortunately, the things scientists discover tend to subvert the uninformed 'commonsense' view of the world held by non-scientists. This has a profoundly disorienting effect in Elias's view.

The point is that scientific investigation has given modern human beings further cause to mistrust their perceptions, to doubt the evidence of their senses. Elias argues that modern science destroyed the medieval idea that human beings can directly apprehend God's being, the idea that He is present throughout the whole cosmos.

In the Middle Ages, seeing was believing. People believed what they saw with their own eyes and what they saw was the world of their spiritual beliefs being enacted in daily life. Medieval men and women assumed that the world, their own existence as people seeing the world, and the very process whereby they saw that world were all expressions of God's power and will.

However, the telescope and the microscope have changed things forever. They show a strange and deeper level of reality behind or beyond superficial appearances. Our commonsense observations can be deeply misleading. Human beings can no longer see what they believe or believe what they see.

Elias versus Kant

To summarize, Elias wants to improve our sociological understanding of the way people relate to themselves, to each other and to nature. He pursues this object by exploring the processual development of figurations such as courts, households, or relations between social classes or national states, including the structured transformations in power balances within those figurations. He also looks at the way individuals and groups involved in these figurations acquire a multi-layered sense of identity, distinctive types of habitus and varying degrees and forms of self-control.

As part of this project, Elias considers the way human knowledge of the natural and social world is formed and develops. In approaching these questions, he squares up to Descartes and Kant. Descartes (1596–1650) famously came to the conclusion that the only thing he could be sure of was the existence of his own doubting consciousness. Later, Immanuel Kant (1724–1804) said that in everyone's consciousness there are a number of *a priori* ideas or universal categories such as concepts of time, space and causality.

According to Kant, because we are pre-programmed with *a priori* ideas we are able to make sense of social and natural phenomena. Because we are all pre-programmed in the same way, these understandings are shared by everyone around us. Broadly speaking, we see the world in a similar manner.

This does not satisfy Elias. In his view, evolution has given human beings the capacity to recognise and communicate through symbols.[6] This means we can handle ideas and categories, enabling us to cooperate, compete and survive. So, like Kant, Elias recognizes the importance of shared symbols. However, unlike Kant, Elias does not believe these symbols (categories, ideas, etc.) are a universal given, fixed for all time. They are not '*a priori*'. However, nor are they contingent, arbitrary or peculiar to each individual. On the contrary, knowledge is acquired collectively within groups over several generations.

Elias's point is that our concepts and our knowledge change over time and these processes of change have a structure and pattern with discoverable regularities or principles of development. Kant's so-called 'universal categories' happen to be those learned by human beings at a particular historical phase in their development. In other words, they are not 'universal'. In fact, Elias argues, they ceased to express our understanding of the nature of the world following the discoveries and insights of Darwin, Heisenberg and Einstein.

In Elias's view, Kant's *a priori* categories no longer adequately express our increasingly objective understanding of time, space and causality. In fact, Kant's image of human existence is a prime example of the model of *homo clausus*. It is not, to borrow Elias's term, 'object adequate'. People may still cling to it for emotional reasons but it does not, in Elias's view, capture the reality of figurations and social processes.

Life, Vision, Sociology

Elias's sociology is a sustained attempt to give coherent and detailed intellectual content to his original vision, his guiding intuitions of connectedness and isolation. If we want to understand his sociology, we need to grasp the vision underlying it. If we want to understand the vision, it will be helpful to look at the life in so far as this is possible. In fact, Elias's work makes sense on two levels. It is both global and personal. At one level he is trying to understand the human past and present. At another level, Elias's work is a way of trying to cope with his own personal situation in an upside-down world.

Some ideas about how the two levels may relate to each other may be advanced on the basis of some of the published evidence about Elias's life.[7] These give some information about Elias's early years at home (1897–1915), the period of intense experience and creative energy (1915–40), the following quarter-century of critical neglect and low published output (1940–65) and the final twenty-five years of high output and increased critical attention (1965–90).

A Secure World (1897–1914)

Norbert Elias was born in 1897, the only son of a textile manufacturer who employed about thirty people. His home town was Breslau in the eastern part of Imperial Germany. Breslau is now Wroclaw and belongs to Poland, not Germany. That is just one outcome of the horrific turbulence that disrupted central Europe after 1914, breaking apart the world of Elias's youth.

However, in the years before World War I Elias felt immensely safe. He was cossetted in the warmth of a loving household within a prosperous Jewish community. This community was, in turn, part of the local bourgeoisie in a highly respectable provincial capital of the German Empire.

Elias later recalled that in his parents' household there was 'harmonious inequality' (Elias 1994b, 8). Sex and death stayed 'behind the scenes' and 'as far as I remember it was a secure world. I knew that my father would do anything for me, and my mother too . . . I felt completely protected. I always think that the staying power I had later, when I wrote my books and no one took any notice of them, was due to the very great security I enjoyed as a child' (1994a, 14).

The sense of security was partly deceptive, partly contingent. Elias grew up in a time and place shaped by powerful tensions between social classes, nations, religions and empires. However, during his childhood and adolescence these conflicts were mainly hidden or held in balance. The German Empire seemed stable. The Russians and French were both held at bay. Within the city, class differences and religious hostilities were in a state of equipoise. Anti-semitism was kept in check, at least among the Elias's more prosperous and better-educated neighbours (12).

Within Breslau, aristocratic and bourgeois cultures co-existed. The city had a prosperous Jewish quarter, an impressive commercial centre, a splendid Rathaus with a Knights' Hall, a university, a twin-towered cathedral, a couple of monasteries and several Baroque palaces, one of them owned by royalty.

The presence of the royal palace gives a clue to Breslau's social atmosphere. Elias once wrote that, since at least the eighteenth century, 'Particularly at the smaller and relatively poorer courts of the German empire it was customary to make social inferiors emphatically aware of their subordinate position'. This attitude has 'perhaps passed into the German tradition' (Elias 1993, 95). Breslau must have been a hive of petty snobbery, in some social circles at least.

Elias 'gradually became aware' that he 'belonged to a minority excluded from much that was going on in Germany' (1994b, 128). In Elias's own case, his Jewish origins stood between him and his desire to be a university professor, an ambition already formed by the time he was in his mid teens. This desire to become a leading academic was a typical aspiration at that time for intelligent young Germans who wanted to rise above 'trade'.

When Elias was a young man he joined a Jewish youth movement with Zionist overtones.[8] However, he was not 'simply' Jewish. At least three other dimensions of his situation are important. Firstly, Elias, like many non-Jews, felt both the pride and the feelings of resentment that went with belonging to the bourgeoisie. A textile manufacturer's son would certainly have suffered from the fact that 'in large areas of Europe up to 1918 bourgeois people were regarded and treated by the rulers as second-class citizens, people of lower rank' (17). In Breslau, Protestant and Jewish traders alike must have smarted at the arrogance of the Silesian Catholic aristocracy whose profitable estates surrounded the town.

Secondly, Elias came from a family that was intensely German. His father was 'very Prussian' and wore 'the same moustache as the Emperor' (11). The son 'was steeped in German *Kultur*' (18). Elias was equally conscious of two identities: 'I knew that I was German and a Jew' (10). He had the 'singular experience to belong to a stigmatized minority while at the same time being wholly embedded in the cultural flow and the political and social fate of the majority' (121). In fact, Elias was so embedded in the

German 'cultural flow' that for his *Bar-Mitzvah* he arranged to be given the collected works of Goethe, Heine, Mörke, Eichendorff and other classics in the edition of the *Bibliographisches Institut*.[9]

Thirdly, Elias maintained an emotional distance both from the German state with its calls for patriotism – 'it is not my world', he remembers thinking (19) – and Breslau society: 'I knew I could not live in that world' (15). When he recalls his feelings from this time, Elias evokes the picture of someone inside a *cordon sanitaire* between himself and the society to which he belonged. He gives the impression of an intense personality surrounded by a protective wall, a true *homo clausus*.

If Elias needed a standpoint from which to mount a critique of this setting, he may have found it in the works of Kant, Goethe and Schiller, his 'great men' (18), all central figures in the canon of German *Kultur*. Their theories were a vital influence on his own early thinking. Kant, lifelong inhabitant of another German provincial town, must have been quite familiar with the *cordon sanitaire* which surrounded an intensely preoccupied intellectual in such a setting.[10]

Kant was a great influence upon Goethe and Schiller, both of whom were very interested in the problem of how the self and the world intertwined; for example, how the self could find true expression in a sympathetic social order. They were fascinated by the volcanic passions of human beings. Goethe and Schiller wanted a social order that would foster creativity without letting madness loose. Schiller taught the need to cultivate disinterested enjoyment of beauty. Goethe thought nature's secret laws could be discovered through the workings of the poetic imagination. Both men hoped that by following these paths the principles of truth, beauty, order and freedom could all be combined.

Throughout his own life Elias was deeply interested in the question of what conditions were favourable to order while not being hostile to human creativity. Reading Schiller and Goethe as a young man, Elias will have discovered that these idealists had an overriding fear. They were afraid that their truth, beauty and freedom would be crushed if a new social order rose up based on science, technology and crass materialism. They were concerned that German *Kultur* and the creative imagination might not be able to survive the rise of 'civilization' and its preoccupation with technical prowess, trivial bodily comforts and petty politeness.

In *Modernity and Ambivalence* (Bauman 1991), Zygmunt Bauman comments (without particular reference to Elias) that 'The most representative spokesmen of pre-Nazi German Jewry saw in the holy trinity of Goethe, Schiller and Lessing (supplemented on occasion by lesser but equally revered saints like Kant, Fichter or Herder) not only the warrant for . . . [an] alliance between German and Jewish cultures, but also vivid and clinching evidence that, in fact and by their own nature, the two cultures are immanently alike and guided by the same spirit' (140).

However, a careful scholar such as Elias would have noticed where his cultural heroes saw the main danger coming from. In their eyes it came from France, England and the Jews. As Marshall Berman puts it, the issue was: 'Should German society throw itself into "Jewish" material and practical activity, that is, into economic development and construction, along with liberal political reform, in the manner of England, France and America? Or, alternatively, should it hold aloof from such "worldly" concerns and cultivate an inward-looking "German-Christian" way of life?' (Berman 1982, 47).

Ironically, Elias's favourite authors directed their critical fire against his own ethnicity and his own class. They also despised France, the society Elias knew and cared for most after Germany. He 'had from early on a deep love of French culture' (Elias 1994b, 56).

The conflict between *Kultur* and civilization had deep personal relevance for Elias. The issues surrounding this conflict, perhaps only half-formed in his mind, were dramatized by the celebrations held at Breslau in 1913 to commemorate the Prussian victory over Napoleon's army at nearby Leipzig a century before. This was celebrated in retrospect as a memorable victory of *Kultur* over civilization. For the occasion a festival hall was specially built. However, the Kaiser refused to take part in the opening ceremony. This was because he disapproved of the fact that Breslau was staging a play by Gerhart Hauptman, one of its native sons. Hauptman gave support to all persecuted peoples, including the Jews. Elias vividly recalled these events over seventy years later (18).

The World Turned Upside Down (1914–40)

There are two ways of telling the next part of the story. First, the bare biographical facts can be set out as follows. In 1915, at the age of eighteen, Elias joined the German army and went off to France with a unit maintaining telegraph lines. The front was 'a big shock . . . a horror' (Elias 1994b, 27).

After the war was over, Elias returned to a very different Breslau. The German empire had been overthrown and French forces occupied the region. Germany's aristocracy had withdrawn from its leading position in politics. This brought increased political and cultural freedom. However, neither the bourgeoisie nor the working class had been able to take the aristocracy's place. As a result, the Weimar Republic stood on very shaky foundations.

Elias looked for a place in this new world. He enrolled at Breslau's university where he began training in medicine and philosophy. Elias dropped medicine after a while, and finished up taking a doctorate in philosophy which he completed in 1924. By this time inflation had eaten up the family fortune so, short of money, Elias became under-manager in a metal goods factory, an episode that has already been mentioned. As his financial prospects improved, Elias moved briefly into journalism and then, in his late twenties, back into academic life. This time he was employed as a

sociology teacher, first at Heidelburg, then at Frankfurt. He worked closely
with Karl Mannheim. As German society became increasingly violent and
private armies roamed the streets, Elias wrote *The Court Society*, which he
submitted in 1933 as his *Habilitationsschrift*.

By the end of 1933 Elias was in Paris. Two years later he was in the
United Kingdom where he eventually got a research position at the London
School of Economics. During these years of turmoil *The Civilizing Process*
was written, as was his long essay called 'The society of individuals' (Elias
1991b). When war broke out the LSE was evacuated to Cambridge. This
life was soon rudely interrupted. As an enemy alien Elias was interned in
1940, first at Huyton and then, for several months, on the Isle of Man.

There is another way of telling the story of the years between 1915 and
1940, one that places Elias's intellectual and imaginative response to
Germany's transformation at the centre of the picture.

The vacuum left by Germany's military defeat in 1918 was not just political
but also moral and intellectual. Germany's soldiers had been told they were
armed representatives of German *Kultur*. However, the war's cruelty made
many survivors utterly cynical. Elias's own loss of faith in *Kultur* was gradual
and partial. He never lost his love of Goethe's poetry or his commitment to
the ideal of balancing order and spontaneity. Nevertheless, by the mid-1920s
he had been 'driven out of the ivory tower' (1994b, 91).

By the time he finished his doctorate at Breslau, Elias no longer accepted
the Kantian idea of *a priori* truth, nor its model of the isolated individual
enclosed within walls beyond which lay nature and society. The protective
walls of his own prewar existence had certainly come tumbling down. As a
Jewish intellectual, Elias was unavoidably caught up in the frightening
maelstrom of German society as it rapidly disintegrated.

Two matters were equally urgent for Elias. One was how to secure his own
physical survival. The other was how to equip himself with new intellectual
tools and a methodological strategy for carrying forward the intellectual agenda already implicit in his prewar reading. The problem could be
stated as follows: what was the relationship between German *Kultur* on the
one hand and German society and politics on the other?

Before 1914 this issue had been implicit in the sharp conflict between
Elias's two loyalties. One of these was his strong attraction to the philosophy and poetry of the German idealist tradition. The other was his deep
involvement in a provincial culture – Jewish, manufacturing, and, in his
own case, Francophile – condemned by those same philosophers and poets
for its triviality and materialism.

By 1924 Elias had detached himself from Breslau and from idealist
philosophy. He was 'outside' both. Before the war Elias's acquaintanceship
with Schiller and Goethe must surely have raised the question of the
relationship between German *Kultur* (the works he was reading) and
Germany's social and political order (the life he was living). However, by
the 1920s Elias's changed situation and changed beliefs are likely to have
disposed him towards other ways of interrogating the relationship between

his class and his inherited culture. How could Elias have avoided wishing to know the answers to two questions: why had 'Kantian' values, the philosophy of *homo clausus*, taken root so strongly in German *Kultur*, the culture of the German bourgeoisie? What part did that social class and that world view play in the violent disintegration of the German nation-state after World War I?

It is interesting to notice that another German textile manufacturer's son, Friedrich Engels, had been faced with a broadly similar intellectual challenge eighty years before. There is an obvious difference between the two cases, apart from the historical gap. This is that in the 1840s Engels was mainly concerned to bring about the overthrow of an unjust socio-political order whereas in the 1930s Elias was preoccupied with understanding the roots of a prevailing *dis*order that brought terror and misery.

Nevertheless, the similarities between the two men are intriguing. Like Elias, Engels came from a bourgeois background and set out to be a philosopher. Like Elias, Engels became deeply aware of violence and oppression in German life, and wanted to understand their causes and effects. Engels's strategy was to begin by looking at another society, similar enough to Germany to be relevant, different enough from Germany to be interesting. The point of adopting this methodology was that the counter-example would help him make sense of Germany. Elias followed a similar strategy, deliberately or not.

Britain and France were the obvious candidates for comparative treatment with Germany. Engels made a detour through British history with his *The Condition of the Working Class in England* (Engels 1969), which appeared in 1845. Elias made a different choice: 'I had an emotional preference for France, not for England . . . England I didn't like' (1994b, 19). *The Court Society*, written in 1933, and *The Civilizing Process*, completed in 1939, are both focused mainly on the case of French society. Although the second is about Europe as a whole, its source material is heavily, although by no means exclusively, based upon the French case.

In *The Court Society*, Elias shows that the development of French 'civility' was closely connected with the gradual eradication of localized violence from French society. The book was written in an atmosphere thick with the constant threat of street violence in German cities. Hitler is a large unspoken presence in the book, especially in Elias's comparison between absolutist kingship and charismatic leadership.

Elias argues that, unlike absolutist kingship, charismatic leadership is extraordinary and daring, creating and thriving upon social disorder. The charismatic leader's personal command is the basis of order and action. A leader such as Hitler draws a central group around him that acts vigorously on society, overthrowing old authorities and established practices. This opens up new channels of promotion for ambitious men and women from the masses. The willingness to take big risks and the ability to deliver excitement and success keep the leader strong even when he is 'riding on thin ice' (Elias 1983, 125).

Elias argues that Hitler thrived because he satisfied certain desires built into the personality type of the German bourgeoisie, whose habitus and self-image had been shaped by their politically subordinate situation within the *Kaiserreich*. In one respect the German bourgeoisie was like the French nobility: it was a beaten class – resentful, nostalgic, circumspect, and obedient.

At one level, *The Court Society* is a subtle analysis of how the figuration of court society inculcated a civilized habitus in the French nobility. At another level, less overt and perhaps less conscious, *The Court Society* is an evocation of *homo clausus*, the Kantian model of human existence that expressed itself in the ideology and behaviour of the German bourgeoisie.

In fact, although Elias does not make this point, his description of the French court is a sketch of *homo clausus* writ large. Seen in this light, the Sun King is the ruling 'I'. His courtiers play the role of the human consciousness. The well-guarded boundaries of the court are like the walls surrounding *homo clausus*. The country at large is reality 'outside', pressing at the gates but not directly apprehended by the courtiers (consciousness) 'inside.'

Elias hoped that just as the French Revolution swept away the court, so would a new 'Copernican revolution of . . . thought and feeling' (Elias 1991b, 56) eventually sweep away *homo clausus*. He wanted to help bring that revolution about by attacking Kantian philosophy.

The case of France provided Elias with empirical distance from German society. However, to make his new Copernican revolution he also needed theoretical distance from his old philosophical mentors, especially Kant. Engels had faced a similar problem a century before. He wanted to challenge the Christian and Hegelian values of his youth. Engels turned to the ideas of Karl Marx. Nearly a century later Elias turned to Sigmund Freud.

The distinctive appeal of Freud's ideas for Elias can be illustrated, briefly, by comparing Freud with his almost exact contemporary, Edmund Husserl, a philosopher who had been greatly influenced by Kant and Descartes.[11]

Husserl was the founder of phenomenology, which is a technique for discovering how human beings experience themselves, the natural world and other human beings. Phenomenology focuses on the solitary individual alone with his or her consciousness. The basic experimental technique is to 'unthink' all we take for granted about the lifeworld. A person who has 'unthought' in this way would be able to focus their mental attention solely on the way they perceive objects within 'pure' consciousness.

Elias had spent a brief period just after the war studying at Freiburg where Husserl taught. He concluded that Husserl had not 'unthought' enough. In particular, he had failed to 'unthink' modern philosophy's model of the isolated individual. As far as Elias was concerned, Freud's approach was more attractive. Freud refused to isolate a person's mind from his or her body and social relationships. Furthermore, like Goethe and Schiller, Freud was deeply interested in the conflict between passion and order within human beings.

Unlike Husserl, Freud did not spend time on the question of whether or not a real world truly exists outside our minds. Freud's approach was quite practical. He believed that people need accurate perceptions of the world so they can act effectively and stand a good chance of surviving. Unfortunately, conflicts within the psyche mean people often fail to see the world as it is. Therapy can help them readjust. That appealed to Elias, who wanted to create useful knowledge rather than engaging in metaphysical speculation.

Husserl's approach takes as its starting point what we all have in common with each other after the particular influence of a specific culture and history have been imagined away. By contrast, Freud was interested in showing why and how people are different from each other in their perceptions and behaviour. Freud's approach converged with Elias's own interest in exploring differences between societies (like France and Germany) and between different periods (like the eighth century AD and the mid-twentieth century).

This leads to a further point which is that the Freudian approach has a historical dimension. To explain what kind of person someone has become, you need to know about their past life, especially how they got on with their parents. In other words, the present is shaped by the past. Husserl paid little attention to history until his last writings, published in the late 1930s. For Elias, the historical dimension is central to sociology.

In *Civilization and its Discontents* (Freud 1994, first published 1930), Freud argues that social life is built upon constraint. People have to restrain their strong inclination for promiscuous sex and curb their violent urges. Society makes sure these 'thou shalt nots' are obeyed, turning the superego into a powerful force. Civilized life is comfortable in a material sense but men and women lose the pleasure they used to enjoy before their instincts were put in chains.

In a footnote to *The Civilizing Process*, Elias acknowledges 'how much this study owes to the discoveries of Freud and the psychoanalytical school' (Elias 1994a, 249). Elias accepted the ego–superego–id model but used it in his own way. Freud employed the model to account for a wide variety of neurotic symptoms all encountered in the early twentieth century. He traced their origins to particular types of family situation. By contrast, Elias wanted to explain differences between forms of behaviour and types of personality predominant (or 'normal') in successive historical periods. Above all, he wanted to know why German society had turned out differently from French society.

For Elias the problem was immediate and massive. German *Kultur* had not prevented the rise of Nazism. Nor had it placed any significant obstacle against Hitler's attacks on the universities, or his persecution of the Jews on the grounds that they were un-German and a threat to Aryan culture. The German bourgeoisie, guardians of *Kultur*, had failed to protect Jewish intellectuals. As a result, Elias – at once German, bourgeois, intellectual and Jew – had experienced a fundamental crisis of identity.

Writing *The Civilizing Process* was one way of coping with this desperate situation. He later commented that although 'at first the problem of civilization appeared to me as a completely personal problem', he came to realize the need to 'distance oneself sufficiently from the immediate situation' (1996, 444). This was true both physically and mentally. Both forms of distancing took him first to Switzerland, then to France in 1933.

As Elias struggled to survive in Paris, the argument of the book began to take shape. As he said in his preface, he wanted to 'help the reader to see the concepts of *Kultur* and *civilization* as less rigidly and self-evidently opposed' (Elias 1994a, xii). This phrasing suggests Elias had in mind, in particular, his German readers who were, indeed, very likely to see those concepts as not only opposed but also hierarchically ranked, with *Kultur* clearly superior.

Instead of joining the 'Kultur versus civilisation' argument, Elias steps back from it. In *The Civilizing Process* he provides an explanation for *why* the argument happened, *why* the German bourgeoisie erected the totem pole of *Kultur* for themselves and took to mocking the civilization they saw elsewhere, especially in France.

One crucial factor, Elias believes, is how the bourgeoisie developed in each society. In France the royal court at Versailles provided the bourgeoisie with a powerful model of behaviour and attitudes which it desperately wanted to imitate. The French bourgeoisie gradually infiltrated the court and picked up its patterns of thought, feeling and behaviour. As a result, by the time the bourgeoisie was able to elbow aside the aristocracy and became the dominant national class, it had developed a very high degree of self-confidence and self-control.

In other words, members of the French bourgeoisie acquired a civilized personality structure, one which they inherited, so to speak from a thoroughly pacified aristocratic ruling class which had long ago left behind habits of violence in public affairs. However, their German counterparts did not have the chance to go down this road. Unlike France, seventeenth- and eighteenth-century Germany had no centralized royal court providing a centre of 'good society'.

Germany became politically unified much later than France, not until well into the nineteenth century. When a prosperous and educated German urban-industrial bourgeoisie came on the scene, eager for power and social recognition, it did not find itself facing one powerful and supremely confident royal court as in France. Instead, its members went knocking at the doors of dozens of small, aristocratic courts, all competing with each other, in snobby provincial cities like Breslau.

The newcomers were mainly turned away with a sneer. Entry to polite upper-class social life was almost completely barred to most of the bourgeoisie. Local registers of lineage kept out social climbers with the smell of trade. It was very difficult to buy your way in. This situation had a very important consequence. This was that polite culture and the civilized habitus that went with it could not be smoothly transmitted from the established aristocratic class to wealthy bourgeois outsiders.

The German bourgeoisie was an isolated class without social poise or political confidence. When the German state unified in the mid-nineteenth century this happened through a series of wars carried out by a militaristic aristocracy. The Kaiser and his victorious generals used the same forceful means to impose discipline throughout the German Empire. According to Elias, the German psyche was deeply marked by this process. It made 'the drive-control of the individual . . . highly dependent on strong external state power. The emotional balance, the self-control of the individual, was endangered if this external power was lacking'.

Members of the German bourgeoisie were thoroughly cowed and, in response, they shut their eyes and ears to the harsh facts of power. They neglected the political and social skills needed to win influence and, instead, turned away 'from everything to do with the administration of the power monopolies'. Having been denied power, the German bourgeoisie grasped hold of education, high personal ideals and elevated knowledge. Bourgeois intellectuals created a distinctive class culture centred on the universities. They valued personal cultivation, the learning of the isolated scholar. This bourgeois culture was dominated by 'inwardness, and the elevation of spiritual and cultural achievements to a special place in the table of values' (1994a, 512–13).

Elias's own suffering, and his need to escape from the Germany he loved, was the result of a civilizing process that had produced 'too much' isolation and 'too little' interconnectedness in German society. In fact, the inward-turning German bourgeoisie was the embodiment of *homo clausus*. Elias's repeated, somewhat obsessive, attacks upon this philosophical concept are, to some extent, expressions of his anger at the political and moral failure of his own class.

Ironically, *The Civilizing Process* hardly mentions the period beyond 1918. It seems possible that in 1939 Elias was not yet ready or able to confront the contradiction between his youthful ideals and his adult experience, nor that between the culture of his class and the fate inscribed in his Jewishness. Towards the end of this book, he writes in a very sensitive way about 'the inner tension of the individual with himself' (497), and modern 'man's fear of himself, of being overcome by his affective impulses' (520). Elias knew that a 'danger zone' was entered 'if the individual cannot sufficiently restrain himself, if he touches sensitive spots, his own-shame frontier or the embarrassment-threshhold of others' (497). Inter-war Germany was Elias's own danger zone.

Rebirth of a Sociologist (1940–65)

In 1940 Norbert Elias was interned in a British camp for enemy aliens at Huyton. As we have already seen, in the midst of the primitive conditions at the camp Eric Wolf found 'Prof. Elias, drawing lines and crosses on a dirty piece of paper which served as a blackboard', explaining 'how a person is born into the world not as a pristine and isolated individual, but as a nexus in a social network' (Gleichmann et al. 1977, 30).

Elias's situation as an internee in a British prison camp expressed the four core elements of his identity. As a Jew, Elias had fled from Germany. As a bourgeois, his education, contacts and resources made flight possible. As a German, he was locked up in a British internment camp. As an intellectual, he taught his ideas even there.

The pain of Elias's journey from Breslau to Huyton, from a warm cocoon to a cold prison, must have been made desperately vivid when he heard during 1940 that his father had died at Breslau. Tragically, he learned this by letter from his mother, *en route* to Auschwitz where she was killed in 1941. Over forty years later, Elias could hardly bear to talk about this. He told an interviewer: 'I simply cannot get rid of the picture of my mother in a gas chamber. I cannot get over it'. He added: 'I should like to write about the whole Nazi episode, but so much has yet to be clarified' (1994b, 79).

Perhaps the matter needing to be 'clarified' was Elias's own emotional turmoil rather than the historical record. His sense of loss must have been enormous. While he gave all his energies to completing *The Civilizing Process*, in England during the late 1930s he knew 'the situation in Germany was getting worse and . . . was very afraid for [his] parents' (55). They refused to leave their homeland. In fact, his father braved the Nazi authorities to get the necessary permissions so that his son's book could be printed and published.

How could Elias not have made a close association between the writing of *The Civilizing Process* and the death of his parents? He may have even felt half-consciously that the first was achieved by the sacrifice of the second. Elias, perhaps trying to avoid more pain, 'believed for a while that it was time to forget the past' (Elias 1996, 429). It is not surprising he found it difficult to write about the Nazi episode. Nor that his published output during the two decades after 1940 was so meagre.

Elias's key works of the 1930s were almost completely unavailable for over thirty years. Furthermore, new work was very slow to appear. Elias never stopped working. However, he was very unwilling to let go of what he wrote. He imposed extremely high standards upon himself. Until the end of his life, manuscripts for publication had to be extracted under extreme duress.

During the first decade of these years of near-silence Elias worked as a part-time tutor in London. His strongest professional identity during these years was that of group therapist. Along with a small number of psycho-analysts, including S H Foulkes, a friend from Frankfurt days, Elias was a founding member of the Group Analytic Society. However, he eventually found a full-time job and with it a secure place in a new cocoon. This was the sociology department at Leicester University. Elias held a lecturing post there between 1954 and 1962, the year of his official retirement, and stayed on, with an increasing number of trips to the continent, for over a decade after that.[12]

In those days the department was a kind of court society, one whose department head, Ilya Neustadt, was deeply familiar with and sympathetic to the European Jewish background from which Elias came. Neustadt, originally from Odessa, was an expert on the work of Auguste Comte and well versed in French culture. Within this cocoon, as a feeling of security returned and self-confidence increased, Elias developed a fifth element of his identity, his sense of himself as a sociologist.

In fact, Elias did not *finally* decide sociology would be the chosen vehicle for his ideas until quite late in life. He had already turned away from it once before. As has been seen, Elias began as a student of philosophy after World War I. He rejected philosophy in favour of sociology during the 1920s but then found sociology deeply unsatisfactory during the late 1930s.

In *The Civilizing Process*, Elias dismissed psychology, history and sociology. He found that 'the psychologist thinks unhistorically' while 'the historian, preoccupied with what he calls facts, avoids psychological problems'. Elias added: 'The situation is little better with sociology. As far as it is concerned at all with historical problems, it accepts entirely the dividing line drawn by the historian between the seemingly immutable psychological structure of man and its different manifestations in the form of arts, ideas or whatever'. In other words, sociologists were unable to tackle questions relating to long-term processes of historical change in human psychological structure.

In the next sentence Elias called for the creation of 'a science that does not yet exist, historical psychology' or, better still, 'a historical social psychology' (1994b, 484). It was against this background that he undertook his work as a group therapist in London. However, after 1954 Elias's post at Leicester gave him a base from which he could, eventually, launch a new mission. This was the ambitious task of redefining sociology. As Elias came to see it, understanding the civilizing process in all its complex aspects was the key to coping with modernity. Sociology was to be the principal means of achieving that understanding.

The Late Flowering (1965–90)

As he approached then passed the Biblical three score years and ten in the late 1960s Elias was, in some sense, 'released'. After a quarter-century of virtual silence, Elias published a series of books and articles in English and other languages. Essays written and reworked over several years began to appear in print. *The Civilizing Process* was re-published. *The Court Society* saw the light of day at last. New books appeared, including *What is Sociology?* (1978), *The Loneliness of the Dying* (1985), *Time: An Essay* (1992), *The Symbol Theory* (1991) and, posthumously, *Mozart. Portrait of a Genius* (1993) and *The Germans* (1996).

There are several essays also; for example, on the emotions, consciousness, psychiatry, violence, state formation, communities, and the sociology
of knowledge, especially the sciences, including sociology itself.[13] However,
it was not until the late 1970s, over three decades after the trauma of 1940/
41, that Elias could bear to return in print or on a public platform to the
unresolved issue – why did inter-war Germany become such a violent and
repressive society? – that had been the main stimulus for his greatest work,
The Civilizing Process. These thoughts were collected, along with two
unpublished essays from the 1960s, in *The Germans* (1996), a book which
appeared the year before he died.

The Germans will be discussed at length in a later chapter. However, to
oversimplify a subtle work, within this book Elias conveys pity for the Jews,
irritation with the bourgeoisie and sorrow for Germany. The tragic heroes
of Elias's book are named in its title, and it is among them, the Germans,
rather than more narrowly among the German Jews, that Elias implicitly
places himself. 'I knew that I was German and a Jew' he declared in 1984
(Elias 1994b, 10). Both, but in that order. In *The Germans* Elias describes
the history and habitus of his people – the Germans – with all the com-
passion of a caring insider.

Conclusion

This chapter has been concerned with the relationship between Elias's life,
his central vision and his chief works. The intention has not been to give a
fully rounded account of a life and a person but rather to identify certain
tensions and conflicts in both that are relevant to his work. The main point
being made is that a central conflict existed between Elias's strong desire as
a young man to be a university professor, to be active at the heart of
German *Kultur*, and his experience of personal rejection at the hands of the
German bourgeoisie on the grounds that, as a Jew, he belonged to a group
tainted with ignoble 'civilized' traits.

It seems likely that the conflict between Elias's aspirations and his
experience at the hands of others appeared during adolescence as he read
his way into German literature.[14] Elias was able to study the problems of
Kultur and civilization with greater emotional detachment by focusing on
the French case and shifting his intellectual base away from Kantian
idealism to other traditions, including the work of Freud.

The conflict at the heart of Elias's identity was manageable as long he
was able to find cocoon-like environments providing a degree of protection.
He was torn away from his first cocoon, the family home at Breslau, by war
service in 1915. Heidelberg in the 1920s provided one more cocoon,
Leicester in the 1950s and 1960s yet another.

However, during the 1930s and early 1940s Elias was exposed to the full
fury of the conflict which flowed from being defined as unworthy by the
class and the nation to which he wished to belong. His forced separation

from Germany in 1933 was followed in the early 1940s by the loss of his parents. Elias's most creative period, leading to the writing of *The Court Society* and *The Civilizing Process*, came after he left the safe haven of Heidelberg in 1929 and before his parents' deaths.

To summarize, during the 1930s Elias's personal experience was of separation, discontinuity and violence. In his books he stressed interconnectedness, continuity and the increasingly stable control of violence. Elias's personal situation encouraged him to enquire into the nature and development of *Kultur* and civilization. In the course of this enquiry he discovered the civilizing process. Investigating that process and its complex ramifications became his life's work.

In the next two chapters, Elias will be compared with two other brilliant scholars of his generation: Hannah Arendt and Talcott Parsons.

Appendix: The Society of Individuals

This appendix summarizes an essay entitled 'The society of individuals' which was originally intended to appear in *The Civilizing Process*. In this essay, Elias sets out his theoretical understanding of the nature of social processes and the situation of human beings within social relationships. According to Elias, societies have a 'hidden order' (Elias 1991b, 13). We have our functions, our places, as part of a society. We may be forced to lose or change these functions and places but we cannot alter them at will. However, this order is not planned by anyone. We all keep society going by our thoughts and actions, like partners in a dance or players in an orchestra, but we do not invent the dance or the melody. Society is not a separate 'substance' weighing down upon individuals from outside. It consists of the relationships among those very individuals.[1] We depend upon each other. We belong to networks and chains of interdependence relationships. A human being cannot exist outside of these relationships.

Society's order, its tensions and constraints, and the openings for change it offers all reside within those relationships between individuals, in other words within networks or figurations. What happens within a figuration is closely related to the psychic make-up, the tensions and constraints, and the openings for change that reside within the very individuals who are part of it.

'The individual is not a beginning and his relations to other people have no beginnings' (32). When we are born we are plunged, so to speak, into the middle of things. We become part of a group with distinctive functions and interests, related in particular ways to other groups, and with a specific pattern of relationship among its own members. What kind of person we become is influenced by the historical era we are born into, the group to which we belong, and our position within that group. 'Human beings are part of a natural order and of a social order' (40).

As a result of its particular evolution, our physiological and biological constitution has left us partly 'open', unfinished, unprogrammed. It also gives us the ability to make a wide range of sounds and facial expressions. We can make gestures, communicate meaning. Within these biological limits, we are malleable and adaptable. We need to undergo social moulding in order to become functioning persons. There is no pre-ordained plan which prescribes how individuals and societies should develop. The 'society of individuals' is 'simply there – as purposeless really as the stars which together form a solar system, or solar systems which form a Milky Way. And this purposeless existence of individuals in society with each other is the material, the basic fabric into which people weave the varying figures of their purposes' (10).

From the group we learn a specific language and way of speech. We acquire a particular pattern of psychical self-control, a distinctive emotional make-up. As we grow up into adulthood, we obtain a personal past and take into ourselves the past of the group. Our personal habits of speech and facial expressions make each of us recognizable as a unique individual. As more things occur within ourselves and within our relationships, our make-up undergoes further change. This process of individualization cannot occur outside social relationships. People learn to say 'I' at the same time as they learn to say 'we'.[13]

As societies become more complex, the number of specialized functions increase. These typically include economic, military, religious, political and many other occupations. As the structure of communal life becomes more differentiated, so does the human psyche. The ego and superego become more distinct from the id, which expresses instinctual drives. Each of these psychic functions is directed at something else. Their object may be within the psyche, as when the ego tries to control the id or is in turn subject to the influence of the superego which typically embodies social standards of personal behaviour.

Psychic functions may be directed to the network of social relationships to which the person belongs, perhaps taking the form of aggression or sexual desire. Or they may be directed to the natural world, for example in the hunt for food or the pursuit of leisure. The instincts and controls are functions which act within relationships. The psyche is 'the structure formed by these relation-functions' (35). The individual person is the structure formed through the social relationships to which he or she belongs by virtue of the functions he or she carries out within the group. The group is the structure formed by the inter-group relationships to which it belongs by virtue of the functions it carries out within society.

In more complex societies monopolies of economic resources and physical force come into being. As people try to ensure their own survival and manoeuvre for advantage, the superego strengthens and instinct is regulated by foresight. Groups within societies become more tightly bound together. They are interdependent but they also compete. As tensions between them increase, these 'network forces' result in social change which 'can follow a very definite order and direction over many generations' (45). The civilizing process is one example.

Notes

1 Elias developed these ideas in an essay originally intended to be part of *The Civilizing Process* but later published as the first chapter in his book called *The Society of Individuals* (Elias 1991a). For a summary see the appendix at the end of this chapter.

2 Three useful introductory guides to Elias's work are Fletcher 1997; Krieken 1998; Mennell 1998.

3 Late in life Elias commented: 'I should always have liked to live in a college, but it was never offered to me in England' (Elias 1994b, 74).

4 See Elias 1983, 268–76.

5 See the first chapter of *The Civilizing Process*.

6 See Elias 1991e.

7 This is restricted to sources published in English. The main source is Elias 1994b.

8 See Hackeschmidt 1995; Hackeschmidt 1997.

9 See Elias 1994b, 85.

10 Perhaps Kant's personal experience in this setting influenced his philosophical approach since, according to him, we cannot know 'things-in-themselves' in the 'real' world outside the self. However, Kant added, our senses do receive impressions from this outside world which our minds synthesize and organize. We have the capacity to interpret these phenomena; in other words, we can use our reason in an independent and critical way to make sense of our perceptions of the world 'outside'.

11 On Husserl, see, for example, Smith and Woodruff Smith 1995.

12 See Brown 1987.

13 See the bibliography for examples.

14 Did Elias, perhaps, sometimes have feelings similar to those of James Baldwin, the Afro-American novelist, who once commented that although he enjoyed westerns with their exciting contests between brave cowboys and wicked indians, he gradually came to realize that he was one of the indians?

PART 2

THE WIDER DEBATE

3

ARENDT AND ELIAS

Modernity: for Better or Worse?

This chapter takes us immediately into a controversial issue, which is the directionality of modernity. The idea of 'modernity' implies dynamism, movement in an identifiable direction. However, is this movement *away from* a more desirable condition or *towards* a more desirable condition? Theorists are divided on the matter.

Hannah Arendt and Michel Foucault[1] take the former position. They think modernity is making things worse. Their criteria of judgement are deeply influenced by a perception that they share, although with different emphases. They both believe that classical Greece and Rome was an epoch when the citizen was expected to be able to exercise rational self-control and take responsibility for his actions under conditions of relatively high autonomy.[2] They see this as preferable to the situation in modern societies where, in their view, human thought and behaviour are largely monitored and directed by bureaucrats, scientists and professionals.

By contrast, Norbert Elias and Jürgen Habermas take the latter position. They both see the possibility of a 'better' society developing out of elements already present within the modern epoch. Each accords a key role to learning processes within society. Habermas locates this process in the spheres of morality and law, Elias relates it to the spread of sociological knowledge.[3]

The debate between Habermas and Foucault is well known.[4] Far less attention has been paid to conflicts and convergences between the theoretical positions and empirical analyses produced by Elias and Arendt. These are the subject of this chapter. In fact, Elias and Arendt did not discuss each other's work in print. As has already been noted, when they met at Heidelberg in the late 1920s Elias concluded that Arendt was 'on entirely the wrong track'. He rejected her philosophical approach.

Going beyond Particularities

Arendt, Heidegger's pupil, was concerned above all with the advantages and disadvantages of different ways of being in the world. The Greek *agora* and the Nazi concentration camp provided working models of types of human society at both ends of the range. In such cases, Arendt tried to penetrate beyond the historical evidence in order to ascertain the potential for creativity or destructiveness that would be realized if the structural principles implicit in such institutions were implemented to the full.[5]

Like Arendt, Elias wanted to find his way beyond particularities to something more general but he pursued a different strategy. Arendt was mainly interested in the relationship between specific human capacities (e.g. the capacity for meaningful action) and different conditions of the web of relationships within which people and things are located (such as, to take two extreme cases, the Greek *agora* or the concentration camp). By contrast, Elias was primarily concerned with identifying and explaining the patterns embodied in empirical generalizations relating to different types of society at different epochs.

As Elias put it: 'beyond a certain point in the accumulation of material facts, historiography enters the phase when it ought to be no longer satisfied with the collection of further particulars and the description of those already assembled, but should be concerned with those problems that facilitate penetration of the underlying regularities by which people in a certain society are bound over and over again to particular patterns of conduct and to very specific functional chains . . . and by which these relationships change in a very specific direction'. At this stage of investigation the object is to identify 'the structure within the entirety of its interdependencies' (Elias 1994a, 488).

Elias's strategy, then, was to look for empirical evidence of regularities within social processes such as the development or breakdown of stable power monopolies. He regarded sociological analysis of this kind as infinitely superior to philosophy of any kind. Like his doctoral supervisor, Richard Honigswald, Elias found 'Heidegger and existentialism in general . . . not worth discussing, and he had difficulty concealing his contempt for such inexact modes of thinking' (Elias 1994b, 92).

Despite these differences, Elias and Arendt underwent similar experiences, held similar preferences about the kind of society to which they wanted to belong, and were driven by similar feelings of disappointment with the class and culture into which they had been born. Norbert Elias and Hannah Arendt both pursued academic careers during the Weimar Republic, and, like many Jews, fled from Germany in 1933 when Hitler came to power. Elias and Arendt both treated the Nazi episode as a major symptom of the breakdown of civilization.[6] They both wanted to understand how this had come about and how, if possible, the situation could be improved.

The major difference between them is as follows. Elias treated Nazism as an aberration within European development, flowing from certain highly peculiar features of German society and history. Arendt, however, regarded it as prototypical of modernity, an advance warning of the dark future that probably lay in store for most people within modern societies.

There is a fascinating mixture of similarities and differences in the approaches taken by these two writers and not just in respect of their approaches to philosophy and sociology, respectively. As German Jews, they reacted in very different ways to the personal challenge posed by the rise of Nazism. However, one thing they definitely had in common. As 'first generation' Jewish intellectuals Elias and Arendt both responded very positively to the open and relaxed cultural atmosphere of university life, especially at Heidelberg whose 'cosmopolitan and liberal . . . spirit [was] known throughout Germany to be tolerant of innovation and experiment' (Young-Bruehl 1982, 66).

Natality and Civility

Before exploring the interplay between their lives and work in more detail, I want to illustrate the intriguing pattern of opposition and convergence in their ideas. This will be done by identifying a central concept in the work of each writer and noticing that these ideas, developed independently of each other, are both opposite and complementary. The two ideas are civility, or 'civilized conduct' (Elias 1994a, 505), the code of restrained and deliberate behaviour associated with civilized personalities, and *natality*, Arendt's term for creative action in the public sphere.

To begin with civility, Elias believed that the dynamics of the social network or figuration into which people were born had a profound effect on the structure of their personalities. More specifically, he thought that conditions of relative political stability were essential for the development of civilized personalities habituated to the exercise of self-control, foresight and rational calculation.

By contrast, Arendt thought that it was when political order broke down, for example during revolutions, that natality, the 'human capacity of beginning something new' (Arendt 1958a, 9), came into its own. In *On Revolution* (Arendt 1963a), Arendt points out that people's councils organised by local activists appeared spontaneously as part of a number of revolutionary uprisings: for example, during the American revolution, in France during 1789, 1848 and 1871, in Russia during 1905 and 1917, in Germany during 1919 and finally in Hungary during 1956.

These people's councils were, in Arendt's view, 'spaces of freedom' (268). They gave ordinary men and women the opportunity to act meaningfully in the public sphere. Arendt compares the councils to 'islands in a sea or . . . oases in a desert' (279). They were usually reclaimed by the desert or the ocean, overwhelmed by more powerful forces.

The people's councils play a role in Arendt's vision[7] which in some ways corresponds to the part played by early feudal courts in Elias's theory of civilizing processes. To be more specific, Elias shows that in early medieval Europe, in a quite unplanned way, one feudal dynasty or another was able, intermittently, to seize the opportunity offered by a particular balance of military forces to claim overlordship of a substantial territory. Once a relatively stable power monopoly was established within a region, a dynastic court would be established as a centre of administration and display.

In Elias's view, such courts were vital arenas for the gradual development of civilized behaviour, just as people's councils were crucial for nurturing the habits of action in the public sphere, according to Arendt. In most cases, the councils, like the courts, were short-lived. Arendt and Elias were both aware of the numerous false starts littered throughout history.

Ironically, the revolution which held most promise in Arendt's view, the American revolution of 1776, was one in which control was held for a substantial period by patricians such as Jefferson who were, to use Elias's terminology, highly civilized.[8] This is an important point of convergence between Elias and Arendt. Natality and civility are, in fact, *both* important ingredients for one outcome valued highly by Elias and by Arendt which will now be discussed.

As already mentioned, both Elias and Arendt attach great importance to pacified, agonistic arenas of discourse and action. This is evident from Elias's study of the absolutist court in *The Court Society*, and also in his statement in *The Germans* that 'a conflict-free society may appear to be the very pinnacle of rationality, but it is also a society of the silence of the tomb, of the most extreme emotional coldness and utter boredom – a society, moreover, without any dynamic' (Elias 1996, 292–3).

Elias clearly favoured a political 'regime of the parliamentary type', one which encouraged non-violent forms of struggle fought out in the form of discussion or 'word duels'. In such a setting, conflicts would be conducted according to clear rules and a high degree of self-discipline. This recalls Arendt's admiration for the Greek *polis*, a sphere of action above the realm of 'sheer violence [which] is mute, and . . . can never be great' (Arendt 1958a, 26). She explored this political form in the early chapters of *The Human Condition* (Arendt 1958a).

In *Rahel Varnhagen* (Arendt 1958b), Arendt explored yet another setting for peaceful competition, the Enlightenment salon. In all these cases – court, salon, *polis* and parliament – the figurations concerned are sufficiently centralized and integrated for stable human interaction to be possible. However, at the same time, they are not so completely centralized as to deprive people of the chance to express their capacity to act. Furthermore, these settings are not so completely integrated as to remove the psychological and political space for doing and imagining things differently.

Arendt's positive evaluation of these agonistic arenas is manifest and frequently asserted. Elias's similar evaluation is latent and breaks surface only occasionally. However, there is clear convergence between the two writers on this matter.

At this point it is worth quoting Elias's comment that during the late 1920s 'Heidelberg was more than ever before a place where one could match one's strength with one's contemporaries and either be reassured or defeated in friendly rivalry with equally intelligent people' (Elias 1994b, 36). This city at that time gave both Elias and Arendt practical experience of the kind of non-violent but agonistic setting they both subsequently valued highly. They each spent half a decade in this environment before the full blast of Nazi repression changed their lives.

The disintegration of German society and the rise of Hitler set the intellectual agenda for them both, even though they approached this agenda in different ways. As has already been noticed, they both thought that Nazism and the Holocaust were symptoms of the breakdown of civilization. However, the ways Elias and Arendt approached these problems will be more understandable if we first consider some aspects of their lives in Imperial Germany and during the Weimar period. This will be done in the second part of this chapter.

The third part will consist of a comparison of the arguments presented by Arendt and Elias, respectively, in *The Origins of Totalitarianism* (Arendt 1973) and *The Germans* (Elias 1996). The final part of the chapter will argue that Elias and Arendt have similar ideals of how a 'civilized' society 'should' be but differ in their analyses of the master trends within modernity. However, taken together, their analyses provide the elements of a much broader and more comprehensive understanding of 'decivilizing' processes than is provided by *The Germans* alone.

Outsiders and Pariahs

Arendt was born in 1906 in Königsberg,[9] like Breslau in the eastern part of the German Empire. She and Elias both came from well-off Jewish families, although the Arendt family was much richer. As has been seen, Elias's father was a medium-sized textile manufacturer.[10] Arendt's maternal grandfather, a tea trader, owned the largest firm in Königsberg, itself 'the most important tea-trading centre on the continent' (Young-Bruehl 1982, 6).

Elias's parent were solid members of the commercial middle class. By contrast, the household in which Hannah Arendt was brought up was professional rather than commercial. Her father, who died when she was seven, was a graduate engineer. Her mother had studied French and music in Paris.[11] Both parents were strong socialists. Arendt's mother had welcomed the 1919 uprising in Berlin.[12]

As the daughter of a prosperous professional couple with left-wing leanings, Arendt was not strongly pulled in her youth towards either Zionism or the values of the Imperial German establishment. Elias, by contrast, felt pressures in both directions. For example, his father, to whom he felt very close, 'was a patriot'.[13] As a child, Elias was not impressed by the Kaiser but 'loved Germany very much' (Elias 1994b, 6, 10–11, 18). He developed 'an enormous admiration for the German landscape'.[14] Elias seems to have relished both aspects of his identity. He accepted that he was both 'a German and a Jew [and] . . . the two things were not competing in any way'.

Jörg Hackeschmidt has recently shown that Elias joined the Zionist youth movement called *Blau-Weiß* before World War I and 'was much more deeply involved in the intellectual debates of this Zionist *Jugendbund* and its "*bündisch*" projects than he admitted in later life' (Hackeschmidt 1995, 4). Elias did later recall that when he was at Breslau University after World War I he joined a Jewish student association.

However, joining this association was not an expression of Jewishness in opposition to Germanness or to the culture of the imperial establishment. On the contrary, the Jewish association was 'more or less modelled' on the duelling societies of well-born Germans.[15] Elias became one of its first officers.[16] In *The Germans*, Elias explores the important part played by the student duelling societies in forming the culture and habitus of the Imperial German establishment.[17] He participated in that culture, at least vicariously.

Elias went to Heidelberg in the late 1920s to build an academic career for himself in sociology and began working with Alfred Weber and Karl Mannheim.[18] Hannah Arendt also spent the late 1920s in Heidelberg. Nine years younger than Elias, she was only a year or so behind him in terms of academic career by that time. Before coming to Heidelberg she had been at Marburg for a year with Martin Heidegger, then spent a semester at Freiburg with Edmund Husserl.

By the late-1920s, Elias and Arendt were both disillusioned with the inward-looking tradition of *Kultur* and *Bildung*. As has been seen, the liberal wing of the German bourgeoisie believed in self-cultivation through literature and philosophy. Pride in *Kultur* compensated members of this class for their political weakness within the German state. Ironically, it also ensured that they were not disposed to acquire the particular knowledge and skills needed to remedy this weakness, including the social graces and polished etiquette which gave access to the courts of the powerful.

Elias and Arendt had both been shocked out of their belief in *Kultur* at the age of eighteen. In Elias's case, the key event was World War I. For Arendt, it was her affair with Martin Heidegger, the 'hidden king [who] reigned in the realm of thinking' (Arendt 1971, 51). Elias was called up in 1915 and served in the front line. The German public had been told the war was a battle to defend German *Kultur* against the base materialistic values of French, British and American 'civilization'. However, widespread disillusionment flowed from the war's futility and the demoralizing defeat of 1918.

As has been seen, Elias's own response was to turn to the study of philosophy. By the time he took his doctorate in 1924 he was seriously at odds with the neo-Kantian orthodoxy which lay at the heart of *Kultur* as an intellectual system. He felt that a universalistic *a priori* approach gave no guidance about the nature of social reality or how it changed over time. Meanwhile, at Marburg in 1924 and 1925, Arendt was learning from Heidegger that all Western philosophy since Socrates was wordy metaphysics obscuring the true character of being.

Disillusioned with the worldview they had inherited, Elias and Arendt both turned to the immediately pressing task of making intellectual sense of the situation of Jews in German society, especially educated middle-class Jews such as themselves. Elias's approach to this question reflected the practical challenges directly confronting him in view of his background and career aspirations.

Elias very much wanted to join the German establishment as a university professor. However, at an early age he had become aware that his Jewishness was a serious obstacle. The question of how relations between established and outsider groups developed was therefore a very practical matter for him. During the late 1920s Elias seemed to be on an upward trajectory as an outsider seeking acceptance by the academic establishment. At Heidelberg he regarded himself as a full member of a very congenial, open, competitive society of equals.

Later, in *The Civilizing Process*, Elias argued that it was quite normal for rising outsider groups to benefit from the 'clear tendency for standards of living and conduct to be equalized and contrasts levelled out' (Elias 1994a, 507). However, although this process had seemed to be underway in Heidelberg, Elias found a very different situation when he went to work at Frankfurt during the early 1930s.

By this time Jews were being violently excluded from German life. Elias's reaction was to stand back from the situation, to search for a point of comparison. As we have seen, he turned to the case of France, a society in which, as Elias saw it, relations between established and outsider groups had developed more continuously in the direction of increasing equalization and inclusiveness. He studied the processes and figurations which intertwined the fates of the French monarchy, aristocracy and bourgeoisie during the seventeenth and eighteenth centuries. This was the subject of his *Habilitationsschrift*, completed in 1933.

During the early 1930s Arendt was in Berlin. She had experienced exclusion in a more direct and personal way than Elias. Heidegger had ended their physical relationship in 1928. Shortly afterwards, he had become a full professor at Freiburg University. By 1933 he was rector of Freiburg and in that year he joined the Nazi party. These events may have some bearing on that fact that Arendt's research topic was Rahel Varnhagen, a woman who had an unhappy affair with a German aristocrat.

Rahel Varnhagen, a prominent female member of salon society in Berlin during the late eighteenth and early nineteenth centuries, was, like Arendt, an intellectual Jewish woman from a bourgeois background. Like Arendt, she came to feel betrayed by a powerful male Gentile establishment.[19] Rahel's response, after much suffering, was to embrace her own Jewishness wholeheartedly, encouraged by the poet Heine, a fellow 'galley slave'.

Arendt set out 'to narrate the story of Rahel's life as she herself might have told it' (Arendt 1958b, xv). Like Elias, Arendt looked for a comparable situation in order to make sense of her own. However, unlike Elias, who sought detachment from the emotions aroused by his personal predicament, Arendt used comparison as a way to sharpen self-consciousness of the feelings aroused by her own involvement in a highly troubled situation. She speculated on the significance of such feelings – for example, how they related to the sense of personal identity, and the experience of powerlessness as opposed to being able to impose one's will.

Elias's strategy was to explore 'outwards', so to speak, along the chains and networks of human interdependence in order to discover how, in certain circumstances, these figurations shaped 'civilized' personalities. By contrast, Arendt moved 'inwards', to discover resources for resisting the *persona* German society was forcing on her as a Jew.

Instead of thinking, as Elias did, in terms of the long-term dynamics of established-outsider relations, Arendt focused on the capacity of each Jewish outsider to choose, so she believed, between being either a *conscious pariah*, actively resisting the society which denigrates them, or a *parvenu* seeking assimilation within that society.[20] Arendt wanted to understand the potentiality for human action to create meaning, and the mental and social conditions which shaped the expression of this potential.

To summarize the difference between them: Elias's object was to obtain knowledge of social processes in order to help prevent the worst evils they might produce. In his view, the social processes which shape the human figurations in which we participate, the nations, classes, ethnic groups and so on, have regularities which are blind and unplanned. However, if we increase our knowledge of those processes by detached observation and reasoning, we can respond in a realistic way and even make limited interventions to change how the processes occur.

By contrast, Arendt believed that when confronted with a hostile world you always had the option of acting so as to help create alternative meanings, standards and realities. At best, those actions took place within a web of social relationships among people able and willing to share the continuing task of creating and maintaining a common world.[21]

How did Arendt and Elias react to the rise of Hitler? Elias's visit to a Nazi rally disguised as an aristocrat, his timely sweep of the sociology department, clearing out all incriminating material, and his later brush with the SS have already been recounted.[22] At about that time Hannah Arendt was arrested by the Nazi authorities in Berlin. She had been working in the Prussian State Library gathering evidence about anti-Semitic attitudes in German business and professional life. This was done for the German Zionist Organization which she had very recently joined. Arendt was taken to the police headquarters at Alexanderplatz, interrogated and imprisoned for eight days. The police searched her flat and poured over her notebooks.

Not long before, Arendt's flat had been a hiding place for left-wing enemies of the regime but, fortunately, it was empty at the time. She was also lucky that the person in charge of her case was very inexperienced and unsure what to do. He let her go.[23] By the autumn of 1933 she, like Elias, was in Paris.[24] In one key respect, Elias and Arendt behaved quite differently from each other. While Elias was busy destroying all compromising material and doing his best to protect himself and his colleagues, Arendt deliberately took risks on others' behalf and acted so as to attract police attention. Elias tried in all he did to keep his profile low but Arendt headed straight for the point of danger.

These two sets of incidents indicate the different orientations of Elias and Arendt. For his part, Elias was quite prepared to take carefully calculated risks. He exploited any opportunities that came his way to get knowledge and insight about what was happening to German society around him. To give another instance, in 1932 Elias attended a meeting at the Frankfurt *Gewerkschaftshaus*.[25] He asked the workers there what preparations they had made against a possible armed attack. By listening to the discussion he learned some of the reasons why the right was so successful against the trade unionists. The 'picture which emerged' pointed to 'some of the structural characteristics of Hitler's victory which could easily be overlooked', not least the workers' conviction that, in spite of everything, 'reason' would prevail (Elias 1996, 221).

Norbert Elias believed his own role was not to get directly involved in the struggle but rather to obtain sociological knowledge about civilizing processes, decivilizing processes and the extent to which rational human intervention might be able to influence them. As he wrote in at the end of *The Civilizing Process*, although 'civilization' is 'set in motion blindly, and kept in motion by the autonomous dynamics of a web of relationships, . . . it is by no means impossible that we can make out of it something more "reasonable," something that functions better in terms of our needs and purposes'. He envisaged that in the future there might be 'greater scope for planned intervention into both the social and the individual structures[26] – intervention based on a growing knowledge of the unplanned dynamics of these structures' (Elias 1994a, 445).

Elias decided that the 'great breakdown of civilized behaviour' in Germany could only be understood 'if, as a social scientist, one could distance oneself sufficiently from the immediate situation'. As has been seen, distancing meant looking at another society, France, to get a comparative viewpoint. It also meant carrying out historical research on medieval and early modern Europe to trace how relatively stable and controlled societies and personality structures came into being.

Elias believed that 'one cannot understand the *breakdown* of civilized behaviour as long as one cannot understand and explain how civilized behaviour and feeling came to be *constructed and developed* in European societies in the first place' (Elias 1996, 444–5; emphasis added). He spent the rest of the 1930s carrying out the first part of this programme. *The Civilizing Process* (Elias 1994a) appeared in 1939. It was intended to prepare the ground for a more detailed analysis of the German case. As it turned out, half a century passed before Elias completed that part of the programme. *The Germans* (Elias 1996) was finally published in 1989.

The significance of the events of 1933 was quite different for Arendt. As she later put it, she decided that '"When one is attacked as a Jew, one must defend oneself *as a Jew*." Not as a German, not as a world-citizen, not as an upholder of the Rights of Man' (quoted in Young-Bruehl 1982, 109; emphasis in original). She took positive action as a conscious pariah working against her oppressor. To borrow Albert Hirschman's terminology in his book *Exit, Voice and Loyalty*, Arendt turned her 'exit' into a positive rejection of German society. She withdrew 'loyalty' from Germany and transferred it to the Zionist project. Finally, she exercised 'voice' very loudly both against Germany and in favour of her version of Zionism.

Matters were much more complex for Elias. He found that being German and being Jewish were in equal measure parts of his social identity, his self-image and his *habitus*. They were equally inalienable. When he was asked, fifty years later, whether he saw himself as a Jew, Elias replied: 'Yes – that is, I am a Jew, a German Jew. In my whole make-up and also in my appearance. The way you put the question, it sounds as if I had a choice . . . I am not a Jew because I want to be but because I am'. The questioner then asked if Elias was 'a German in the same way'. He answered: 'A German Jew, that is correct' (Elias 1994b, 79).[27]

Unlike Arendt, Elias experienced exit from Germany as a traumatic rupture of his *persona*. His life goal, to be a German university professor, was put beyond his reach. He was separated from Germany, a country to which he retained a deep loyalty. He had to cope with his parents' deaths, his mother a concentration camp victim. One consequence of these successive shocks was that Elias lost his voice, so to speak, for two decades after the appearance of *The Civilizing Process* in 1939, years during which he published hardly anything

Why the Germans? Why the Jews?

Elias and Arendt responded to the crises of the 1930s and early 1940s by moving towards opposite poles of the involvement–detachment continuum.[28] Their trajectories are starkly diverging. In the early 1930s, while Arendt was researching the personal dilemmas of a middle-class Jewish female in late eighteenth-century Berlin, Elias was exploring the seventeenth-century French court. By the late 1930s, while Arendt was helping Jewish refugees in Paris, Elias was in the British Museum reading about table manners in early modern Europe. In 1941, while Arendt was campaigning for the formation of a Jewish army, Elias was entering his long period of near-silence.[29]

Elias did not turn back to the question of Germany till the early 1960s and then only gradually. Detachment from this particular issue became extreme, a way to avoid touching a sore place, a means of psychological self-protection. Arendt's situation was different. Whereas Elias had to overcome extreme detachment to write about Germany in the 1930s, Arendt had to pull back from her stance of intense involvement in order to be able to do the same thing. Totalitarianism was an enemy she 'felt engaged to destroy'.[30]

In both *The Origins of Totalitarianism* and *The Germans* a balance between involvement and detachment is achieved. However, the different directions from which the authors have travelled to achieve this balance is evident in the texts. Arendt self-consciously adopts the role of all-seeing interpreter so as to maintain distance from issues where her previous inclination has been to act, to intervene, to try to make a difference. Equally self-consciously, Elias reminds the reader that he was there, he took part, he experienced the tensions, as if he is manipulating his own imagination, deliberately plunging himself into scenes he would rather forget.

Arendt's book is written from 'above' the events it analyses. It conveys an atmosphere of deep and settled moral certainty. Arendt's underlying anger is kept under rigorous control, never allowed to disrupt or displace the argument. By contrast, Elias's book is written by someone reporting from 'within' a situation he finds deeply troubling. His sorrow and anxiety keep breaking through: for example, when he laments for 'poor, self-destructive Germany' (433), or when he remembers 'my schoolfellow, Bernhard Schottländer, a completely unathletic, highly intelligent person, who, with his thick spectacles, looked like a young scholar even as a first former, and who tended to communism after reading Marx, and whose corpse, if I remember rightly, was found in the Breslau city moat, tied up with barbed wire' (Elias 1996, 187).

It will be argued here that the perspectives from which Elias and Arendt tried to make sense of Nazism and the Holocaust are complementary. Each adds a dimension that is missing from the other. With some modifications, *The Origins of Totalitarianism* and *The Germans* can be read as if they are two volumes of the same book. At the centre of both books there are three themes: the brutalization of the bourgeoisie; the destruction of the nation state; and the social and political effects of territorial expansion linked to ethnic or national aggrandisement. The main difference is that while Elias focuses on Germany, Arendt gives her analysis a European and colonial context.

While Elias is concerned above all with social processes in Germany that created the 'space' for Nazism and the Holocaust, Arendt is concerned with the processes that went on within that 'space'.[31] More specifically, the two issues Arendt regards as most problematic are: firstly, why did Jews became victims of the Nazis? and secondly, how did genocide fit into the rationale and *modus operandi* of totalitarian domination?

By contrast, Elias largely takes it for granted that Jews were an outsider group and high on the list of potential victims. He treats genocide as a particularly horrific instance of the more general category of irrational, unrealistic and emotion-laden behaviour. These particular issues are not, in fact, his main concern. The question he is most concerned with is what aspects of German society gave the Nazi movement its moment of opportunity.

The two books are written from perspectives informed by two different interests, expressed between the lines, so to speak. As far as Elias was concerned, Nazism was part of a highly painful disturbance *within* 'his' society. For Arendt Nazism was a highly threatening movement directed *against* 'her' people.[32] Arendt asks: why the Jews? For Elias, the question is: why Germany?

The Germans

In *The Germans*, Norbert Elias repeatedly emphasizes the peculiarity of German state-formation and the national *habitus* which resulted from it.[33] The comparison, sometimes implicit, sometimes explicit, is with France, Britain, the Netherlands and other European nations. Elias stresses Germany's special characteristics. For example, the German-speaking people were, geographically, in between two other competing language groups fighting for position within the European landmass. Unlike the tribes whose language were derived from Latin and those to the east who spoke Slavonic languages, the Germans were always fighting on two fronts, living in a constant atmosphere of threat and aggression.

Furthermore, the German (Holy Roman) Empire underwent progressive decline during the early modern period, especially the seventeenth century, while Germany's neighbours such as France, England and Sweden became more tightly integrated absolutist monarchies. In other words, Germans lived 'in the shadow of a greater past' (Elias 1996, 4). The long trajectory of decline was broken by the military and diplomatic manoeuvres of the Hohenzollern monarchy. These culminated in the German Empire, founded in 1871, but this brief reversal of fortune ended in the defeat of 1918, a disaster repeated in 1945.

A further peculiarity is that, unlike France or Britain, German state-formation was plagued by breaks and discontinuities. This unhappy past shaped the Germans' self-image, their 'we-ideal' (137). The German psyche was characterized by unhappiness, self-pity, the wish for revenge, and a 'yearning for the spectacular' (326).[34] German people were deeply discontented with their political weakness and insecurity. They had a strong but unrealistic wish to see their medieval greatness restored, even at a high cost to themselves. Their songs harped on about 'heroic death' (333).

Finally, relations between the aristocracy and bourgeoisie in Germany followed a course quite different from France. As has already been seen, in Germany there was no socially confident model-setting court at the national level, as in absolutist France, where aristocratic and bourgeois interests were equally powerful, and ambitious members of the bourgeoisie could gradually infiltrate into the nobility. Germany's warrior nobility was pacified and civilized to a much lesser degree than the French equivalent schooled in flattery and intrigue at the Versailles court.

Local courts throughout Germany were contemptuous of trade and rigorously excluded the bourgeoisie. During the eighteenth and early nineteenth century, part of the bourgeoisie responded by developing a liberal ethos linked to an idealistic German nationalism. Ironically, a unified Germany was delivered in 1871 not through a nationalist uprising of 'the people' but by the military efforts of the aristocratic old guard, most of whom found Goethe contemptible and Kant unreadable.

This situation split the bourgeoisie. A minority, which included Max Weber's circle and many Jews, clung to the neo-Kantian tradition of *Kultur* and *Bildung*. However, most of the German bourgeoisie transferred their loyalty to the militaristic values of the aristocracy. They imbibed these values in a coarsened form by becoming members of student duelling societies. For the socially ambitious a scar on the cheek became a distinct social asset. As Elias put it, the bourgeoisie was moving from the social and moral world that produced Kant to the world that shaped Nietzsche: from the categorical imperative to '"virtue free of moral self-righteousness"' (Elias 1996, 119).[35]

Membership of student 'fighting fraternities' gave an *entrée* to at least the fringes of the imperial establishment. The *satisfaktionsfähige Gesellschaft*[36] joined together all sections of that establishment from the court in Berlin to 'good society' in university towns like Marburg. It imposed a code of strict hierarchy, discipline, violence and cruelty.[37] Its pitiless habitus was inculcated through the rituals surrounding drinking bouts, duelling contests, and sexual liaisons.[38]

Elias sums up the dominant code of values as follows: 'Adult life is a constant war of all against all. One has to be a tough customer to win through in this struggle. The untamed warrior ethos comes to life here once again in a bourgeoisified version . . . The harshness of human relationships which finds expression in the use of physical violence, in people being wounded or if need be killed by other people, spreads like an infection even to those areas where physical fights do not occur at all' (108–9). Later, he adds: 'Underlying both the training provided within the student fighting fraternities and the life as a member of the imperial upper classes at which it was aimed is an implicit picture of human social life as a struggle of all against all which was almost Hobbesian in character' (112).

In the *Kaiserreich*, the military establishment regarded itself as 'the real Germany' (69), as opposed to the mass of the people.[39] However, the domination of this establishment became increasingly insecure. The expansion and consolidation of German territory brought about by the Empire meant that Germany's capitalist economy flourished, the working class became increasingly well organized, and large industrialists grew more powerful.[40] These challenges confronted a population that had become used to relying on some form of external authority to guide their thoughts and behaviour. This external authority might be, for example, the immediate social group, the employer, the policeman, local 'good society', the nation-wide *satisfaktionfähige Gesellschaft*, or the Kaiser himself.

In Elias's view, the personality structure of the German people required direction from external authority. It was attuned to 'an absolutist-monarchic or dictatorial regime' which 'allows great scope for a readiness in the individual person to accept orders . . . Under a regime of this type, the individual person still remains in a child-like status in relation to the state'.[41] Elias argues that the specific German personality structure helps explain the decivilizing process that occurred after the German Empire, 'like a runner colliding at full pace with a wall' (183), collapsed in 1918.

Germany's defeat, the Kaiser's abdication and the installation of the Weimar Republic made life meaningless for many in the officer class and the student associations. Their feelings are caught in a semi-autobiographical novel, quoted by Elias, which was set in that period: 'We . . . lit a funeral pyre, where . . . our hopes were burnt, our longings; there burnt the bourgeois tablet, the laws and values of the civilized world; there burnt everything that we still dragged with us like dusty junk of the vocabulary and beliefs in the things and ideas of the time that now dismissed us' (195).[42]

Some people, like the author of those words, resorted to terrorism on the grounds that the 'only hope of a more fulfilling, more meaningful life lies in the destruction of the society . . . He who destroys is all-powerful' (226). After 1918 parliamentary government was weak. Class tensions repressed during the previous regime found overt expression. Murder and street violence became endemic, often pitting armed bands led by ex-officers against groups of workers. The people at large felt belittled and directionless, deprived of the strong external authority they required.[43]

Hitler filled the gap left by the collapse of the old establishment. Elias argues that for most citizens he became the symbol of a Germany capable of greatness but under intense threat: 'the belief in the Führer and the power which he exerted over the population right to the end . . . were grounded essentially in the simple needs of simple people'. Hitler 'had the aura of a saviour'. His attributes 'dovetailed with their needs' (390).

Hitler made skilful use of the national self-image and the national habitus, especially the German 'lust for submission' (378), to achieve power. The ideal of the *Kaiserreich* establishment was broadened to include the whole population, and its ethos was made even more brutal. The whole of the German people were to be part of an Aryan master race destined to rule by force. In these respects, Elias argues, 'The National Socialist vision of a Third Reich was the culmination of a long tradition of beliefs and behaviour' (377).

The Origins of Totalitarianism

Turning to Arendt, like Elias she examines processes of territorial expansion driven partly by capitalist greed and partly by ethnic or racial aggression.

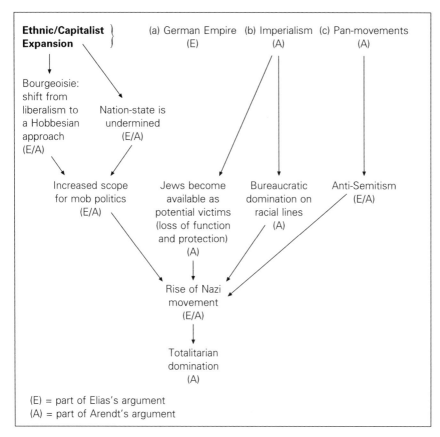

Figure 3.1 *Some central themes of* The Origins of Totalitarianism *and* The Germans

However, while Elias looks at the German Empire in Europe, Arendt focuses on European colonialism in Africa and Asia (see Figure 3.1). Imperialism plays a key role in her analysis of the processes that eventually produced a confrontation between, on the one hand, the Nazi movement whose leaders were drawn from the 'mob',[44] and, on the other side, the Jews as its victims.

In Arendt's view, imperialism fundamentally undermined the liberalism of the modern European bourgeoisie and the European nation-state. Like Elias, Arendt sees the bourgeoisie as split between two tendencies: towards liberalism and towards a Hobbesian view of society. However, while Elias concentrates on the manifestations of this tension in Germany alone, Arendt believes it can be observed throughout Europe. She explores in much more detail than Elias the way Jews were affected by the changing balance between these two tendencies.

Arendt believes the world described by Hobbes contains the essence of modern capitalism: dynamic accumulation, cut-throat competition, instability, and underlying violence. Here, also, she argues, is the fundamental bourgeois character: self-centred, vain, insecure, and cowardly. The bourgeois is a 'poor meek fellow who . . . submits to any existing government and does not stir when even his best friend falls an innocent victim to an incomprehensible *raison d'état*' (Arendt 1973, 146).

However, bourgeois members of respectable society liked to think of themselves as humane and decent. This was due to the influence of the liberal state which, in the wake of the French Revolution, accorded citizenship rights of various kinds to many adult males, irrespective of social rank, religion or ethnicity. By the late nineteenth century, in many European states, there was widespread, relatively peaceful bargaining between organized class interests within a framework of rights. This did not interfere too seriously with profits, so it suited the bourgeoisie to be seen as the upholders of liberal principles.

Jews were a transnational ethnic group, not a national class. As a group they did not fit into the framework of the liberal nation-state. However, as has been seen, Arendt believed an individual had a choice between being a pariah or a parevnu. The most privileged pariahs provided financial services and international contacts for the state. These included well-connected Jewish families such as the Rothschilds. However, both strategies became increasingly difficult to follow from the late nineteenth century. They were undermined first by imperialism, then by World War I.

During the 1870s business people with surplus capital and social marginals seeking their fortunes turned to colonial ventures. Business interests in league with demagogic politicians persuaded governments to provide credit, organizational back-up, and military support 'in the national interest'. The state's need for credit from Jewish banking houses was greatly reduced as governments started raising taxes more effectively on their own account to support colonial expansion.

The pragmatic alliance between the European bourgeoisie and the liberal state transformed both partners. The state's main task was to apply force against other national or ethnic groups, either as rivals or victims. For its part, the bourgeoisie cast off its liberal mask in the colonies and became Hobbesian. Imperialism was racist and bureaucratic, a violent contest for gain minimally regulated by governments. Non-whites had to endure systematic exploitation and submit to violence.

This 'tribal nationalism' (153) was dynamic and expansive. Cecil Rhodes wanted to 'annex the planets' if he could. The national spirit was not to be fettered by any consideration of 'universal human rights'. This approach was not restricted to the colonies. It spread through Europe during the 1880s and 1890s. Its impact was greatest where the liberal state was weakest: in Austria-Hungary, and Russia.

The aim of pan-Germanism was to unite rootless German minorities in all parts of Europe. The Jews were the prototypical rootless pan-European people. As a result, they were the most obvious rival to pan-Germanism and became its principal enemy. Furthermore, Jewish bankers lent money to hated ruling houses such as the Hapsburgs. As a result, Jews attracted the enmity of all groups with grievances against oppressive governments. This odium continued, even when governments dispensed with the services of moneylenders. Jews continued to be stereotyped as rich and parasitical but lost the governmental protection against attack they had previously enjoyed.

The weak position of European Jews was disguised for a while. Imperialism brought renewed prosperity and greater social peace for a decade and a half before World War I. By that time many Jews had moved out of banking into trade and industry. Others were making their mark on intellectual life or in 'Society'. However, after World War I, Europe became a swirling sea of nationalities released from Hapsburg, Romanov or Ottoman rule.

New governments in new states such as Czechoslovakia, Poland, Yugoslavia and Romania failed to anchor themselves within this torrent and were torn apart by the politics of ethnic hate. Within existing liberal states, including Weimar Germany, the entire apparatus of peaceful bargaining within a framework of rights fell apart. There was a constant temptation to take direct action, resorting to violence. People felt unprotected and isolated. They were unsure whom to trust, what to believe, or where to run for cover.

Making Sense of Genocide

At this point, Arendt's analysis re-establishes contact with the argument made by Elias. As has been seen, he persuasively suggests that the national habitus of the German people made them highly vulnerable to the skilful appeal made by Hitler to their collective self-image. Elias's detailed and painstakingly constructed case provides an answer to a question Arendt neglects, which is: why did the European-wide processes she delineates crystallize in the successful rise to political power of a *German* Nazi movement whose first major target was *German* Jews?

However, at the same time, Arendt's analysis of imperialism, pan-movements, the increasingly 'Hobbesian' character of the European bourgeoise, and the undermining of liberal nation-states after World War I provides something Elias does not offer: a possible explanation for the status of Jews as potential victims and for the existence of movements led by people attracted to the idea of using systematic violence against ethnic or racial enemies.[45]

Arendt, like Elias, sees the prevailing mood following World War I as being 'self-centred bitterness' and a taste for 'destruction without mitigation' (Arendt 1973, 315, 329). However, in Arendt's view, these feelings were not specifically German but part of a more general 'psychology of the European mass man' (315) and its new demagogic leaders. These leaders were drawn from the mob of desperate misfits and *déclassés* left over from the old order shipwrecked in 1918, successors to the cut-throats and desperados who had ravaged Africa, whipped up anti-Semitic feelings in central Europe during the 1870s and 1880s, and shouted '"Death to the Jews"' (111) at the height of the Dreyfus affair.

Arendt places much less emphasis than Elias on Hitler's charisma.[46] Instead, she stresses the capacity for domination of a powerful organization designed for two purposes: to impose a specific ideological view of the world upon everybody within reach; and to deploy violence in order to reshape the world, making it consistent with that ideological view.[47]

Arendt shows how the Nazi organization consisted of a number of circles: from the inner core of power-holders, ranged in warring factions, to the outer circle of relatively passive Nazi sympathisers in society at large. In between were the ordinary party members, and various elite groups of highly committed party workers. Each circle provided protection for members of smaller, more exclusive circles nearer the heart of the movement. Organized violence provided a 'fire wall' round the whole movement. The Führer's word was the sole source of authority.[48]

The organization's main objective was knowledge and control of all aspects of society. This would enable it to treat all people according to categories based on the movement's ideology, its source of 'knowedge' about the world. On this basis, for example, Jews were to be destroyed. Any resistance to the movement's programme was to be overcome by overwhelming force. In Arendt's view, the concentration camps were the Nazi's first major experiments in the technology of total domination. They provided experience in the systematic use of terror to destroy communities and undermine the *habitus*, self-image and personality structure of the victims who fell into their power. A new reality was to be created through an act of will.

For Arendt, the camps provided a glimpse into the future which modernity was probably going to hold for all, not just a minority of chosen victims. Arendt sees the Nazis and the Holocaust as prototypes for advanced modernity. By contrast, Elias treats this movement and its leader as throwbacks to a much earlier stage in the civilizing process. In Elias's view, Hitler was 'an innovative political medicine man' (389) who appealed to popular emotions, including hatred and fear. In this way he was able to demand enormous efforts and sacrifices in pursuit of irrational objectives. These objectives included 'enormous mass murder . . . in the service of . . . the dream of a great empire in Europe under the rule of . . . people of German descent'. The sheer irrationality of such action severely tests Elias's patience. He deplores 'the simple pre-industrial mind-set of Hitler and his generals' (371).

Elias suggests the Nazi leaders were confronted by the dilemma that any future empire they created through conquest would be full of hostile elements upon whom they would have to depend for economic services. He concludes: 'One sometimes has the impression that all the rage which the Nazis could not afford to discharge against their other enemies and victims because they needed their labour or because the groups involved were too powerful was released against the Jews, who, of all their declared enemies, were the weakest . . . The Nazis acted like a man who, prevented from destroying his real enemies, discharged his pent-up rage against enemies who represented a predominantly imaginary danger for him' (371).

Elias's explanation for Nazi genocide is that it was the result of a decivilizing process within German society that permitted the release of very high levels of aggression against a set of victims that happened to be available, without rational consideration of the likely consequences. However, Elias admits to being very severely tested by this issue. He writes that the 'mixture of quasi-scientific, pseudo-rational ideal and absolutely uncompromising violence – whose human victims were for those who perpetrated the violence really only impersonal things, treated like materials in a factory in order to turn them into useful objects such as soap, bone-meal or animal food, and were basically only symbols in a theory for those who killed them – remains an open question to this day' (286).

Elias finds it very difficult to identify the regularities which characterize genocide as a particular type of social process. In effect, he subsumes it under the very large category consisting of the many types of irrational behaviour made possible by a fragmentation of social ties and a weakening of controls on thoughts, feelings and behaviour.

Elias describes the concentration camps as places where the feelings generated by 'the enormous pressure of the tensions and conflicts . . . behind the monolithic facade' were released: 'It was as if the whole mixture of thwarted and contradictory feelings for which the regime left few outlets elsewhere revealed itself in all its fury in the treatment of the concentration camp prisoners: "For once the enemies are in our hands and no one is watching. So long as it lasts, let us show them who the masters are." And so they inflicted on them everything they had secretly wished to inflict on others. They did to them things which in ordered societies even children are forbidden to do and took revenge for all the disappointments they had suffered' (Elias 1996, 382–3). The implication is that the camps express the disintegration of society.

Arendt, on the other hand, sees the concentration camps as proving grounds for a highly regulated society in which all aspects of everybody's existence are to be regulated according to the categories in which they are placed by the regime, and the rules pertaining to those categories. From this point of view, the camps were blueprints for the highly centralized and disciplined social order which the Nazis hoped they were bringing into existence.

For Arendt, the concentration camp represents the opposite pole to the *polis*. In the Greek city-state public life centred on the *agora*, where issues of peace, war and public policy were decided. The *agora* provided a space for peaceful rivalry among citizens trying to outdo each other in memorable words and deeds. High standards of performance, in terms of both form and content, were imposed upon all participants.

At the other end of the scale, concentration camps destroyed the human capacity for meaningful action. In the camps inmates were transformed into passive victims. their interests were denied and their lives and deaths rendered meaningless. The Nazis' systematic use of terror and violence was part of a strategy for total domination, one involving complete eradication of the space for public action by citizens.

A Typology of Decivilizing Processes

Elias and Arendt agree that the rise of National Socialism was a decivilizing process. However, while Elias describes it in terms of a breakdown of controls, Arendt sees it as involving a tightening of controls. This difference in emphasis between them runs throughout their work. Arendt is especially sensitive to the threat posed by a radical increase in political centralization and integration, accompanied by feelings of isolation among the fragmented masses. By contrast, Elias is concerned about the opposite tendency, in other words, a radical decrease in political centralization and integration leading to fragmentation and breakdown.

These contrasting sensibilities may be related to their differing experiences of disorder during the 1930s and 1940s. To put it crudely, disorder was Arendt's friend and Elias's enemy. Social and political upheaval brought Elias personal disaster: loss of country, career and family. By contrast, disruption, ambiguity and confusion repeatedly allowed Arendt to preserve her life and freedom, rescue her dignity and resume the struggle for new political structures.

In 1933 at Alexanderplatz police station it was the breakdown of official routine, her captor's inability to categorize her, that kept her from imprisonment. In Paris during the 1930s, Arendt's life of political debate and campaigning went on in a shadowy world whose inhabitants lacked official papers. In the 1940s it was the disorder caused by the German invasion of France that gave her the chance to get out of the internment camp in which she had been confined. By escaping, she saved her own life since those who did not leave were later shipped off to the gas chambers.[49]

The difference between them is not absolute. The very title of Elias's *The Loneliness of the Dying* (Elias 1985a)[50] indicates his awareness of the depersonalizing, isolating tendencies of modernity. Similarly, in *On Violence*, Arendt argues that street violence in the United States during the 1960s illustrates 'the disintegration processes which have become so manifest in recent years' (Arendt 1970, 84). Nevertheless, Arendt argues that the dominant trend since the French Revolution has been towards centralized control over urban-industrial populations by bureaucrats, scientists and professionals. This is likely to produce 'the deadliest, the most sterile passivity history has ever known' (Arendt 1958a, 322).

On the one hand, Elias argues that the civilizing process generally leads towards increased functional democratization, a pervasive equalization of

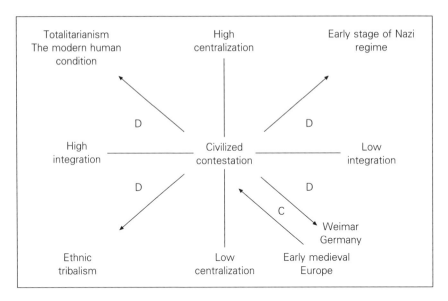

Figure 3.2   *Civilizing and decivilizing processes in the work of Arendt and Elias. (Arrows indicate direction of processual change; C = civilizing process, D = decivilizing process.)*

power balances rooted in increasing interdependence within the complex division of labour within urban-industrial societies. On the other hand, Arendt argues that as modern societies become integrated in an increasingly complex way, power becomes more centralized.

The question of how the tendency towards functional democratization is related to the trend identified by Arendt, which might be labelled 'functional centralization', is an empirical one which cannot he decided here. However, the two dimensions of 'degree of integration' and 'degree of centralization' provide the basis for a possible way of thinking about decivilizing processes.

The directionality of social processes may be described, in an over-simplified but systematic way, by focusing on, firstly, the extent to which resources and opportunities are monopolized at a central point, for example by a ruler, as opposed to being widely distributed through the population, and secondly, the extent to which institutions and groups are tightly bound together as opposed to being fragmented and discontinuous (see Figure 3.2).

At the beginning of the chapter it was seen that Elias and Arendt were both favourably disposed towards figurations such as the court, salon, *polis* and parliament, which encouraged and allowed the exercise of both natality (stressed by Arendt) and civility (emphasized by Elias). These figurations had the following characteristics. They were: sufficiently centralized and integrated for stable human interaction to be possible; not so completely centralized as to deprive people of the chance to express their capacity to speak, debate, argue and act; and not so completely integrated as to remove the psychological and political space for doing and imagining things differently from the status quo. They may, perhaps, be collectively labelled as situations of 'civilized contestation'.

The Civilizing Process largely describes figurational transformations whose overall tendency is away from a situation of decentralization, fragmentation and instability of controls and towards increased centralization and integration. According to Elias, the tendency towards centralization is modified by the counter-tendency of functional democratization.

Arendt's *The Human Condition* complements this analysis by considering the implications of a continuation of the tendency towards increasingly complex and tightly integrated figurations during the modern age under conditions of functional centralization rather than functional democratization.

Decivilizing processes may occur in four directions. In every case the movement is away from what has been labelled civilized contestation. The first type of decivilizing process is the one described by Elias in *The Germans*, that is, a decrease in integration and centralization, as occurred in Germany after World War I, leading to a breakdown of parliamentary politics and widespread street violence.

Three other types of decivilizing process are described by Arendt. One type of decivilizing process entails a decrease in integration combined with an increase in centralization. This includes the early stage of the Nazi regime as described by Arendt; in other words, the phase when the structures of parliamentary government and trade unionism were being 'atomized' by a new dictatorial regime. Other examples include the dismantling of parliamentary regimes by invading armies in the early phase of World War II.

Another type of decivilizing process described by Arendt involves an increase in both integration and centralization. This results in the oppressive and comprehensive system of organization from above characteristic of totalitarian regimes (and, indeed, advanced modernity in general according to Arendt).

Finally, there is a type of decivilizing process which involves increased integration combined with a decrease in centralization. This variant includes violent conflict between warring ethnic groups, each bound tightly together. Arendt describes how tensions of this kind developed between the two world wars following the collapse of the Austro-Hungarian, German and Ottoman Empires. Other, more recent examples have occurred following the breakup of the Soviet Union and Yugoslavia.

This typology does not try to build in the dimension of changes in personality structure. However, it is worth noting that within a society, movement along the dimensions of centralization/decentralization and integration/disintegration may occur quite quickly, producing rapid changes within the course of single generation. Changes in personality structure may occur more slowly or, at least, may occur at different rates in different parts of the society.

This means that decivilizing processes are likely to impact upon personality structures which, in many respects, remain civilized in an Eliasian sense. In fact, that is why they are *experienced* as decivilizing processes by the people concerned. They entail, in Elias's terms, a transformation of the figurational context and, in Arendt's terms, the loss of a 'world'. In so far as 'decivilizing' changes occur in personality structure, a distinction should be made between the loosening of internal restraints, as emphasized by Elias, and the inculcation of passivity, which is the process emphasized by Arendt. They are both decivilizing in the sense of eroding the conditions for civilized contestation but they move away from these conditions in two opposite directions: in one case towards disruptive violence; in the other case towards apathy.

Conclusion

The argument of this chapter has probed beyond the overt theoretical disagreements between Elias and Arendt and showed that the patterns of sensitivity embedded in the particular 'antennae' they developed converged in respect of the sociopolitical ideal to which they were both attracted. Their work was also complementary in respect of the empirical processes to which they gave most attention. Arendt and Elias provide particular 'Jewish' and 'German' perspectives, respectively, upon the 'breakdown of civilization' which accompanied the rise of Nazism.

It has been possible to combine insights from both writers in two respects. Firstly, by considering *The Origins of Totalitarianism* and *The Germans* together, a set of arguments has been identified that offer an explanation not only for the selection of Jews as particular victims of the Nazis and the rationale of Nazism as a totalitarian movement but also for the fact that Nazism and the Holocaust were rooted in Germany rather than any other particular European society. Secondly, different ways in which 'decivilization' may occur have been identified by distinguishing social processes in terms of their implications for changes in the level of centralization and degree of integration within socio-political figurations.

To conclude, three comparisons have been carried out in this chapter: between two German Jewish intellectuals born in the latter phase of the German Empire; between two analyses of Nazism and the Holocaust; and between two interpretations of modernity. The challenge has been to account for three things: major differences in intellectual orientation between a philosopher and a sociologist very similar in generation, class, occupation, ethnicity and nationality;[51] important similarities in the empirical analyses of German development provided by two writers with very different intellectual orientations; and profound differences between the interpretations of modernity in general offered by two intellectuals whose interpretations of the case of Germany in particular are very compatible.

In answering these questions, two methodological operations have been carried out. Firstly, categories introduced to establish the relevance of a specific comparison, for example, in this case, the categories of bourgeois, intellectual, German and Jew, have been undermined or broken down to expose complexities hidden within or behind them. Behind the category 'bourgeois' lies the inter-generational shift from commercial to professional and in many cases, academic careers. The term 'intellectual' leads towards the competing paradigms attempting to occupy the ground left void by the weakening grip of *Kultur* upon the German intelligentsia. Interwoven with these processes was the increasingly difficult struggle to reconcile Jewish and German social identities.

Secondly, concepts and social processes from apparently unrelated contexts have been brought together and compared in order to demonstrate an unexpected degree of complementarity between them or to show that they converge as particular variants of a more general category. For example, complementarity has been shown in the case of civility and natality; convergence has been shown in the case of the variants of decivilizing processes explored by Elias and Arendt.

In the next chapter the argument turns to another sojourner at Heidelberg during the late 1920s: Talcott Parsons.

Notes

1 To be discussed at greater length in Chapter 5.

2 See Arendt 1958a; Foucault 1978; Foucault 1987; Foucault 1988a. Note that Foucault gave priority to the private sphere in his analysis whereas Arendt emphasized the public sphere.

3 See, for example, Habermas 1991, 95–129; Habermas 1996; Elias 1978.

4 See, for example, Habermas 1987, 238–93. Foucault's Howinson lectures on 'truth and subjectivity' refer to Habermas. See Macey 1993, 431; Miller 1993, 456–7. The ramifications of this particular debate extended far beyond the question of whether modernity represented a move towards or away from a 'better' society.

5 She believed Hobbes had displayed analytical skills of this kind. In her view, he was able to anticipate the character of the modern bourgeoisie centuries before it came to full flower. See Arendt 1973, 139–47, 155–7.

6 Elias stressed in the preface to *The Civilizing Process* that 'the issues raised in this book have their origin . . . in the experiences in whose shadow we all live, experiences of the crisis and transformation of Western civilization as it has existed hereto' (Elias 1994a, xvi). In *The Origins of Totalitarianism*, published twelve years later, Arendt remarked that 'there prevails an ill-defined, general agreement that the essential structure of all civilizations is at the breaking point' (Arendt 1973, vii).

7 Arendt accepted that vision had a part to play in grasping and communicating key aspects of human experience but she thought it was dangerous to rely on it too heavily as a means of intellectual orientation to the world. She recognized that 'the speculative, non-cognitive way of thinking' was 'loyal to the fundamental experiences of the thinking ego' but was suspicious of relying on metaphor to carry meaning. See 'Metaphor and the ineffable' in *Thinking*, the first volume of Arendt's *The Life of the Mind*. Arendt 1978a, 110–25.

8 In fact, the '*hommes de lettres*' who made the American revolution came from a group whose 'members had started their career by withdrawing from society, first from the society of the royal court and the life of a courtier, and later from the society of the salon' (Arendt 1963a, 118).

9 Now Kaliningrad in Russia.

10 His commercial premises were on the main square, near the Rathaus. According to Elias, 'he had probably started about 1880 or 1885 and was carried along by the prosperity

which had come after 1870. It was a kind of factory but with relatively few machines, mainly people working by hand, about thirty people, including tailors, making clothes for the wholesale trade' (Elias 1994b, 5).

11 Young-Bruehl 1982, 10.

12 In fact, Arendt's second husband, Heinrich Blücher, had participated in the 1919 uprising. Young-Bruehl 1982, 125–6.

13 He seems to have been inclined to support the Wilhelmite establishment. Significantly, he gave his only child the distinctively German name of a twelfth-century saint with a noble pedigree, a man who had been Archbishop of Magdeburg. Magdeburg was a central point for propagating the Catholic faith among the Poles. Its charter inspired the Magdeburg Law, a code of municipal government adopted throughout eastern Europe during the thirteenth century. Norbert of Xanten was born into a noble family in north Germany and founded a community of canons in 1120 at Prémontré near Laon on northern France. The Premonstratensians, or 'white canons' followed a monastic rule. Their task was to stamp out heresy. Norbert won the support of both the Pope and the German Emperor, a considerable achievement in the early twelfth century in the wake of the 'investure context'. This helped gain him the position of Archbishop of Magdeburg. He was later canonized.

14 See also Hackeschmidt 1997; Hetherington 1994; Mennell 1996, vii; Elias 1994b, 35. Elias's love of the German countryside encompassed 'a very intimate knowledge of all the cathedrals . . . I knew all the buildings by heart, all the styles' (Elias 1994b, 19). Years later, at Marianne Weber's seminar in Heidelberg, Elias gave a talk in which he 'spoke of the differences in the structures of the German and French societies and their reflections in the structures of their cathedrals' (98).

15 To anticipate a later argument, Elias's incisive assaults on chosen opponents such as Talcott Parsons and Karl Popper later in his career sometimes bring the image of a duel to mind: Elias 1994a, 185–204 (on Parsons); Elias 1985b (on Popper; the present author has not read the German translation but heard Elias deliver the original English version in a seminar at Leicester University in 1970).

16 Such societies, he recalled, 'were not taken seriously; they were not entitled to demand satisfaction,' that is, to duel (Elias 1994b, 35).

17 When Elias uses the term habitus or social habitus he is usually referring to the distinctive code of feeling and behaviour instilled in members of a particular group. For a discussion see Fletcher 1997, 10–15.

18 Alfred Weber, brother of Max, agreed to sponsor his *Habilitation* at some point in the future, and Elias began research on Renaissance artists such as Galileo and Uccello whose experiments on perspective promised to give insights into the transition from pre-scientific to scientific thinking. Later, at Frankfurt, Mannheim became his sponsor. Elias 1994b, 95–6; Mennell 1998, 14.

19 Rahel Varnhagen, a brilliant leader of salon society in Berlin during the late eighteenth and early nineteenth centuries, had an affair with a German aristocrat which ended unhappily. Arendt had an affair with Martin Heidegger whuch affected her deeply. There were two serious difficulties in the relationship between Arendt and Heidegger. He was married, and his wife was inclined towards National Socialism. The impressions of Arendt's first husband in this respect are reported by her biographer. Despite this, the affair was intensely pursued for a year at Marburg. In 1925, Heidegger encouraged Arendt to move away from Marburg, where he taught, to Heidelberg. They continued to meet until 1928 when he ended the relationship. Shortly afterwards Heidegger became a full professor at Frieburg. By 1933 he had become rector of Frieburg University and joined the Nazi party. See Ettinger 1995, 13–37; Young-Bruehl 1982, 48–50, 59–62, 108.

20 See Lazare 1949; Bernstein 1996, 14–45.

21 She accepted that actions within this web of relationships could easily have unpredictable and unintended consequences. See her passages on 'The process character of action', 'Irreversibility and the power to forgive', and 'Unpredictability and the power of promise' in *The Human Condition*. Arendt 1958a, 230–47.

22 See page 12.

23 Arendt later told Elizabeth Young-Bruehl, 'He . . . said: "Normally when I have someone in front of me, I just look up the case in our records and I know what to do. What am I supposed to do with you?"' (Young-Bruehl 1982, 106).

24 Young-Bruehl 1982, 105–15. Arendt was later to have other narrow escapes, managing to evade deportation to Germany, and secure a passage to the United States with her second husband. Young-Bruehl 1982, 153–63.

25 Trade union headquarters. Elias was there to discuss a student scholarship.

26 The context makes it clear that by 'individual structures' Elias is referring to 'the structure of the personality, . . . human mentality, . . . the malleable psychological apparatus' (Elias 1994a, 445).

27 'I don't think one can say one ever chooses things' (Elias 1994b, 3).

28 Elias argues that the social scientist must, quite self-consciously, combine both involvement and detachment. Involvement makes empathy possible. However, it carries the danger that one's perceptions, and the actions governed by those perceptions, might become totally dominated by heightened emotions relating to the self. The risk of extreme involvement is that what one sees and does becomes no more than an expression of one's own deep wishes and fears. Elias contrasts involvement with detachment, which occurs when feelings about the self are rigorously excluded from the process of perception and do not interfere with actions based on those perceptions. Complete detachment and complete involvement are at either end of a continuum. In *On Violence*, Arendt writes: 'Absence of emotions neither causes nor promotes rationality. "Detachment and equanimity" in view of "unbearable tragedy" can indeed be "terrifying," namely when they are not the result of control but an evident manifestation of incomprehension. In order to respond reasonably one must first be "moved," and the opposite of emotional is not "rational," whatever that may mean, but either the inability to be moved, usually a pathological phenomenon, or sentimentality, which is a perversion of feeling' (Arendt 1970, 64).

29 Elias was by no means inactive. While in London he helped to found the Group Analytic Society and led therapeutic groups. Elias 1994b, 63–4. On Arendt's campaign for a Jewish army, see Young-Bruehl 1982, 173–81.

30 Replying to a critical review of *The Origins of Totalitarianism*, Arendt wrote that she had difficulty knowing how 'to write historically about something – totalitarianism – which I . . . felt engaged to destroy' (Arendt 1953, 77). Quoted in Canovan 1992, 17.

31 References to the Jews, National Socialism and Hitler can be found on fewer than fifty pages of *The Germans*. At the same time, Germany, as distinct from the Jews, National Socialism and Hitler, is mentioned on fewer than seventy-five pages in *The Origins of Totalitarianism*. Both books are about five hundred pages long.

32 In the mid-1930s in Paris Arendt took private lessons in Hebrew from a Polish Jew recently arrived from Palestine: '"I want to know my people," she told him' (quoted in Young-Bruehl 1982, 119).

33 See, for examples, Elias 1996 2, 31, 51, 63, 64, 65, 73, 97, 162, 285–6, 338, 343, 362, 401, 411.

34 Elias 1996, 6–7, 319–20, 324–8, 331–3, 343, 377.

35 Elias writes: 'Nietzsche was certainly not aware that, with his elevation of power in the scale of human values, with his belittling of the socially weak and of the middle-class code of morality, he was giving philosophical expression on the level of the highest philosophical universality to developmental tendencies which, unintentionally and with little discussion, were becoming dominant in the German society of the *Kaiserzeit* which he so often attacked' (Elias 1996, 118).

36 The strictly hierarchical establishment of those who had the right to 'demand satisfaction' of other members of this establishment in the form of a duel. Elias 1996, 106–13.

37 Elias 1996, 47–8, 77–85.

38 Elias shows how these practices expressed the distinctive *'formality-informality span'* of German society (Elias 1996, 28; see also 41–3). This concept allows him to explore differences between societies, and between particular societies at different times, in the degree and scope of formalization in everyday life, and the degree to which a relaxation of psychic and social

controls is permitted in certain situations. Elias's discussion of the way duelling societies ritualized the practice of deliberate transgressions against inhibitions instilled from childhood takes him into areas which also fascinated Foucault. See Elias 1996, 106–8; Foucault 1977a, 49–54; Smith 1997. On drinking, sex and duelling in Imperial Germany, see Elias 1996, 35–6, 49–50, 65–72, 97–8, 107–8. See also Wouters 1977; Wouters 1987.

39 Or even the state apparatus. Elias notes that by persisting in duelling, which was technically illegal, members of the aristocracy were asserting their position as the real lords of the land. Elias 1996, 52–3.

40 See, for example, Elias 1996, 54.

41 Elias adds: 'The personality structure of the individual person may be adapted to a hierarchy of command and obedience; but in order to make quite sure, autocratic rulers usually use their unrestricted right of disposal over the state's monopoly of force to create the most airtight surveillance apparatus possible, an apparatus that ensures that the individual does not go astray' (291). Elias saw this configuration as being quite specific to the German case. However, writers such as Foucault, and Arendt, believe it has a more general applicability. Elias argues that, by contrast, 'a multi-party parliamentary system . . . requires a correspondingly more complex and more differentiated personality structure' (291–2). Also compare the view expressed by Elias in *The Civilizing Process* fifty years before where he writes that in Germany 'habituation to a strong external state authority became deeply ingrained in the bourgeoisie'. He adds that 'The emotional balance, the self-control of the individual, was endangered if this external power was lacking. From generation to generation a super-ego was created in the bourgeois masses which was disposed to relinquish to a separate, higher circle the specific form of foresight demanded by the ruling and organization of society at large' (Elias 1994a, 512).

42 The quotation is from Ernst von Salamon's *Die Geächteten* (The Outlaws). Von Salamon 1931, 144–5. Von Salamon was implicated in the murder of Walter Rathenau, a liberal politician. Elias 1996, 186, 191.

43 Elias notes that 'as the wider world lost its trusted form,' for many Germans 'Their private worlds became increasingly the one firm element in their lives' (Elias 1996, 399). This went with the grain in the sense that the German bourgeoisie was already predisposed 'to a cultivation of inwardness' (Elias 1994a, 512). During the Hitler regime, according to Arendt, the behaviour of the bourgeoisie was 'philistine'. She writes: 'The philistine is the bourgeois isolated from his own class, the atomized individual who is produced by the breakdown of the bourgeois class itself . . . Nothing proved easier to destroy than the privacy and private morality of people who thought of nothing but safeguarding their own private lives.' Arendt contrasted the 'philistine' bourgeois with the 'bohemian' Nazi mob leader such as Goebbels. This distinction between the 'philistine' and the 'bohemian' may owe something to the Chicago School of Sociology. The terms are used in, for example, *The Polish Peasant in Europe and America*. See Thomas and Znaniecki 1927, 1868–71. See also Smith 1988, 107–8.

44 The mob consists of *déclassés*, that is, failed businesspeople, out-of-work artisans, criminals, gentry fallen on hard times, unfrocked professionals, unemployed students, disenchanted intellectuals, and so on, including those Elias refers to as 'half-educated people and social outsiders' (Elias 1996, 376). These people, all outsiders, regarded decent society as a giant confidence trick. The mob contained 'the residue of all classes' (Arendt 1973, 107) ready to rally behind a strong leader.

45 Also, as will be seen, Arendt's analysis of the modus operandi of the Nazi movement complements Elias's own discussion of it within the framework of decivilizing process.

46 See Arendt 1973, 361–2. Compare Elias 1983, 121–6.

47 Elias emphasizes the part played by political and social fragmentation in permitting the release of frustration, hatred and anger through violence. By contrast, Arendt stresses the calculated way in which terror and organized violence were used to destroy the remains of an existing order and begin to construct a new one, at level of both society and the personality.

48 Arendt 1973, 364–88.

49 By contrast, it was Elias's prolonged stay in a British internment camp during the 1940s that gave him his first real opportunity to play the role of teacher in a secure and stable setting,

however primitive. There he could be 'Professor Elias', the title by which Eric Wolf first knew him in 1940. See Wolf 1977, 30.

50 This could almost be the subtitle of *The Origins of Totalitarianism*.

51 The obvious gender difference between Elias and Arendt is difficult to tie in systematically to specific aspects of their intellectual approaches, although for interesting and insightful comments on this theme see Eyerman 1995; Benhabib 1995.

4

PARSONS AND ELIAS

Biographical Parallels

Parsons, born in 1902, was five years younger than Elias. Both men had early aspirations to a career in medicine, both were influenced by Freud and both trained as psychoanalysts (of different kinds) in their forties, in Parsons's case at the Boston Psychoanalytic Institute.[1]

Another parallel with Elias is that Parsons, too, was keenly interested in the fate of democracy and the liberal freedoms within Germany. This theme will be picked up again at the end of the chapter.[2] Parsons's interest in Germany was reinforced by visits he made there between the wars. During the 1920s both he and Elias spent time at Heidelberg trying to build academic careers. Parsons and Elias probably never knowingly met during those years. At least, if they did, neither mentioned the fact later. However, they had overlapping social circles. Parsons, like Elias, made the acquaintance of Marianne Weber (the widow of Max Weber), knew the philosopher Karl Jaspers and had academic links with the sociologist Alfred Weber.[3]

Elias was at Heidelberg between 1925 and 1929, working as an assistant to Mannheim. During this time Parsons made two, briefer, visits, to the city. During the second visit, in the summer of 1927, he successfully defended his doctorate which was a study of Brentano, Sombart, Marx and, especially, Max Weber.[4]

Parsons's response to the neo-Kantian element of Weber's work was a positive one. By contrast, Elias, who had received his doctorate at Breslau in 1924 following studies in philosophy, reacted negatively to the neo-Kantian tradition and had a serious disagreement with his supervisor, Richard Hönigswald, on this matter.[5] These differences of opinion at Heidelberg had an interesting sequel nearly half a century later.

High Noon at Varna

In 1970 Norbert Elias made a large exception to his practice of ignoring rival sociologists. He singled Talcott Parsons out for a special honour: he attacked him. He criticized Parsons's ideas directly and at some length, itemizing the fundamental inadequacies, as he saw it, of Parsons's intellectual system. In effect, in a rather Heidelbergian way, he issued Parsons with a challenge to an intellectual duel. That duel never took place, for, as far as I know, Parsons never replied directly to Elias's criticisms, at least not in print. However, the challenge itself was significant.

It is appropriate to talk of challenges and duels in this particular context. Elias had a continuing fascination with the student fighting fraternities of Imperial Germany. He wrote about them at length in *The Germans* (Elias 1996). As a young man in Breslau Elias even joined, for a time, one of the 'Jewish associations which tried to imitate them'. He became one of its first officers and wore a 'strange uniform'. However, members of the Jewish associations 'were not entitled to demand satisfaction' (Elias 1994b, 35), that is, issue challenges and engage in duels. They were outsiders.

Half a century later, Elias's long period as an outsider was coming to an end. Stephen Mennell describes the historical context well. He writes: 'For fifteen years after the war, German sociologists had (like the rest of Europe and much of the world) been orientated to American-style sociology, dominated by number-crunching empiricism and the conceptual schemes of Talcott Parsons. The year 1968, the year of student revolutions, marked an intellectual sea-change. *The Civilizing Process* suddenly fell on fertile ground, and became something of a cult book among German and Dutch sociology students' (Mennell 1989, 24).

The late 1960s was an encouraging period for Elias. In 1969 *The Civilizing Process* was republished in German after thirty years during which it had been virtually unobtainable. In the same year *The Court Society* (Elias 1983), written in the early 1930s, appeared for the first time, also in German. The original German-language version of *What is Sociology?* (Elias 1978) went into the bookshops in the following year. Elias was finally being accepted by the country of his birth, by a society that had previously rejected him. An important part of educated German society was beginning to open up its arms and welcome him in.[6]

By 1970 Elias was beginning to be recognized as an important sociologist. In that year both he and Parsons attended the Seventh World Congress of Sociology held at the Black Sea port of Varna. In his presentation at the Congress Elias adopted the manner of someone asserting the right to 'demand satisfaction' not just in Germany but on the larger international stage. Elias is claiming intellectual territory and telling his chief rival, the man in possession, to move aside. This is a rare and highly significant episode, a major compliment from Elias to Parsons, and a rare public act of self-assertion by the challenger. At Varna, Elias is demanding satisfaction from an opponent he takes to be his equal, or, at least, almost his equal.

Reading the text of Elias's talk, I am reminded of a passage Elias quoted in *The Germans* taken from a novel about German student life published in 1900: 'With regally uplifted nose, Werner strode past the tables of the gymnasts and nationalist fraternities, with solemnly doffed cap . . . [he went] . . . past the Hessian and Westphalian groups, . . . [and then] smiling but with a ceremonial bow . . . [he] came up to the table of [his own fraternity] . . . where he was made welcome . . . with the studied cheerfulness which the corps students always affected when they knew they were being watched' (Elias 1996, 102).

There is an echo of Werner's style in Elias's presentation at Varna. The main theme of his talk is the need for 'a developmental sociological paradigm', one that enables us to examine long-term nation building and state formation processes. He comments that this type of theory 'does not correspond to the ideal image of a theory which the most prominent theoretical sociologists of our time appear to take for granted and which is a kind of philosophical hangover from the time of classical physics'. You can almost see the coat being dragged along the floor, teasingly.

Elias then turns directly in Parsons's direction: 'Take one of the best known examples of an essentially static sociological theory of our time, the theory which tries to come to grips with the problems of society by presenting society as a "social system". I am glad to find that the leading exponent of contemporary social system theories, Talcott Parsons, is among us. I am critical of the intellectual system he has built up. A Round Table discussion at a World Congress is, it seems to me, the right place for stating some of the reasons for my critical attitude – only some, for my time is strictly limited, and I like to combine my critical remarks with at least a few hints about the positive aspects of a developmental sociological theory which alone can justify criticism' (Elias 1970, 276).

Elias proceeds in a courtly fashion, beginning with the statement that 'my critical attitude towards Parsons' intellectual system is qualified by my respect for his person [,] . . . his intellectual sincerity and integrity . . . [and] his power of synthesis which is one of the qualifying gifts of the distinguished theory maker' (277). However, despite this graceful overture (doffing his cap), Elias is soon haughtily dismissing Parsons's 'teleological perspective'; in other words, his assumption that all institutions exist to keep 'the system' functioning well. Elias then proceeds to score a number of elegant hits with his rapier on the body of Parsons (or rather upon his theories).

Finally, Elias pushes Parsons aside, so to speak, with the exasperated comment: 'One does not know what to admire more, the patent sincerity and goodwill or the disarming naivety and incomprehension which one encounters here' (281). Here, in all its magnificence, is the 'regally upturned nose' mentioned previously. It is a clear instance of what Elias calls, in the duelling context, 'ritualized sneering behaviour' (Elias 1996, 102). And, to reiterate the point, it is a rare and considerable compliment from Elias to Parsons. He is 'calling out' a worthy opponent in one of the highest public forums available to them both within their shared profession.[7]

Elias's Case against Parsons

Elias's main charge against Parsons is that his conceptual apparatus is profoundly misleading.[8] For example, Parsons breaks societies down, analytically, into 'elementary components' (Elias 1968, 185). Two of these elementary components are human acts and the values that guide those acts. Parsons treats '"actions" [as] . . . a kind of atoms of human societies' (Elias 1970, 277). These 'atoms' and the societies to which they belong are like players in a card game. They can only play the cards they are dealt. These cards are the values or 'pattern variables' that give acts meaning and direction. Elias comments: 'every type of society, in Parsons's view, represents a different "hand". But the cards themselves are always the same; and their number is small, however diverse their faces may be' (185).

Elias takes a different approach: 'Why put "actions" in the centre of a theory of society and not the people who act? If anything, societies are networks of human beings in the round, not a medley of disembodied actions. Nor is it easy to see how the atomism of such a sociological action theory can run in harness, as a horse from the same stable, with a decidedly not atomistic theory according to which everything in a society is a dependent part of a highly integrated and normally smoothly functioning whole. This, too, . . . is rather remote from the rough and tumble of men's social life, as one can actually observe it' (Elias 1970, 277).

According to Elias, Parsons's theory is abstract, idealistic and misleading. It consists of 'barren generalizations too remote from research tasks to be either confirmed or refuted by reference to observable data'. At the same time, its abstractions are 'in the service of a specific ideal'. This ideal is the 'unified, equilibrated and well functioning social system' which 'often appears as the purpose and aim towards which all part-events are directed'. Parsons's theories with their 'purely descriptive character' and 'strong teleological undertones' are, 'without doubt unintentionally . . . disguises for subject-centred values' (278).

Parsons's work, in Elias's view, represents 'an unnecessary impoverishment of sociological perception' (Elias 1968, 186). In effect, he cannot see the world properly. Because of his impoverished capacity to perceive reality, Parsons is unable to recognize that long-term social processes such as state formation and nation building have occurred over past centuries and are still underway in the present. Parsons reduces this movement to 'static chunks' which he analyses in terms of 'law-like abstractions from selected aspects of contemporary "advanced" societies', as if the present stage of development was 'a stage without future, . . . an end-stage' (275).

Parsons and those who see the world as he does cannot understand the need for theories and concepts which 'include spatial figurations and time sequences of long duration' (276). They are stuck in a world of 'short-term statics' (274) and when they write about 'the social system' they are evoking, consciously or not, their vision of a unified and harmonious nation-state. They are blind to the 'structured backbone' of 'development' (276) with its 'long-term dynamics'. Instead, for them 'the concept of social change refers . . . to a transitional state between two normal states of changelessness, brought about by malfunction' (Elias 1968, 188). The 'unstructured flow' of '"history"' intervenes between these 'normal states of changelessness' (Elias 1970, 276).

The Knowledge/Understanding Model

Confronted with this mind-set, Elias calls for a 'restructuring of the socio-logical imagination' (Elias 1970, 274). His strategy has three stages: first, acquiring *knowledge*; second, changing *perceptions*; and third, posing the challenge of *explanation* in order to improve *understanding*. This is clearly expressed in the following statement:

> [The question of how and why long-term processes of integration occur] . . . comes to life only if one has at one's disposal a sufficiently wide and vivid long-term *knowledge* which enables to look back through the continuity of the development of societies and to *perceive* the continuity of the development of societies which led, say, from the multitude of relatively small, loosely integrated dynastic states of the 11th and the 12th centuries, by way of a great number of integration and disintegration spurts, gradually to larger, more populous and more closely integrated social units . . . – unless one is able to perceive this long-term process, one does not become aware of the problem. How is it to be *explained* that a development of societies went on in this case for centuries, through all the fissions and fusions, through all the disintegration and integration spurts, in the direction towards the formation of larger and more closely knit societies? (278; emphasis added)

In his 1968 preface to *The History of Manners*[9] Elias emphasizes, repeatedly, that in *The Civilizing Process* he is, above all, concerned with establishing facts. For example, in the course of four short paragraphs Elias refers to 'the discovery and elucidation of what actually takes place', 'the discovery and definition of factual connections', 'the discovery and eluci-dation of factual connections', the collection of 'reliable empirical evidence', 'an approach directed at factual connections' and 'the attempt . . . to isolate the factual core' (Elias 1968, 182–3). This is a message he is determined to get across.

By insisting on the scientific investigator's capacity to acquire knowledge of 'things as they are' in the world, past and present, Elias is, indirectly at least, reasserting his long-held opposition to the Kantian position on this matter.[10] As is well known, Kant argues that we cannot have direct knowledge of things in the world as they ('really') are. What we experience are the impressions registered within our senses. These impressions give us intuitions about things in the world.

These intuitions are synthesized by the imagination and then our under-standing imposes conceptual order on the synthesis. Our understanding is 'pre-programmed' with built-in concepts and categories, common to all humans. These features of the understanding enable us to 'build a picture', so to speak, which has temporal and spatial dimensions, regular patterns, law-like relationships, sequences of cause and effect, and so on. Our understanding provides us with an explanation for the world so that it makes sense to us.

From a Kantian point of view, organized social life is possible because human beings perceive the world and act within it on the basis of a universal conceptual order that exists even before they begin perceiving and acting, an order that is, in fact, the very condition of human beings being able to act and perceive. In other words, our *understanding*, which gives the capacity to *explain*, allows us to *perceive* the world as having order and enables us to *know* how the things we perceive fit together.

Obviously, these assumptions are diametrically opposed to those of Elias who reverses this sequence (see Figure 4.1). As has just been seen, Elias assumes that *knowledge* shapes our *perception* and presents the challenge of *explanation* to our *understanding*. For Elias, the understanding is confronted with the challenge of perceptions which are produced as a result of the acquisition of knowledge about the real world.

Elias

Knowledge → Perception → Explanation → Understanding

(Knowledge shapes Perception which presents the challenge of Explanation to the Understanding)

Kant

Understanding → Explanation → Perception → Knowledge

(The Understanding provides an Explanatory framework or conceptual order that shapes our Perception and provides the Knowledge or 'know-how' that enables society to function)

Figure 4.1   *The knowledge/understanding model*

As Grathoff puts it, Kant asked himself 'how it is at all possible that men's perceiving, cognitive constructing and experiencing can reach the world as an empirical world of vivid creatures. Kant proposed that this can be achieved by the application of what he called "schemata" of understanding [which are the mind's] . . . means to reach the world of objects as objects known . . . However the origin and constitution of these schemata remain [for Kant] an open problem, which Kant refers to as a secret of the human soul' (Grathoff 1978, xiv).[11]

Parsons was much more sympathetic to the Kantian approach than was Elias. Parsons's quest was to understand the built-in principles of order that, in his view, made society possible. He wanted to decode the universal concepts and categories embedded and expressed in human action and perception. In Roy Fitzhenry's words, 'Parsons' whole work is an attack, from a highly abstract base, upon this "open problem". For him the symbolic orders in culture are the empirically discoverable schemata, governing what an actor can know about his social world and hence, how he may act' (Fitzhenry 1986, 173).

Similarities and Differences

Parsons and Elias can both be aligned to the Knowledge/Understanding model. However, they drive it in opposite directions. To oversimplify, for

Elias the acquisition of knowledge is the principal 'driver' in our attempts to make sense of the world. This is because it makes possible an increase in our understanding, especially our understanding of the unplanned but structured social processes of development.

For Parsons, however, the conceptual apparatus built into human understanding is the main 'driver'. This is because, as he sees it, the schemata embedded in our minds at any point in time define what is valid and relevant knowledge. They also guide our interpretation of that knowledge, and make it possible for us to behave knowledgeably, especially to apply knowledge about how integrated and harmonious societies function.

Elias and Parsons are similar in the utter confidence with which they present their findings. Parsons displays a very high degree of optimism about his personal capacity to identify the 'empirically discoverable schemata' from which, in his view, social order originates. Elias is equally optimistic that he is able to identify the 'factual' content, boundaries and interconnectedness of social processes, mechanisms and figurations.

This confidence and optimism can be seductive. It wins followers. However, other writers such as Foucault and Arendt have produced competing versions of 'empirically discoverable schemata' and alternative depictions of social processes, mechanisms and figurations. They have offered them to us with equal confidence. How does one choose between these alternatives?

For example, on what grounds would one choose between Parsons's account in *The Structure of Social Action* and Foucault's very different analysis in *The Order of Things* (Foucault 1974)? What reasons are there for having greater confidence in Elias's version of the development of the European nation-state during the nineteenth and early twentieth centuries rather than, say, the one given by Hannah Arendt in *The Origins of Totalitarianism* (Arendt 1973) which contradicts Elias's account in important respects?

My answer is that one does not make an absolute choice. It is much more useful to bring the different works together in a reasoned debate from which none is likely to emerge as an outright 'victor'. I take a similar view of the contest between the Eliasian and Parsonian versions of the Knowledge/Understanding model. There is no need to make a choice, since our knowledge and our understanding are in continual dialogue, each modifying the other.

One 'Eliasian' response is to assert the conceptual right of way on the grounds that the Parsonian approach is 'philosophical' (and 'metaphysical') whereas the Eliasian approach is 'sociological' (and 'empirical'). This is not a satisfactory response, for two reasons. One is that Elias's approach, like that of Parsons, is based upon philosophical assumptions. The difference between them is that Elias makes the opposite philosophical assumptions, as has just been seen.[12]

Another reason for pausing before rejecting Parsons on the grounds that he is 'metaphysical' is as follows. In the classic work establishing his approach, *The Structure of Social Action* (Parsons 1968), Parsons makes it clear that he has produced 'an empirical work in a double sense. First, it is very much oriented to problems of the macroscopic developments in Western society, especially as seen through the eyes of the . . . authors discussed in the study. Secondly, it [is] . . . an empirical study in the analysis of social thought. The writings treated are as truly documents as are manorial court rolls of the Middle Ages' (vii) – or, one may add, as truly documents as are the manners books examined by Elias in the first volume of *The Civilizing Process*.

The quotation just given from *The Structure of Social Action* is taken from the preface to the second edition published in 1968. This was the same year in which *The History of Manners* was republished with Elias's equally trenchant insistence on his work's 'factual' concerns. In fact, the original publication of this first volume of *The Civilizing Process* also coincided with the original appearance of *The Structure of Social Action* in 1937. Coincidences of this kind strengthen my reluctance to make a radical choice between the two texts, abandoning one and concentrating exclusively on the other. It seems likely that something may be learned by looking at the two together.

It is worth considering the possibility that Elias has vastly oversimplified matters, that he was wrong to represent himself and Parsons as belonging to two completely different universes. In fact, I want to suggest that – in the late 1930s at least – these two scholars were to a great extent concerned with the same problems and were implementing analytical strategies that complemented each other to a significant extent.

The Structure of Social Action and *The Civilizing Process*

When he wrote *The Structure of Social Action* (1968), Parsons was trying to understand the built-in principles of order that, in his view, made society possible. He wanted to decode the universal concepts and categories embedded and expressed in human action and perception. Discovering that abstract order involved an empirical study of several theories of society.

In the preface to the second edition of his book in 1968, Parsons wrote that 'A major one-sidedness of the book is its relative neglect of the psychological aspects of the total conceptual scheme – a balance which a thorough revision would certainly have to address. Here . . . Freud . . . looms up as having played a cardinal role . . . as a vital part of the same general movement of thought' (xvi). Freudian ideas were, of course, very important in Elias's work.[13]

The rationale for Parsons's study was that if a number of theories produced in very different socio-historical settings – but without significant contact between their authors – were found to converge on a particular constellation of ideas, this would be an important reason for believing that those ideas were part of the core conceptual order that made society possible.

Parsons traces the structure of one aspect of the process whereby, as he sees it, the 'voluntaristic theory of action' emerged from two co-existing traditions: the positivist tradition which included work by Marshall, Pareto and Durkheim, and the idealist tradition whose most important representative was Weber. The aspect of this process upon which Parsons focuses is the development of theories as intellectual systems. He traces the effects of tensions and contradictions within the positivistic and idealist traditions and the partial resolution of these tensions by a process of convergence between the two traditions.

Parsons emphasizes that the process he is tracing is an unplanned one. However, one outcome of the process is that the voluntaristic theory of action has become available to human beings. In other words, this theory has become part of the stock of scientific knowledge, a fact that, by implication, increases the scope of human control over social life. As Parsons puts it, 'What has happened in the minds of these men is not the appearance of an unorganized mass of arbitrary subjective judgements. It is part of a great deep stream of the movement of scientific thought . . . extending far beyond the works of the few men here considered . . . What has been traced is not merely a movement of thought of major proportions; it is scientific progress; indeed, notable scientific progress. One of its main aspects is a clearer, sounder understanding of a broad range of the facts of human action' (Parsons 1968, 775).

Elias makes similar claims for his analysis of the civilizing process. In his view, it is an unplanned process but one of its results is to increase the capacity of human beings to plan their actions on a rational basis. Parsons emphasizes the development of theory from its medieval origins in Christianity but especially since the seventeenth century, tracing this development through to the cognitive reorientation which, he believes, occurred in the early twentieth century. For his part, Elias analyses the development of a civilized habitus as an aspect of the reconfiguring of human styles of thinking, feeling and acting from the medieval period onwards.

The analyses are complementary rather than competing. For example, both *The Structure of Social Action* and *The Civilizing Process* derive their dynamism from the tension between the Germanic and French socio-political, cultural and intellectual traditions and the social formations in which those traditions were embedded. This is, perhaps, not surprising in works produced during the late 1930s. In Elias's case, this tension is explored in part one of the first volume of *The Civilizing Process* which is concerned with the distinction between the German concept of *Kultur* and the French concept of *civilization*.[14] The equivalent distinction in Parsons's work is between the positivistic tradition represented by Durkheim and the idealistic tradition represented by Weber.[15]

I will return to the comparison with Elias shortly, but at this point a brief analytical summary of Parsons's argument will be useful.

Order and Freedom

Like Elias in *The Civilizing Process*, Parsons in *The Structure of Social Action* relates his analysis to profound social changes going on around him. Elias refers to 'the crisis and transformation of Western civilization' (Elias 1994a, xvi), Parsons to 'a basic revolution in empirical interpretations of . . . social problems' (Parsons 1968, 5), one of 'such magnitude' that no equivalent could be found since the sixteenth century.

Parsons means by this a sustained attack on individualism, rationality and science, widespread anti-intellectualism and the growth of 'socialistic, collectivistic, organic theories of all kinds' including socialism and fascism. Like Elias, he is responding to the social and political changes that, for example, took the National Socialist party to power in Germany. Parsons believes that, although, to some extent, the intellectual movement he describes is 'an ideological reflection of certain basic social changes', a large part is also played by 'an "immanent" development within the body of social theory and knowledge of empirical fact itself' (5).

To anticipate the argument, Parsons claims that his empirical investigations show that an important aspect of the intellectual movement under way is a process of convergence on what he calls '*the voluntaristic theory of action*' (11; emphasis in original). In other words, theorists from different traditions are coming to understand that when people act (for example, marry, vote, drive a car, buy a house or start a revolution), their actions are not simply shaped and conditioned by the means or resources at their disposal (good looks, political connections, money, weapons, and so on), and the 'scientific' knowledge and powers of reasoning they possess.

They are also influenced by social norms specifying how people 'should' behave. This is important because if there are no norms in the picture, the theoretical consequences are nasty. Two outcomes are possible. One alternative is to accept that people are free to choose but are not morally restrained: producing freedom at the cost of disorder. Another is to factor out the freedom to choose and turn people into ciphers acting out the prescribed behaviour for someone with their social characteristics: producing order at the cost of unfreedom.

The voluntaristic theory of action avoids both these unpleasant alternatives. This theory can allow action to be 'voluntary' because it subjects that action to normative control or, at least, guidance. By putting norms into the picture it introduces some predictability into the model while allowing people to be intelligent choosing creatures. The result is freedom combined with order. This is the social outcome that Parsons (and, incidentally, Elias) wants to see.[16]

Positivism and Idealism

The process of theoretical development analysed by Parsons has four phases, although he does not demarcate them explicitly. I will label them the medieval phase, the early modern phase, the bifurcation phase, and the convergence phase.

The medieval phase: Parsons argues that thinking in terms of 'the action schema', in other words, thinking in terms of individuals who act within particular situations to achieve specific ends or goals, is 'deeply rooted in the common-sense experience of life' (51). This experience was coloured by the fact that 'In an ethical and religious sense Christianity has always been deeply individualistic' (53), a trait inherited from Greece and Rome and reinforced by the Protestant Reformation. Parsons adds that 'Germany is the principal exception' (52) to these generalizations.

The early modern phase: In this phase, beginning in the seventeenth century, individualism was reinforced by rationalism, producing a model in which the human actor was 'analogous to the scientist whose knowledge is the principal determinant of his action' (58). This positivistic model reflected the great prestige of the physical sciences, especially following the decline of the religious worldview that had predominated in the Middle Ages.

The bifurcation phase: During the nineteenth century there was 'an increasingly clear differentiation' between a positivistic and an idealistic trend within European culture, with the former becoming 'increasingly predominant' (62). Each of these tendencies had deep internal tensions. For example, one of the main forms of positivism was utilitarianism, an approach which argued that individuals would take those actions they believed would gain them benefits and avoid costs.

However, utilitarianism had to accept that actors were to be treated as free and independent agents, able to choose their own goals and pursue their own interests. This meant that scientific enquiry must not try to predict or control those choices, for example by explaining them in terms of factors such as heredity or environment. Putting these features out of bounds was a large and very unwelcome restriction upon science which naturally sought to explain as many aspects of social life as possible.

This 'utilitarian dilemma' (64) made that schema inherently unstable. A related problem was that when resources were scarce it was unrealistic to expect people to work together peacefully as if they had a 'natural identity of interests' (97). Parsons reviews the twists and turns that occur as these problems are identified clearly (for example, by Hobbes) and as alternative solutions are tried by thinkers such as Malthus and Darwin. Malthus stresses the need for regulatory institutions like marriage and private property. Darwin, on the other hand, turns the Hobbesian state of disorder into an 'orderly' struggle for survival in which the success of the fittest may be confidently expected and scientifically understood.

Meanwhile, thinkers in the idealistic tradition, influenced by Kant, argued that purposive human action could not be understood by using the intellectual tools of positivism and the natural sciences. Acts of the human mind, like making meaningful choices, were expressions of the human spirit and could not be 'reduced' to the level of material changes of the kind studied by physics or biology. Nor could they be made subject to law-like generalizations of the kind pursued in those disciplines. Idealist scholars concentrated instead on identifying such factors as the unique 'spirit' of particular cultures or epochs. They also, like Ranke, produced detailed histories that accumulated a wealth of detail without attempting to make empirical generalizations.

As Parsons puts it, 'there was no general analytical theory in terms of which to organize discrete observations, and to evaluate their scientific significance. Hence the necessity for recognizing a source of knowledge with little place in the repertoire of science as generally understood – a kind of "intuition" for the peculiar structure of a whole which could neither be "observed" in the usual operational sense, nor constructed by the ordinary theoretical processes' (481).[17]

The convergence phase: *The Structure of Social Action* is mainly concerned with this phase which began in the latter part of the nineteenth century and which, by implication, includes the work of Parsons himself. Tensions and dilemmas within both positivism and idealism led to the appearance of residual categories in theories produced within both traditions. These are categories containing facts and empirical observations that were clearly important but which could not be fitted elegantly into the core propositions of the theory. A major example of this is Pareto's concept of nonlogical action which did not fit easily into the utility theory he had borrowed from Marshall.[18]

According to Parsons, the voluntaristic theory of action emerged as the joint product of two developments. On the one hand, key writers in the positivistic tradition such as Durkheim drew upon concepts rooted in the idealistic tradition. On the other hand, and at the same time, leading inheritors of the idealistic tradition such as Weber drew upon certain aspects of positivism. The details of this convergence process are not directly relevant here. Many of Parsons's specific interpretations are disputed[19] but the point here is not the accuracy or persuasiveness of these interpretations but the fact that Parsons was describing what he considered to be the latest phase of a long-term process of theoretical development.

The flavour of Parsons's analysis is conveyed in the following passage: 'The ultimate-value element came into Weber's work in the first instance with the systems of value attitudes associated with religious ideas . . . Its institutional relation to the intrinsic means-end chain is expressed in the concept of legitimate order, the direct equivalent of Durkheim's rules possessing moral authority. Its nonempirical "religious" reference is formulated in the concept of charisma, corresponding to Durkheim's sacred . . . In all these respects there is a remarkable point-for-point correspondence between Weber and Durkheim' (717).

One aspect of the voluntaristic theory of action is worth noting. Parsons is well aware of 'the fundamental difficulty of atomistic theories when applied to organic phenomena' (740) such as markets, bureaucracies or other 'figurations', to use an Eliasian term. To cope with this matter, he uses 'the figure of a "web" of interwoven strands', arguing that a particular 'concrete immediate end' pursued by a specific actor 'may be thought of as a means to a variety of ultimate ends, so that from this point ahead the "threads" branch out in a number of different directions' (740–1).

Parsons is clear that the web of interconnected actions is the empirical reality encountered in experience. The individual acts can only be isolated conceptually, not in real life. As he puts it, 'A given concrete act is to be thought of, then, as a "knot" where a large number of . . . threads come momentarily together only to separate again, each one to enter, as it goes on, into a variety of other knots into which only a few of those with which it was formally combined enter with it . . . The web must be thought of as composed only of analytically, not in any sense concretely separable units' (741).

This passage from the late 1930s suggests that Elias and Parsons could have engaged in a fruitful interchange exploring the links between the former's dynamic figurations linking interdependent people, groups, institutions and processes, and the latter's dynamic webs linking human acts and their complex, interlocking ramifications.

The Dynamics of Intellectual Development

The Talcott Parsons who emerges from the pages of *The Structure of Social Action*, arguably his greatest work, is not the process-reducing model-monger, largely preoccupied with short-term statics, to whom Elias issued his challenged at Varna.[20] On the contrary, Elias and Parsons could almost have been a double act in the late 1930s. Indeed, the courtiers at Versailles, representatives of the civilized habitus in its early modern blossom-time, might almost have read *The Structure of Social Action* themselves, since their habitus embodies aspects of the voluntaristic theory of action.[21]

As Elias explained in *The Court Society* (Elias 1983), whose findings were incorporated into *The Civilizing Process*, advancement at court depended upon pursuing your interests in a rational and calculated way, using all the relevant means at your disposal while collecting as much information as you could about your environment, especially the activities and interests of your rivals. The choices and initiatives of people at court were additionally guided and constrained by the prevailing norms of the court, expressed, for example, in a rigid code of etiquette. The main features of the voluntaristic theory of action are there.

Of course, that does not mean that Parsons provides an explanation for the emergence of the habitus expressed in civilized courtly behaviour in European society during the early modern period. However, he does make a contribution to a problem identified by both Elias and himself. This is the issue of why an objective or scientific understanding of the civilizing process and the voluntaristic theory of action, respectively, has not been achieved until the twentieth century although the process (as understood by Elias) and the theory (as understood by Parsons) were, supposedly, in operation many centuries earlier.

Parsons's answer is that by the nineteenth century human understanding of the world was split between positivistic and idealistic (or aprioristic) theories each of which was incomplete and subject to internal tensions.[22] Only when the two theoretical traditions converged and reconfigured did a unified approach emerge that, in his view, clarified the nature of human action. Elias also recognizes the dominance of the two traditions but sees them both as fatally disabled because, as he puts it, they accept an atomistic model of 'the individual' rather than seeing that human beings 'live from the first in interdependence with others' (Elias 1994a, 203).[23] In his view, no convergence between the two traditions could overcome these fundamental flaws.

Elias has no truck with 'The image of the individual as an entirely free, independent being, a "closed personality" who is "inwardly" quite self-sufficient and separate from all other people'. He thinks it leads into an 'epistemological impasse. Thought steers helplessly back and forth between the Scylla of positivism and the Charybdis of apriorism . . . We have here an example of how closely the inability to conceive long-term social processes (i.e. structured changes in the figurations formed by large numbers of human beings) or to understand the human beings forming such figurations is connected to a certain type of image of man and self-perception' (203). Elias goes on to name Descartes, Weber and Parsons as being guilty of having this erroneous image of the individual.[24]

Parsons clearly does not examine social processes of the kind defined by Elias in the last paragraph. It is not necessary to accept Parsons's conclusion that the voluntaristic theory of action which, in his view, emerges in the latter phase of this process, provides 'a clearer, sounder understanding of a broad range of the facts of human action' (Parsons 1968, 775). However, *The Structure of Social Action* is certainly the study of a process of theoretical development that is related to, or part of, broader social processes, as Parsons recognizes early in his text.[25]

Parsons describes his work as representing; 'scientific progress; indeed, notable scientific progress'. He is right but for the wrong reasons. In the last few pages of his book Parsons gives the impression of a man who has found a great treasure at the end of a long, patient and systematic search. This treasure is the voluntaristic theory of action and having 'discovered' it, so to speak, Parsons goes on in his later works to elaborate and build upon this idea. However, in taking away his 'treasure' Parsons left behind the substance of his real achievement, which was to trace a major movement of ideas in a way that explained the tensions and contradictions pushing it forward across several generations and through the work of several writers.

It is quite possible to reject the suggestion that the voluntaristic theory of action gives us a scientifically verified account of human action, while accepting that Parsons has advanced our understanding of the development of theory as a long-term process. Parsons's analysis of selected items from the stream of theoretical writings, especially from Hobbes onward, may be placed alongside Elias's analysis of selected items from the stream of manners books during the medieval and early modern period.

One challenge this would pose is to trace the interplay between two sub-processes: on the one hand, the development and enactment of a 'civilized' habitus as an unplanned consequence of long-term transformations embedding people in increasingly dense and interdependent figurations; and on the other hand, the development and enforcement of discourses which rule out some forms of behaviour while constraining people to act in certain patterned ways. As an example of the latter, consider the impact of Malthusian thought on the treatment of the poor in nineteenth-century Britain (not least Ireland) and, more recently, the role of the World Bank in developing countries or the impact of neo-liberal orthodoxies in eastern Europe. The 'thou shalt nots' of the political economists are just as important as the 'thou shalt nots' of the manners books.

Parsons's work alerts us to the possibility that the long-term sequences of development that Elias captures in his term 'the civilizing process' are interwoven with long-term movements in intellectual understanding that are not adequately grasped by consigning the relevant theorists to a box labelled 'homo clausus' or treating them as an ideological reflection of other aspects of society.

The theories Parsons writes about are relevant because the works of Hobbes, Locke, Ricardo, Marx, Marshall, Durkheim, Weber and so on have contributed to the strategies and legitimizing ideas employed by the powerful in government, the professions and business.[26] If the powerful believe in 'the voluntaristic theory of action', then those 'below' who wish to survive and prosper are likely to behave as if they believe it also, and, indeed, to believe it in fact, eventually. The same applies to the Christian idea of 'the soul', the capitalist idea of 'the free market' and the idea of 'the nation'. This perception is expressed more strongly in the works of Foucault than in those of either Parsons or Elias. However, Parsons provides a reasoned account of the 'immanent' dynamics of long-term processes of intellectual development which is missing from either Foucault or Elias.[27]

Parsons and Foucault

In fact, writing during the early 1940s, Parsons displayed an insider's knowledge of many aspects of the forms of control through discursive practices that Foucault later attacked in the adopted role of outsider. The difference between the two men is that whereas, as will be discussed in the next chapter, Foucault wanted to resist these practices, Parsons wished to exploit them more efficiently on behalf of the established social order.

This comparison between Parsons and Foucault is worth briefly pursuing further. In an article entitled 'Propaganda and social control' published during World War II, Parsons argued in favour of a propaganda programme within American society with the object of 'strengthening attachment to the basic institutional patterns and cultural traditions of the society' (Parsons 1942a, 569). This programme would be 'a kind of "social psychotherapy"' designed to cultivate 'maturity' in the population.

Parsons argued that 'the structure of Western society in its relation to the functions of social control provides an extraordinary opening for the deliberate propaganda of reinforcement as an agency of control'. Such propaganda would be 'simply an extension of the automatic but latent functions of many institutional patterns' (570). These patterns turn out to be similar to those identified by Foucault decades later.

Parsons begins by noticing that 'control functions' exist in 'the most ordinary patterns of interaction between persons' in order to overcome, as a matter of routine, the 'essential factor of "resistance" to the fulfilment of normative expectations and obligations' (556). He then turns to the therapeutic situation and argues that the analyst's authority is based upon the patient's trust or confidence. By systematically questioning or refusing to accept any rationalizations and motivations that appear to be immature or lacking in reality, the analyst 'allows' the patient to adjust to his or her personal situation.

Analysts draw upon the generalized authority of the medical profession which is 'a particularly striking case of relatively unconscious automatic control mechanisms in society' (561). Medicine, in turn, derives its authority from science. The authority to provide or criticize 'definitions of the situation' does not simply belong to science. Historically, the clergy, the law and academics have had similar influence.

In a strikingly Foucauldian passage, Parsons comments on 'the similarities in the ways in which the medical, the academic, and the clerical roles exert a steady discipline on the people to whom they are subjected. The church service . . . exerts an important influence in this way. By the doctrinal content of its sermons and scriptural readings it serves to stabilize the definition of the situation, while at the same time through the collective ritual observance in hymn-singing, prayer, and in other ways, it has an important influence on attitudes' (566–7).

The authority and influence of the cleric, the doctor, the professor and, by the same token, the government official, are greatly reinforced by the impersonality enshrined in the 'office' each fills. The authority each exercises is not personal. To put it in a more Foucauldian way, the authority resides in the discourse with its 'official' tone. As Parsons puts it, 'control mechanisms, the operation of which is not a matter of the deliberate "policy" of any group, or even of their manifest functions, pervade the whole structure, and play an essential role in the functioning of the social system' (568).

In order for a propaganda programme to work, 'it is essential to establish a position of impersonal authority' based upon 'technical competence and moral integrity'. However, Parsons adds, no professional group was recognized by the public as having technical competence in '"social psychiatry"

– perhaps someday some of the social sciences will achieve this – . . . [and] the next best seems to be the deliberate cultivation of a reputation for scrupulously truthful reporting of information the sources of which the public cannot have direct access to'.

Parsons concludes that the main task of the propaganda agency would be 'to "refute" undesirable opinions and definitions of the situation', keeping more desirable opinions and definitions 'continually, but not too obtrusively, before the public. In detail just how it should be worked out is a very complicated and technical subject' (571).

Parsons and Germany

Part of the rationale for Parsons's proposed agency to transmit 'propaganda of reinforcement' was that it would counter the 'disruptive' propaganda of the Nazis.[28] This was designed to subvert the democracies. However, while reinforcement propaganda was intended to encourage 'maturity' and development of 'the reality principle', disruptive propaganda by fascists 'exploits precisely the opposite elements of character structure, those most closely bound up with "neurotic" types of reaction pattern, ideological distortion and affective overreaction' (570).

It is clear from passages such as this that by the early 1940s Parsons had encountered the works of Freud. Like Elias, he incorporates a Freudian dimension in his sociological analysis when trying to make sense of the way German society had developed in the early twentieth century.

Parsons's explanation for the rise of fascism emphasized the psychological and social instability caused by the process of rationalization. By this he means the 'cumulative social change' associated with advances in science and technology and the shift towards defining a whole range of 'action patterns and contexts of human relationships' in contractual terms oriented to 'relatively specific and limited goals'. Other aspects of rationalization were the codification of individual rights, the development of modern forms of private property freed from feudal or other types of traditional obligation, and the rise of a spirit of 'critical rationality' (1942b, 141) directed against all aspects of culture.

The consequence of this 'very central dynamic process' (140) was widespread anomie and psychological insecurity: 'The personality is not stably organized about a coherent system of values, goals and expectations. Attitudes tend to vacillate between indecision which paralyzes action – and all manner of scruples and inhibitions – and on the other hand compulsively "overdetermined" reactions which endow particular goals and symbols with an excess of hatred, devotion or enthusiasm over what is appropriate to the given situation' (139).

Parsons argues that the development of the utilitarian tradition of social thought was one aspect of this process of rationalization. One of its early expressions was classical economics. Later, it took the form of socialism and Marxism.[29] Unfortunately, this tradition of thought, as it became 'leftist' and 'positivistic', was not 'adequate to formulate all the important values of our society, nor its cognitive orientation to the world'. It ignored or debunked the 'non-logical' aspects of human behaviour, including religion, friendship, and the traditions of family, class, ethnicity, region and nation. It even debunked rationalism itself.

The inadequacies of utilitarianism enabled opposing 'anti-intellectualist' movements, especially fascism, to take root and grow strong. It appealed to specific groups placed under intense strain by the uneven process of rationalization, including females, the young, the lower middle class and 'traditional elements' especially in rural areas. Parsons concludes that 'In the complex process of interaction in Western societies between imperfectly integrated institutional structures, ideological definitions of the situation, and the psychological reaction patterns typical of anomie, at a certain stage in the dynamic process of its development this new structured mass movement has come upon the scene and at certain points has gained ascendancy'.

In Parsons's view the possibility of fascism was 'as deeply rooted in the social structure and dynamics of our society as was socialism at an earlier stage' (145). Parsons's analysis of fascism emphasizes that it is a political tendency present in a large number of Western societies, not simply Germany.

Towards the end of the war, the question of what to do with the defeated enemy came onto the agenda. Parsons gave his views at a conference of psychiatrists, anthropologists and sociologists held in New York in 1944 (Parsons 1945). The conference agreed that the war was not caused simply by the Nazi regime or the specific situation of Germany in the 1930s. Instead, it was the result of 'a typical German character structure which predisposes people to define all human relations in terms of dominance, submission and romantic revolt'. This character structure was 'supported by and closely interdependent with, an institutional structure of German society' (78).

Parsons had his own version of this general argument. He stressed that to understand German society it was essential to understand the historical roots of the German character structure and how this affected the way Germans defined their own situation as a nation. He argued that the German character structure had a 'striking dualism'. One component was 'emotional, idealistic, active, romantic', the other was 'orderly, hardworking, hierarchy preoccupied, methodical, submissive, gregarious, materialistic' (85). This second component gave a 'peculiar prominence' (86) to authority relations.

The Prussian state had made effective use of the orderliness and submissiveness in the German character, especially in its civil service and military organization. Both institutions supported a culture that put great emphasis on 'prestige status' and 'militaristic values' emphasizing hierarchy and formalism. However, 'Every at all complex society contains very important elements of internal conflict and tension' (84) and Germany is no exception. For example, the traditional patriarchal family pattern was put under strain when 'an authoritarian father in the family [is also] a subordinate whose subordination is continually rubbed in outside' (87).

Another serious difficulty was that the culture of the Prussian state 'took precious little account' of the emotional, romantic and idealistic component of German character. This was diverted into religion and 'various forms of a-political romanticism – in the arts and philosophy. Germany as a land of poets and idealistic dreamers fits into this situation' (97). At this point, Parsons is referring to the division between the politico-military and academic-professional wings of German society, a distinction also analysed by Elias, although in a different way.[30]

Parsons argues that the dualism in German character structure is expressed not only in the differentiation of militaristic and academic cultures but also within each individual. For example, despite their 'orderliness, industry and methodicality . . . there has been little romanticization of *success* in Germany' (86; emphasis in original). The efficiency of German bureaucrats is linked to a culture that is unsympathetic to individualistic money-making and easily mobilized against capitalism. Here Parsons is tuning in to the tension that Elias discusses at the beginning of *The Civilizing Process*: the antipathy between German 'seriousness' and French, British and American 'triviality', 'materialism' and 'corruption'.

Elias focuses in particular on the debate surrounding the supposed virtues and vices of *Kultur* and civilization, respectively, going back to the eighteenth century. Parsons shows that it is still very much a live issue in the 1940s. For example, he proposes that the victorious allies should encourage Germans to adopt such values as those of 'science and free enquiry, the dignity and freedom of the person . . . [and] equality of opportunity'. However, he adds, care should be taken not to associate these values with 'those aspects of "Western" societies which have served as widespread negative symbols in Germany. Thus, expressions of the values of freedom should not emphasize freedom to make profits, or even, in many contexts, of trade' (100).

The Nazis exploited the German desire for order and security while also providing channels of expression for both sides of the dualistic German character. They used the desire for hierarchy, subordination and methodicality. They also 'harnessed [the] . . . romantic dynamism to an aggressive, expansionist, nationalistic political goal' (85). The Nazis provided the Germans with an 'ideological definition of the situation' (96) which identified the Germans as a master race with a special mission in a corrupt world. The result was a message with 'an extraordinarily wide combination of symbolic appeals calculated to catch virtually every main strain of German sentiment with which it is difficult for Anglo-Saxons to cope' (98).

In practice, instead of providing order and security, the Nazi regime did the opposite. It '"atomized" the society wherever its older groupings conflicted with the Party, which involved an exceedingly wide area' (91). However, writing as the war was in its final stages, Parsons recognized that the Nazi synthesis remained powerful at the ideological level. How was it to be destroyed?

Parsons had six specific proposals. Find non-political outlets for the romantic, idealistic yearnings of the Germans, for example by integrating their professional class into broader international networks. Encourage the emancipation of women. Undermine the old Junker class.[31] Encourage industrial production and the development of a socially mobile urban population. Introduce greater equality of opportunity into the higher civil service.

And, finally, a most interesting idea: 'The fundamental remedy [for] . . . the German tendency to be fascinated by power' is to undermine 'the system of competitive politico-military power relationships' and 'so define the situation that the international order is a cooperative order and . . . Germany is not primarily a competitive unit. The moral foundations for such a definition exist but have been overlaid by the competitive power pattern. They must be brought again to the fore' (88).

In this last suggestion Parsons was participating in the strengthening of a political mood that helped to lay the foundations for a range of institutions from the United Nations to the European Union, a topic which returns in a later chapter.

However, before discussing that issue, Elias will be compared with two writers from the generation born in the 1920s, beginning with Michel Foucault.

Notes

1 This shared background helps explain a belief they both shared. It was expressed by Parsons as a 'conviction of the fundamental continuity between the living systems of the organic world and those of the human sociocultural world'. Like Elias in this context, Parsons was interested in the role of 'the "symbol"' (Parsons 1970a, 831) although their particular analyses differed. A further coincidental similarity is that both men were afflicted with deaths in their close family during the early 1940s. Parsons lost both parents and an elder brother in this period. Like Elias he had trouble completing work for publication at this time although he emerged from these difficulties far more quickly than Elias. See Parsons 1970a, 839–40.

2 It is worth also mentioning that they had a similar scholarly habitus. A.J. Heerma van Voss and A. van Stolk, the editors of Elias's *Reflections on a Life*, describe his work pattern as one that was maintained 'seven days a week . . . until ten at night' (Elias 1994b, 2). Edward Shils recalls that 'when collaborating with Parsons we often worked until midnight discussing and drafting, discussing and redrafting; then often as early as seven o'clock in the morning of the next day, he would be on the telephone with me, raising a question about what we have done the preceding day, suggesting a new formulation, a new distinction, or a new connection which we had failed to make. He sought to find systemic patterns and the interconnectedness of all things in society' (Shils 1981, 192).

3 For an interesting commentary on some of Parsons's formative experiences, see Szakolczai 1996, 64–94. See also Parsons 1970a.

4 For some additional comparative comments on Parsons and Elias, see Robertson 1992a, 219.

5 Elias 1994b 30, 88–9, 91–2.

6 Years later, Elias commented in passing: 'It gives me a certain satisfaction to be thought of as a German sociologist' – although he added 'but, of course, I am more than that' (Elias 1994b, 75).

7 Furthermore, Parsons was clearly a 'gentleman'. Edward Shils recalls his first meeting with Parsons in the mid-1930s as follows: 'The first thing that struck me about Parsons was the look of refinement on his face, which was not common among [American] sociologists. He looked well-bred, and gave the impression of pacific concentration of mind. Most sociologists looked very ill-assorted . . . they were gawky, awkward country boys, however old they were. Parsons looked a little like a genteel easterner, although . . . he [was] born in Ohio' (Shils 1981, 191, quoted in Smith 1988, 141).

8 In this section I will also draw on the critical comments about Parsons made by Elias in the preface to the 1968 edition of *The History of Manners*, volume 1 of *The Civilizing Process*, which is reprinted as an appendix in the 1994 edition. See Elias 1994a, 181–215.

9 First volume of *The Civilizing Process*.

10 Elias takes the view that inaccurate perceptions are largely to be explained in terms of the 'subject-orientation' of the perceiver; in other words, the tendency for perceptions to express the involvements, desires and self-image of the observer. In Elias's approach, two important and, by implication, related, factors tend to make perceptions more 'object-adequate', i.e. lead them to express the actual character of the object to a greater extent. These factors are the competitive advantages flowing from having accurate knowledge (for example, in war or in the contest for limited food resources) and development of detachment, the ability to reduce or eliminate the influence of subject-oriented emotions and drives upon the process of perception. Detachment is not easy to achieve, as he sees it, and is subject to 'double-bind processes' such as the difficulty of resisting the tendency for emotional and fantasy-ridden perceptions to take hold when control is difficult to achieve or maintain in competitive situations where a great deal is at stake. See Elias 1971; Elias 1987c; Fletcher 1997, 58.

11 Quoted in Fitzhenry 1986, 172–3.

12 As Parsons puts it, 'It is a corollary of the immanent tendency of reason to a rational integration of experience as a whole, that a scientist as well as other men may be presumed to have philosophical ideas and that these will stand in determinate reciprocal relations to his scientific theories' (26–7).

13 Parsons's subsequent use of Freudian ideas will be discussed later in this chapter.

14 Elias 1994a, 3–41.

15 Marshall and Pareto, English and Italian respectively, are aligned with Durkheim, a grouping that mirrors traditional Germanic contempt for the Latin and Anglo-Saxon preoccupation with materialism, industry, etiquette and social superficiality as opposed to the deep and soulful concerns of writers such as Goethe and Schiller.

16 Elias concludes *The Civilizing Process* with his vision of a future in which 'the common pattern of self-control expected of men can be confined to those restraints which are necessary in order that men can live with each other and with themselves with a high chance of enjoyment and a low chance of fear' (Elias 1994a, 524).

17 Elias has a certain sympathy with the idea that a kind of intuitive penetration beyond particularities is possible. To recall a point quoted early, he believed that 'beyond a certain point in the accumulation of material facts, historiography enters the phase when it ought to be no longer satisfied with the collection of further particulars and the description of those already assembled, but should be concerned with those problems that facilitate penetration of the underlying regularities by which people in a certain society are bound over and over again to particular patterns of conduct and to very specific functional chains . . . and by which these relationships change in a very specific direction'. At this stage of investigation the object is to identify 'the structure within the entirety of its interdependencies' (Elias 1994a, 488).

18 See Parsons 1968, 454–60.

19 See, for example, Giddens 1971, 106; Mestrovic 1993, 46, 60; Scaff 1989, x; Turner and Factor 1994, 175 and Tenbruck 1987, 262–3.

20 See also Kilminster 1998 for a discussion of Parsons and 'Parsonianism'.

21 Not that people develop a habitus simply by reading books, although 'manners books' were presumably intended to mould behaviour and attitudes. These books were also an indication of standards, perceptions and forms of behaviour already well-established in the society at the time they were published.

22 In fact, the two traditions were well represented at Heidelberg in the 1920s, as Elias acknowledges, in the persons of Alfred Weber, exponent of idealistic *Kultur*, and Karl Mannheim, who had strong leftist tendencies. Elias was teaching assistant to Mannheim. Weber was Elias's first sponsor for his *Habilitation* candidature. Later, Mannheim took on that role. See Elias 1994b, 102–20.

23 This quotation and those in the next paragraph come from the preface to the 1968 edition of *The History of Manners*.

24 See Elias 1994a, 204.

25 Discussing the 'basic revolution in empirical interpretations of some of the most important social problems that has been going on', Parsons states that 'It is, of course, very probable that this change is in considerable part simply an ideological reflection of certain basic social changes . . . It is no less probable that a considerable part has been played by an "immanent" development within the body of social theory and knowledge of empirical fact itself' (Parsons 1968, 5). Parsons also assumed that the dominant theoretical understandings within a society had great influence upon the way people in that society defined and used 'knowledge'.

26 Exactly how influential, by what routes and on what time-scale are issues that cannot be discussed here.

27 In *The Order of Things*, for example, Foucault does not explain the shift from one episteme to the next. Foucault 1974.

28 Parsons also refers to a third type of propaganda that he labels 'revolutionary' (Parsons 1942a, 568). This is designed to convert people to values and definitions that are in conflict with existing institutions.

29 Compare Elias's reference to the 'utilitarian, rationalist humanists of the left' (Elias 1994b, 103).

30 Elias pays attention to the effects of the particular pattern of provincial and local courts in German society. Traders, manufacturers and shopkeepers, however wealthy, were excluded. Many such families encouraged their offspring to go into professional careers, including the universities. Elias himself falls into this pattern. See Elias 1996.

31 'It may well be that the bulk of what is left [of the Junker class] . . . will be adequately cared for by Russian occupation of Northeastern Germany. Since the Soviets have not the same tradition of respect for established property rights as the Americans, the moral dilemma for them of direct expropriation of Junker estates would not be nearly so serious' (Parsons 1945, 88).

5

FOUCAULT AND ELIAS

The Great Escape

On 2nd December 1970 French riot police were out in force on the Parisian Left Bank. Michel Foucault was at the Sorbonne to give his inaugural lecture as Professor of the History of Systems of Thought. Everyone going to hear him passed uniformed officers and police cars in siege formation.

Suddenly, Foucault appeared at the rostrum. He was an intense-looking man in his mid-forties, head completely shaven. *Le Monde*'s reporter described him as 'a hairless personage, of ivory tint, Buddhist in demeanour . . ., Mephistophelean in . . . gaze'. His lecture was a dazzling 'high wire act' (Miller 1993, 183).

It so happened there was 'student trouble' that day in Paris. The police presence was not for Foucault. But everyone must have made a connection between the lecturer inside the hall and the noisy scenes outside. Foucault had faced police tear gas. About a year before, along with others, he had taken over the main campus buildings at the University of Vincennes in the Parisian suburbs. When police tried to dislodge them, Foucault and a few last-ditchers retreated to the administrative building roof, then threw bricks at the officers below.

Foucault was an activist, a thinker and a performer. In all these roles he was a challenging, subversive, master of the unexpected. He once compared his lectures to stage shows: 'My relation with the people there is like that of an actor or an acrobat'. Or, he might have added, an escapologist. There was something Houdini-like about Foucault, in more ways than one. Michel Foucault and Harry Houdini were both highly professional performers drawing big crowds. Both were driven men, eager for acclaim. Both died in their fifties, at the height of their fame.

Both had a deep interest in escape techniques: physical escape in the case of Houdini, mental or spiritual escape in Foucault's case. Only a few hundred metres from where Foucault gave his inaugural lecture, sixty years earlier Houdini had leapt into the Seine wearing only a bathing suit and a pair of handcuffs attached by a chain to his neck. Miraculously, or so it seemed, he had survived.[1] Houdini showed the world he could escape from handcuffs. Foucault wanted to show his audience they could escape the imprisoning society.

The need to make a 'great escape' from a 'great confinement' is at the heart of Foucault's vision. This confinement is not physical, not like an eighteenth-century madhouse. It is mental confinement, constriction in the straitjacket of the self. This straitjacket is woven and fitted during those many moments when we are taught 'what is proper' at the meal table, in the playground, in the classroom, at the workbench, and so on.

Discipline moulds us: as children, as pupils, as patients, as conscripts, as welfare claimants and so on. When learning these roles we are taught to accept certain discursive practices, particular routines for interpreting and dealing with the world in speech and thought. Once society has given us a self (an identity, a sense of who we are), it is difficult to be any different. The assumptions and habits embedded in speech and thought infiltrate our feelings, our perceptions, our sense of reality.

Foucault's instinct was to challenge this process. How exciting, how dangerous, he thought, to deny the self imposed by society, to rip off the straitjacket, release explosive and unpredictable energy, let our own true being speak. That form of speech would be challenging, creative, violent, unpredictable, disruptive: in other words, a threat to established order. In Foucault's opinion, that threat is feared by all people and institutions with an interest in the established order. So discourse is kept in chains.

We have to obey specific rules of grammar, conform to particular styles of reasoning, follow certain research topics, avoid others, and so on. Under this regime, each published text must have its clearly identified 'author', directly responsible for it, someone to punish if necessary. Foucault's mission was to wage war against these constraints, break out of culture's prison, restore the dangerous, untamed power of true discourse. That was the message of his inaugural lecture.

In the Hothouse

Foucault is an interesting test case for Elias's theory of the civilizing process. He was a product of the society that had provided Elias with his principal example of that process in operation. Foucault came from a solidly conventional family belonging to a solidly conventional class living in a solidly conventional part of France: Poitiers, 'a petit bourgeois, provincial milieu' (Foucault 1996, 371) three hundred kilometres southwest of Paris. Foucault's father was a highly distinguished local surgeon: a surgeon's son, he had married a surgeon's daughter. He wanted his son to be a surgeon.

When *The Civilizing Process* was published in 1939, Foucault was thirteen. Had he read it at the time, which he almost certainly did not, he might have found the following passage relevant to his personal situation:

> [I]t is precisely fears of the loss of distinguishing hereditary prestige . . . that have to this day a decisive part in shaping the prevailing rule of conduct. Precisely those fears . . . are particularly predisposed to internalization; they, far more than the fear of poverty, hunger or direct physical danger, become rooted in the individual member of such classes, through his upbringing, as inner anxieties which bind him to a learned code almost automatically, under the pressure of a

strong super-ego, even independently of any control by others. The continuous concern of parents whether their child will attain the standard of conduct of their own or even a higher class, whether it will maintain or increase the prestige of the family . . . fears of this kind surround the child from its earliest years . . . They continuously add fuel to the fiery circle of inner anxieties, which hold the behaviour and feelings of the growing child permanently within definite limits, binding him to a certain standard of shame and embarrassment, to a specific accent, to particular manners, whether he wishes or not. (Elias 1994a, 521–2)

As a child, Foucault felt himself to be under seige from punishing pressures and demands coming from two directions: the external world and his own psychic drives. He later recalled that the 'obligation of speaking, of making conversation with visitors [was] . . . very strange and very boring. I often wondered why people had to speak'. At school he was a loner, always at his books.

The atmosphere in Poitiers was oppressive. Religious bigotry, class envy, war and (after 1940) foreign occupation all added to the social and psychological tension. Also, Foucault got crushes on other boys. This whole milieu taught him 'there were many different ways of speaking as well as many forms of silence'. He discovered, for example, that 'some kinds of silence . . . implied very sharp hostility' while 'others . . . meant deep friendship, emotional admiration, even love' (Foucault 1996, 371).

There are some interesting resemblances between Foucault's 'respectable' background and Elias's own in Breslau some decades before.[2] However, while Elias's household provided him with a relatively pleasant cocoon Foucault found himself stifling in a hothouse.

These early years gave Foucault great self-discipline. His writing was a defiant answering thrust against the shaping pressures imposed by society and culture on our bodies and minds. He was determined to hold these pressures at bay, revealing them for what they are. This process helped him make sense of his own inner drives, especially his homosexual inclinations and fascination with suicide.

In fact, it is important to emphasize the centrality for Foucault of the creative tension between the need for order and the desire to overthrow it. On the one hand, he wanted to make a 'great escape' from pressure and constraint. On the other hand, he had a powerful 'bourgeois' urge towards discipline and hard work. This gave him the capacity to spend long periods buried in the archives, and allowed him to contemplate huge research projects such as his multi-volume history of sexuality.

Foucault shared Elias's bourgeois work ethic but in other respects his situation was very different. In fact, Foucault's problem was precisely the opposite of Elias's. From a very early age Elias knew what he wanted to be: a professor in a German university. Creating this future identity for himself was a project that required German society to remain relatively stable and open. In fact, it became less stable and increasingly closed to Jews such as himself. Elias wanted an explanation for the violent and oppressive nature of German society.

Elias believed the Germans' consciousness of themselves was profoundly affected by the lateness and instability of Germany's political unification. Unfortunately, 'for centuries the question "What is really German?" has not been laid to rest' (1995a, 5). In Elias's eyes, the case of the French seemed different. They did not worry about their identity. Social peace prevailed. *The Civilizing Process* was, in large part, an attempt to discover what long-term social processes had removed the question of national identity from the French agenda.

By contrast, Foucault wanted the question of identity put right back onto the agenda. He took on the task of exposing and attacking the discursive practices which, as he saw it, closed down inquiry into the nature and boundaries of human experience. Ironically, the routines of etiquette, for Elias such a key expression of the civilizing process in French society, were a torment for Foucault as a child.

Elias knew from an early age what he wanted to be. By contrast, Foucault knew from an early age what he did *not* want to be. He did not want to 'accept' the identity that was being foisted on him by a society that was all too solid and stable and, in conventional terms, offered him an open door to worldly success.

Three Strategies of Resistance

There were three strategies available to Foucault if he wished to avoid accepting the identity that society offered him. One strategy was to remove himself from this painful and oppressive setting. As a young man he attempted suicide on more than occasion. A less drastic version of this strategy was exile. Near the end of his life Foucault remarked: 'I have suffered and still suffer from a lot of things in French social and cultural life. That was why I left France in 1955' (Foucault 1988b, 4–5; Eribon 1991, 74). Between 1955 and 1970 Foucault spent only eight years in France.

Five years were spent teaching French culture in Uppsala, Warsaw and Hamburg (1955–60). These years allowed Foucault to make a 'great escape' from a society he found oppressive. As a leading light in the Maison de France (Uppsala), the French Centre (Warsaw) and the French Institute (Hamburg), Foucault had a new freedom to interpret France in his own way. This neatly turned the tables: in these years, Foucault was defining French society rather than French society defining Foucault.

A second strategy was resistance and transgression. At first sight this seems to put Foucault in the same camp as Sartre who taught that people were able to make existential choices even under the most oppressive cir-cumstances. However, Foucault was much more sensitive than Sartre to the 'invisible hand' of discursive practices: assumptions and habits embedded in speech and thought. These guide our behaviour even when we think we are making free choices. Sartre argued that human freedom is inalienable – no matter how oppressed we might seem to be. Foucault counter-argued that discursive practices always shape and discipline our feelings, perceptions, and sense of reality – no matter how free we might seem to be.[3]

In Foucault's opinion, the bonds of inhibition and restraint can be radically loosened through calculated violence or subversion directed at the self, society, or both. For example, some forms of physical restraint or abuse such as sado-masochistic sexuality may push the consciousness over the edge and lead to psychic release, escape from the oppressive regime of normality.

In fact, any kind of limit-experience, real or imagined, could lead towards liberation. Political resistance provides another route to the same goal.[4] So do 'alternative' art forms such as the theatre of the absurd. The object is to subvert the discursive and non-discursive practices shaping 'normal' identity and stimulate feelings and insights that are normally blocked. If this is successful it provides the participant with new insights into the 'unprocessed' existence that is behind or beyond human culture and language.[5]

A third strategy for Foucault was to protect himself from society's worst oppressions by rising within it, by achieving worldly success. His inaugural lecture at the Sorbonne, with which this chapter began, marked the achievement of a status that provided him with the protection he needed from French society. He began to resist more openly. In 1971 Foucault founded the Prison Information Group (*Groupe d'Information sur les Prisons*) which campaigned against inhumane prison conditions. In 1972 he was arrested following a demonstration against police brutality. In 1975 he published *Displine and Punish* (Foucault 1977a).

Very soon after finishing *Discipline and Punish* Foucault began work on his multi-volumed *History of Sexuality* (Foucault 1978; Foucault 1987; Foucault 1988a). This took him off the streets and into the archives, out of modern society and into the villas of ancient Greece and Rome. It was another escape.

The Maelstrom and the Panopticon

The difference between Elias and Foucault could be summarized in the aphorism: Elias tried to swallow the world, Foucault tried to spit it out. They both worked hard to identify, as far they could, the processes and mechanisms that produced the situations in which human beings found themselves. However, their intentions were different. Foucault's objective was to subvert those processes and mechanisms or get himself beyond their reach.

Elias, however, did not consider that was a viable option. Instead he wanted to be able to understand or 'know' the forces that made the world turn so that he and others could adapt their behaviour in the light of this knowledge. Elias's object was to work towards producing scientific knowledge of social processes and figurations so that some of their worst consequences for human beings could be avoided by rational action.

As I have argued elsewhere,[6] the contrasting approaches of Michel Foucault and Norbert Elias can be summed up in two images. One comes from Bentham's plan for a Panopticon, a building designed to allow all its inhabitants to be visible from a central point. Foucault borrows this idea in his *Discipline and Punish* (Foucault 1977a). The other image comes from a story by Edgar Allen Poe. This story, which refers to two fishermen caught in a maelstrom, is recalled by Elias in his *Involvement and Detachment* (Elias 1987c).

The Panopticon is designed to monitor and control its inmates who are, virtually, its prisoners. Each of the prisoners is totally exposed, completely controlled, and deprived of the chance to be free or exercise any initiative. These prisoners may be contrasted with the fishermen Poe writes about. They are brothers caught in a highly dangerous and uncertain situation. The whirlpool is pulling their boat down into the watery depths and death seems a very likely prospect.

However, Elias's point is that even a serious situation like this is not irretrievable if you remain cool. Unfortunately, one of the brothers is unable to do this. He panics and, as a result, gets sucked down beneath the waves. The other brother manages to control his emotions and stay detached. By using his eyes and brain, and weighing up the evidence available to him (small objects float to the surface, large objects get sucked under the water) he manages to act rationally (tie himself to a small barrel) and survive. If we want to understand Foucault we have to realize that he empathizes with the prisoner trapped in the Panopticon. If we want to understand Elias it helps to think of the surviving fisherman.

Foucault, the prisoner in the Panopticon, would find the maelstrom a more congenial place to be but he would be more interested in the experiences of the drowning brother, the one slipping free of society's oppressions. Similarly, Elias, the endangered fisherman, would appreciate the more orderly and controlled existence of the Panopticon but he would be keen to share the perspective enjoyed by the observer in the watchtower who was, supposedly, able to obtain something approaching object-adequate knowledge of the surrounding world.

Elias looks for the principles of order within the world. Foucault cares about this too (although his analysis is different) but he is equally, perhaps more, interested in the creative chaos that lies, in his view, beyond, behind or somewhere deep within the world of oppressive discursive practices. This takes him into areas and assumptions that Elias rejected.

Nietzsche, Husserl and Bachelard

Foucault turned, for example, to Friedrich Nietzsche who deplored any suggestion (he was thinking of Hegel) that the human record was a story of increasing rationality and continual progress. According to Nietzsche, events are made by the hazardous encounter of active and reactive forces, partly influenced by a few noble human beings able to influence the shape of morality and knowledge. The natural and social sciences plough ahead relentlessly, without vision, without regard for human interests. Christianity offers no more than arid dogma for the servile and small-minded.

Nietzsche says: do not accept the promise of order and comfort in these false systems of thought. Instead, confront directly the hostile chaos of existence. Not everyone has the courage to do this but some, at least, can reach knowledge of primal being. One route is through intoxication, involvement, and self-forgetfulness. This 'Dionysian' approach leads to a state of passionate release. We see things as they truly are, bringing ecstasy and joy mixed with horror and agony.

The only way to bear this terrible, dangerous knowledge is by mixing the Dionysian spirit of headlong involvement with an Apollonian spirit of dream-like detachment. If we can manage to find a balance between Dionysian involvement and Apollonian detachment, then the restless flux of life can be at least partially expressed in terms of principles of aesthetic order, through music, sculpture, drama and so on. The challenge is to find this balance between the Dionysian and Apollonian spirits and discover a way of conveying the knowledge they lay bare. Both spirits have their source beyond the normal waking state. They can best be experienced by a consciousness that is both heightened and relaxed, as in a dream.

Foucault was very interested in dreams as a possible route beyond the imprisoning structures and practices of modernity. In 'Dream, imagination and existence' (Foucault 1993), Foucault comes down squarely on the side of Husserl over Freud, the opposite choice to the one made by Elias.[7] Husserlians treat each dream as a meaningful total experience which is unique to a particular person and has to be understood in its own terms as the projection of a specific consciousness.[8] Foucault wants to go further still. He argues that to dream is to plunge into a hidden or forgotten reality. Freudians are wrong to interpret dreams as the expression of fears and wishes in an unreal fantasy world where the impossible happens. On the contrary, the state of consciousness engendered by dreaming propels us towards reality, towards existence.

The dreamer returns in imagination to the point *before* his or her intentions and actions have taken effect, *before* they have helped make a world in which that person feels either fulfilled or alienated. The dream 'discloses the point of origin from which freedom makes itself world' (Foucault 1993, 51). In other words, in their dreams human beings and the world they inhabit are both restored to the condition of flux and openness from which they came, returned to a condition of 'becoming' not yet frozen into the fixed forms of 'being'.

In Foucault's view, dreaming lets us see more easily the difference between the contingent effects of discursive practices, which differ between epochs and cultures, and the 'fundamental coordinates' (60) of existence which human beings cannot change. These basic parameters of being, space and time are also expressed in traditional art forms, to which dreaming is

closely linked.[9] Dreaming empowers imagination. It draws us close to the
core of existence. It allows us to imagine a complete merging of the self and
the world.[10]

Foucault's interest in Husserl and Nietzsche was reinforced by contact
with the work of French historians of science such as Gaston Bachelard.[11]
Bachelard did not accept the conventional scientific ideal. For him, as for
Nietzsche, there was no 'universal truth' progressively uncovered by
cumulative discoveries, valid throughout time and space. His approach was
more 'geological': as he saw it, different worldviews, different knowledge
formations, different 'sciences', and so on, were pushed to the surface in
successive eruptions during the turbulent onrush of life. The sciences of
every age were embedded in a larger mass made up of culture, philosophy,
religion, ideology and the human imagination.

Bachelard and his colleagues thought that the creative imagination of
poets and other artists should not be simply treated negatively, as an
obstacle to disciplined scientific thinking, but positively, as an alternative
route to understanding reality. They also thought that intellectual and
cultural life are subject to massive and sudden ruptures, 'epistemological'
breaks, seismic shifts in the way knowledge is organized and reality
perceived.

They also assumed that within each of the distinct historical periods that
occurred between these fundamental cleavages, similarities could be found in
the internal structures of different sciences: their concepts, their methodologies, their discourses. Each epoch had its own 'take' on the world, so to
speak, and this permeated all aspects of its knowledge and thought.

However, only detailed empirical research could yield information about
the sciences and other knowledge formations of each epoch. This meant
undertaking a careful process of excavation, working through sedimented
layers, piecing together evidence. By this process the historian could
discover the structural principles which made each epoch distinctive and
also investigate how these structures were produced and transformed.

Some of these ideas influenced structuralists[12] such as Louis Althusser
(disciple of Bachelard and friend of Foucault). However, although, for a
while Foucault allowed himself to be identified as a sort of structuralist
'fellow traveller', in practice he distanced himself from that movement in
various ways.

Foucault put at the centre of his work not 'structures' but 'practices': the
way people think, feel and act in a range of particular situations. Practices
are both mental and social. They involve material resources as well as
emotions and perceptions. Foucault was interested in the structuring process which actively shapes specific practices – for example, the way we treat
the mentally sick, deal with criminals, or manage our sex lives.

Foucault makes an implicit distinction between two kinds of structuring.
On the one hand, there is the structuring of human existence by its universal 'fundamental coordinates' such as the interplay of nearness and
distance, light and darkness, or rising and falling.[13] On the other hand,

there is the structuring of social and mental practice within particular historical epochs by specific institutional discourses (for example, in schools, law courts and clinics) which penetrate and control the psyche.

The two kinds of structuring have different consequences. Epic, lyrical and tragic art forms give us an expanded sense of the human condition. By contrast, the institutional discourses of modernity, argues Foucault, close off existential options, and reduce the range of possibilities for human experience.

However, this is implicit rather than explicit. Foucault does not strive to reach an elaborate or consistent philosophical position of his own regarding the nature of being (what 'are' structures and practices?) or knowledge (how do we 'know' what they are?). Nor is he interested in producing a 'grand theory'. His theoretical concepts are cutting tools, practical instruments for dissecting his experiences. These tools are created on the workbench and lie scattered about it. They do not constitute a 'system'. Foucault is a historian of systems, not a creator of one.[14]

What does excite Foucault are two related projects – and here we re-establish contact with Elias. The two projects are: to discover through detailed historical research how the structuring of practices has occurred in different epochs (to be discussed shortly); and to evoke and clarify his own fundamental vision of what is most deeply at stake in human life.

The visions, the intuitions about how the world worked and fitted together, pursued by Elias and Foucault are different: in the first case, a fascination with the interplay of interconnectedness and separation and a strong sense of the flows and counter-flows, surges and counter-surges that shaped the tides and maelstroms of life; in the second case, a dialectic between the modalities of oppressive constraint and explosive release.

However, the two thinkers are similar in being both vision-led, so to speak. Elias once remarked: 'My experience is that I am gradually seeing something new, something I did not know, and that I am setting an example: one can do it, and it is worth the trouble . . . It is the normal way of working for a scientist. One has a problem and one day one knows: I have the solution. One has not thought it out – one has it' (Elias 1994b, 75–6).[15]

Some Similarities

Foucault and Elias read the landscape of modernity in different ways. However, they agree about the three most important places on the map. For example, both Foucault and Elias, like Hannah Arendt, have a high regard for conditions of relative stability which allow people to make rational decisions on their own behalf and exercise a high degree of autonomy. This is a shared ideal. The difference between them is that while Elias believes it is a condition that may become more widespread in the future, Foucault believes it is a condition enjoyed by certain groups in the distant past but not on the cards within modern societies.

Foucault and Elias agree that there are two main alternatives to this situation of rational self-control. One is a situation of heteronomy where one is subject to the control of an authoritarian central ruler. Elias finds that Germany's political development is partly explained by the susceptibility of the German habitus and social personality to this kind of external central control. However, as has been seen, he regards the German case as a product of peculiar circumstances that are atypical. In his view, the German case is an exception.

By contrast, Foucault believes that heteronomous control of the body and psyche through the workings of discursive and non-discursive practices is the 'normal' modern condition. This includes France, the heartland of the civilizing process. Foucault reports that after the French Revolution, the police tried to create 'an apparatus . . . coextensive with the entire social body, . . . not only by the extreme limits that it embraces, but by the minuteness of the details it is concerned with' (Foucault 1977a, 213). More generally, he argues, modernity has created 'docile bodies' (135). These bodies are subject to 'uninterrupted, constant coercion' (137), 'objects of a . . . new "micro-physics" of power' (139).

The other alternative that both Elias and Foucault recognize is a situation that combines social disorder with instability at the level of personality. Again the question of context divides them. For Elias, disorder and instability are conditions that prevailed at the early stages of the civilizing process but which are, unfortunately, liable to re-emerge in the course of decivilizing processes such as occurred in Germany. He hopes that such experiences may be avoided.

Again, Foucault differs. If the only practical alternative is the oppressive experience of modernity, then Foucault chooses disruption and, ultimately, chaos. He takes seriously the idea that the powerful drives which flow through us are the backwash of cosmic forces. We should accept that we live in a hostile chaotic world, 'tune in' to these powerful forces shaping our lives, accept the grief that comes our way, and seize what pleasure we can.

Foucault and Elias do not agree about the relative order of desirability in which the three options – rational self-control, authoritarian heteronomy, and disorder – are to be placed nor about the strength of conditions favouring their appearance or suppression in modernity. However, they do agree that, whatever those conditions are, they are mainly influenced by processes beyond the scope of human planning. In other words, societies change in ways that are largely beyond human control.

Turning to the question of social change, there is a surprising degree of convergence between Elias and Foucault. The movement is from Foucault's side and is to be seen in his practice as a historian rather than in any general statements about methodology. Insofar as he did write about methodology, Foucault took a Nietzschean position and asserted the importance of the genealogical approach.

In other words, he argued that historians should see our present condition as the outcome of a dispersed multiplicity of power struggles and accidental happenings. The present should be seen as 'emerging' from a complex 'descent' whose details have to be pieced together by painstaking research.[16] Foucault is here resisting the teleology built into some 'metaphysical' histories: 'In placing present needs at the origin, the metaphysician would convince us of an obscure purpose that seeks its realization at the moment it arises. Genealogy, however, seeks to reestablish the various systems of subjection: not the anticipatory power of meaning, but the hazardous play of dominations' (Foucault 1984, 83).

However, by the time Foucault began work on the second volume of his *History of Sexuality* he had begun to see rhythms and patterns in the 'hazardous play of dominations' that are very similar to those recognized by Elias. One possible reason for this is that in the second and third volumes of this work Foucault transported himself out of the oppressive realms of modernity and into the classical world of Greece and Rome. Having arrived there he produces an analysis which has some astonishing similarities to *The Civilizing Process* and other related works by Elias, notably *The Court Society* and an article entitled 'The changing balance of power between the sexes – a process-sociological study' (Elias 1987a). In the next two sections of the chapter I will explore these similarities.[17]

Husbands and Wives

At first, the signs of convergence do not seem very evident. Anyone who picks up the first volume of *The History of Sexuality*, first published in 1976, two years after *Discipline and Punish*, will soon get the impression that Foucault is deeply unsympathetic to the Freudian analysis of the psyche that is deeply embedded in *The Civilizing Process*.

Foucault's target is probably Marcuse rather than Elias. However, the effect would be extremely negative for an Eliasian reader also. Foucault attacks the Freudian 'repressive hypothesis' and dismisses the suggestion that the workings of modern society can be explained in terms of psychological controls over the expression of libidinous impulses.[18]

In spite of this unpromising background, there is considerable convergence between Elias's work and the second and third volumes of Foucault's *The History of Sexuality*, entitled, respectively, *The Use of Pleasure* and *The Care of the Self*. In these books, Foucault investigates the question of which aspects of sexual activity were regarded as problematic by philosophers and doctors in classical Greece and Rome.

In these volumes Foucault discovers the existence of a non-oppressive form of rationality, one that is different from the monopolistic 'will to knowledge' imposed through professional hierarchies and the state upon clients, convicts, conscripts, pupils and patients within modern disciplinary society. In *Madness and Civilization* (Foucault 1967), Foucault had found an alternative to this deeply flawed modern rationality in the practices of the Renaissance when men and women took irrational feelings and nonrational states of mind seriously as a potential source of truth, a different perspective on the world. They were sources of enrichment, not of threat.

However, classical Greece and Rome provided another model. Foucault found that many citizens within those societies were able, within the limits imposed by their power situation and knowledge, to implement an ethos based on rational self-mastery and the pursuit of pleasure without ill-health. One of Foucault's key findings was that over a period of six centuries from the fourth century BC onwards, Roman wives became more powerful and sexual relations became more austere and restrained.

As he put it, a 'whole corpus of moral reflection on sexual activity and its pleasures seems to mark, in the first centuries of our era, a certain strengthening of austerity themes. Physicians worry about the effects of sexual practice, unhesitatingly recommend abstention, and declare a preference for virginity over the use of pleasure. Philosophers condemn any sexual relation that might take place outside marriage and prescribe a strict fidelity between spouses, admitting no exceptions'[19] (Foucault 1988a, 235).

In Foucault's view, these changes were a product of changes within marriage and in the structure of the Roman Empire. For example, marriage increasingly became a concern of public law. Meanwhile, state business was falling into the hands of a minority of citizens. Most upper-class husbands were not directly involved in public affairs.

By chance, Elias gave the talk on which his article on the changing balance of power between the sexes was based in 1985, the year after Foucault's second and third volumes on sexuality were published.

Elias's argument converges strongly with Foucault's own. He notes that when the Romans were a tribal society wives were usually obtained by taking women by force from their families and, in many cases, giving the process legitimacy by making a payment in exchange. Since the woman became in this way a chattel of her husband he 'could do with her as he liked' (Elias 1987a, 293). 'The Roman Republic did not have the institutional means for bringing people's sexual life and thus also marriage under state control' (295).

There was no marriage law apart from the decisions made by family heads and tribal elders. Matters changed when the republic became an empire. The most successful tribal warriors acquired large estates and turned into an aristocracy. In these new circumstances daughters were pawns in a dynastic game and marriages were used to seal political bargains.

Meanwhile, the Roman state acquired increased influence and became more effective. Marriage was drawn into the orbit of public law and civil administration. As a result, public officials were able to provide some protection for the interests of wives against their husbands. Elias argues that by the first century BC there was 'virtual equality between husband and wife' (300) and that women became 'self-ruling human beings in their marriages' (304). They were better educated, could get divorced more easily and were able to 'develop into what we now call individuals' (310).

Since wives maintained close relations with their own kin, formed their own social networks, and developed the skill of acting collectively, a higher degree of 'self-discipline [developed] . . . in the dealings of married men and women with each other', even 'a curious aloofness' (301–2). The fact that women were not allowed to take part in politics and public business also reinforced the social distance between husbands and wives. Elias argues that the 'Roman heritage' regarding conjugal equality 'was . . . to some extent carried forward by the romanized Church' (313). He finds that 'its influence . . . can be felt . . . on Roman and Church law till far into the Middle Ages' (304). This reflects the fact that equality within marriage lasted a 'surprisingly long' time, persisting even 'when the state organization – particularly in the Western part of the Roman Empire – and thus the condition of the level of civilization that had been achieved began to deteriorate' (309).

According to Elias, the process of equalization produced a 'changed social habitus or personality structure of women . . . which persisted in Rome till late into the Christian era' (301). Foucault takes Elias's argument further, drawing attention to a dimension of the situation to which Elias had not paid attention. This is that during Rome's imperial period ideas of citizenship changed. Specifically, being involved in public life ceased to be thought of as a duty for all citizens but came to be seen as an activity one entered as a 'personal act of choice' (Foucault 1988a, 87). One consequence of this change was that adult males were forced to reflect on which roles in public and private life they would follow.

This problematization of the self spilled over into several areas, including the sphere of sexual behaviour and relations between husbands and wives. Furthermore, Foucault suggests that marriage became less political in the course of the imperial era. As he puts it, 'in the privileged classes, status and fortune came to depend on proximity to the prince, on a civil or military "career," on success in "business," more than simply on the alliance between family groups' (Foucault 1988a, 74). This analysis by Foucault is not unlike Elias's discussion of the situation in which the pacified court aristocracy found themselves in early modern France. To quote Elias: 'By his personal favour the king can alleviate or prevent the impoverishment of a noble family. He can come to the family's help by awarding a court office, or a military or diplomatic post' (Elias 1983, 71).

The processual character of Foucault's discussion of Roman marriage is complemented by figurational passages in which Foucault argues that by the second century BC the Roman empire had become vast, discontinuous, flexible and differentiated: 'It was a space in which the centres of power were multiple; in which the activities, the tensions, the conflicts were numerous; in which they developed in several directions; and in which the equilibria were obtained through a variety of transactions' (82–3).

Rome was no longer a small society of land-holding self-governing citizen-soldiers. Within the Roman Empire, 'the agonistic game by which one sought to manifest and ensure one's superiority over others . . . had to

be integrated into a far more extensive and complex field of power rela-
tions' (Foucault 1988a, 95). Such passages indicate that Foucault moved in
Elias's direction in the period following the publication of *Discipline and
Punish* (Foucault 1977a).

In his best-known book Foucault had described a disciplinary society
and dedicated himself to the task of exposing and subverting it. He claimed
he could already hear 'the distant roar of battle' (Foucault 1977a, 308). By
the early 1980s he was able to adopt a more detached orientation, display
more sensitivity to the complexity of interdependence within human
relationships, and give more attention to the subtleties of historical change
within complex chains or networks of human interdependence.

Sex and Civilization

So far, some major overlaps have been noticed in the arguments Elias and
Foucault use to explain a sequence of social development they both found
intriguing. Now attention will be given to some fascinating parallels in the
way they investigate practices relating to the management of the self in two
different historical eras: the period between the fourth century BC and the
second century AD as analysed in *The Use of Pleasure* and *The Care of the
Self*; and the period between the twelfth and eighteenth centuries AD with
which Elias is concerned in *The Civilizing Process*.

Foucault and Elias both make use of advice books as a way of getting
access to standards of behaviour and the workings of the psyche in these
historical periods. These are contemporary works that cover such subjects
as how to manage your body and your feelings, how to behave with other
people, and how to handle yourself in tricky situations. These books tell
their readers what they 'should' do and, as such, they are a useful guide to
contemporary standards. The 'should' is not necessarily 'philosophical' or
'moral'. Rather, it is a matter of what will work most effectively or produce
the best impression upon others. By the same token, denizens of the French
court took it for granted that a courtier's political career would be
enhanced if he showed he could behave well at the table, conduct himself
properly in dealings with the opposite sex, display good manners at all
times and engage in apt conversation.

A common problem binds Foucault and Elias together at this point. They
are both deeply interested in the links between how we 'manage' or 'cope
with' our bodily urges and how we conceptualize the 'self', its substance,
capacities and obligations. They are both also trying to unravel the complexities of those areas of human conduct in which how human beings
manage natural functions such as sex, excretion, eating and drinking has a
close relationship to the way they try to survive or advance themselves by
managing their health, marriage, patterns of friendship and political
intrigues.

For his part, Elias starts by noticing a set of contemporary attitudes towards 'proper' social behaviour among the German middle class and then sets out to discover and explain how this class came to accept the particular ontology and ethical code that is expressed, indirectly at least, in those attitudes. Foucault takes a similar approach in his analysis of Greco-Roman attitudes towards 'proper' behaviour in the specific area of sexual relations. He begins with the practical question 'how *should* one behave?' and shows that underlying that question are ontological issues and questions about the objects of ethical behaviour.

Early in *The Use of Pleasure*, Foucault quotes Socrates's condemnation of the love of elder men for 'soft boys . . . all made up with rouge and decked out in ornaments' (Foucault 1987, 19). He shows that Socrates's remarks were an expression of 'a thematic complex . . . of sexual austerity' that was to be found 'very early in the moral thought of antiquity' (Foucault 1987, 21) and which grew stronger over six centuries. In other words, rather than take Socrates's remarks at face value, Foucault explores how the moral attitude it expressed was tied to a specific 'axis of experience' and 'cluster of concrete relationships' (23) which changed in a specific direction over time.

In a similar way, Elias digs beneath the the moral critique of French 'civilization' carried out in the late eighteenth century by 'the middle-class German intelligentsia'. According to Kant, he and his contemporaries were 'civilized to a point where we are overburdened with all sorts of social propriety and decency . . . The idea of morality is a part of culture. But the application of the idea, which results only in the similitude of morality in the love of honour and its outward decency, amounts only to civilizing' (Elias 1994a, 7).

Again, rather than taking such a remark at face value Elias goes on to explore how specific experiences within specific figurations in the course of the civilizing process led to the appearance of *civilité* among the French court nobility and *Kultur* among the German bourgeoisie (7). He argued that members of the German bourgeoisie, being largely excluded from 'good society', cultivated 'a very special kind of bourgeois self-image [which entailed] . . . a turning away from everything to do with the administration of power monopolies, . . . a cultivation of inwardness, and the elevation of spiritual and cultural achievements to a special place in the table of values' (Elias 1994a, 512).

How do Elias and Foucault, respectively, make sense of the changes in behaviourial standards that occur during the two historical periods being compared? They refer to changes in political structure that are broadly similar although by no means exactly the same in their character. It is relevant to Foucault's argument that the circumstances of Roman citizens were transformed as the Empire became more centralized and bureaucratic. It is equally relevant to Elias's argument that the secular upper class in Europe found itself in a new situation as feudal society was pacified and a stronger royal authority took shape.

The parallel is not an exact one. The Roman Empire did not acquire a stable centralized power monopoly equivalent to the state in absolutist France. However, the degree of centralization and the complexity of networks of interdependence increased greatly in both cases. In the course of several generations Roman citizens and medieval knights became less autonomous and their lives became less simple. In both cases, they lost many of the social functions that had previously accompanied their elevated status. For example, they were no longer free to govern or fight for themselves.

The response of both citizens and knights was twofold. They concentrated on elaborating the external indications of their social status, and they became very deeply preoccupied with the nature of the self. For example, the French courtier, deprived of his old function as a feudal warrior, sought social prestige. He became extremely self-aware. In the words of La Bruyère, the courtier is 'master of his gestures, of his eyes and his expression; he is deep, impenetrable' (Elias 1994a, 473, 476).

This pattern of behaviour, these feelings, and this self-awareness were all to be found within the propertied Roman establishment in the first two centuries AD: 'On the one hand there is an accentuation of everything that allows the individual to define his identity in accordance with his status and with the elements that manifest it in the most visible way. One seeks to make oneself as adequate as possible to one's own status by means of a set of signs and marks pertaining to physical bearing, clothing and accommodations, gestures of generosity and munificence, spending behaviour and so on . . . But at the opposite extreme one finds the attitude that consists of forming and recognizing oneself as the subject of one's own actions . . . through a relation . . . [that] is fulfilled in the sovereignty that one exercises over oneself' (Foucault 1988a, 85). The search for status and concern for the self are closely related.

In imperial Rome political activity was a vocation deliberately chosen by a minority, and those who took part needed certain skills. These included being able to make rational judgements and take responsibility for them, and being able to find your way safely through complex social and administrative hierarchies. It was also important to keep the public face separate from the inner self, which must be under proper control, and to avoid making enemies since alliances could swiftly change. Foucault often quotes Seneca. For his part, Elias makes good use of the memoirs of the Duc de Saint-Simon, a valuable source of insights about French court life. Both authors emphasize the need to be rational, show sensitivity to others, and restrict oneself to realistic goals.

Elias and Foucault both relate long-term changes in standards of behaviour to changes in contemporary ideas about the nature of the self, the strength of the desire to avoid specific bodily functions or activities,[20] the level of anxiety or fear, the extent of political centralization, and the density and complexity of interdependence chains. With respect to the first of these factors – ideas about the self – Foucault's argument differs significantly from Elias's.

The Self as a Problem

Elias argues in *The Civilizing Process* that over a long period of time as people develop increasing self-awareness and greater self-control, anything directly associated with bodily functions becomes regarded with increasing levels of embarrassment and shame. There is greater pressure to hide such functions and activities behind the scenes, to avoid discussing them, and to feel inhibited about them. As people became increasingly civilized, they became increasingly vulnerable to feelings of shame and repugnance, especially in respect of sexual feelings and sexual activity.

Foucault agrees that the level of self-consciousness increases as does the preoccupation with self-control. However, his argument is significantly different. According to Foucault, the Greeks assumed there was 'a close connection between the superiority that one exercised over oneself, the authority one exercised in the context of the household, and the power one exercised in the field of an agonistic society' (Foucault 1988a, 94). These assumptions worked reasonably well when society was relatively uncomplex and the adult male citizen was in a dominant position.

However, these assumptions were less applicable six centuries later when there was much greater reciprocity and equality in the household and local urban politics were part of a 'far more extensive and complex field of power relations' (95). The advance in socio-political complexity led to an increase in anxiety about the vulnerability of human beings within a social world that was seen as being ever more complex, ambiguous and unpredictable. It was no longer true that the adult male's sense of having command of himself was buttressed by command over his household and regular performance on the public stage as an active citizen.

This disruption of traditional expectations made the self problematic as an ethical project. How should one behave? What should one expect of oneself? Attention was being focused on the self but this did not, in Foucault's view, lead to a fundamental change in attitudes towards human sexuality. Sex did not become magnified in the consciousness as something that was regarded as more evil or more intrinsically dangerous than before.

In fact, according to Foucault's findings, perceptions of sex did not change greatly during the six centuries he studied. It was recognized that it had unfortunate side effects: it was exhausting and tended to upset one's equilibrium for a while. Over the whole period sexuality was seen as a natural force whose capacity to disrupt rationality was recognized. It was treated with great respect. This attitude did not change significantly. What did change over time were popular attitudes towards the rules that governed how one behaved both in public business and in private affairs.

People became increasingly self-conscious about the need to take personal responsibility for choices. They were increasingly aware that all kinds of personal arrangements in life were liable to change quite quickly and without notice. It was recognized that social networks were dynamic and one's situation within them was always temporary. It was not that sexuality was regarded differently. The point was that the consequences of handling it badly could be greater in a more complex world. So it had to be treated with more care and caution.

As Foucault puts it: 'Sexual pleasure as an ethical substance continues to be governed by relations of force – the force against which one must struggle and over which the subject is expected to establish his domination. But in this game of violence, excess, rebellion and combat, the accent is placed more and more readily on the weakness of the individual, on his frailty, on his need to flee, to escape, to protect and shelter himself' (Foucault 1988a, 67).

Foucault argues that the spread of Christianity coincides with a major shift towards perceiving sexuality as repugnant and evil. Christians were preoccupied with sinfulness and learned to fear their own flesh as a source of temptation leading to evil and punishment. Christians were subject 'to a general law that is at the same time the will of a personal god' (Foucault 1988a, 239). According to this law, you could only achieve ethical fulfilment if you renounced earthly satisfactions and made your desires pure. The task of life was to decipher your soul and subject yourself to a regime of confession, penitence and hatred of the flesh. In ways such as this Christianity encouraged a further and even more radical redefinition of the self as an ethical project.

According to Foucault, the inauguration of the confessional regime was part of a long-term social process which could be traced over several centuries. In *The History of Sexuality* Foucault traces a phased transition in Western societies from 'ethics-oriented' moralities to 'code-oriented' moralities.[21] His analysis identifies four phases. In the first phase, ethics-oriented moralities based on rational self-mastery predominated whose focus was *askesis*, in other words, training for self-mastery. During a second phase, these ethics-oriented moralities became more austere. Sexuality came to be seen as something to keep at a distance and treat very carefully. These are the phases that he studies in detail in Greece and Rome.

In the third phase, during the medieval period, 'quasi-juridical' (Foucault 1987, 29) code-oriented moralities became influential under the influence of Christianity. They imposed strict observance, initially in monastic settings but eventually for all the laity. The key practices were confession and penitence, provoking a widespread preoccupation with sex in thought, feeling and behaviour. In the fourth phase, the Church's role was taken over by the bureaucratic state, modern science and the secular professions. Teachers, doctors, demographic planners and other 'experts' used discourse about sexuality as the chief medium of the will to knowledge and will to power.

Conclusion

Elias and Foucault have different analyses of modern society since the French Revolution. However, there is significant convergence in their discussions of the Roman empire. For example, they concur in arguing that as the empire grew larger and more complex and acquired a substantial state bureaucracy, the position of wives was strengthened within Roman households although some details of their two arguments differ.

Elias and Foucault follow complementary paths through the European Middle Ages. To oversimplify, Elias concentrates on the social processes that transform feudal warriors into polite courtiers while Foucault pays attention to the related social process whereby the practices developed within monastic settings are translated into techniques for exercising control by priests over communicants. Between them they cover what Elias recognized were the two main means of exercising social leverage in the pre-modern epoch.

In Elias's words, in societies such as early Rome and early medieval Europe 'Besides fighting potential it was only the possession of magical power that formed a similarly important source of social power – the priestly function hence stood alongside the warrior function' (Elias 1987a, 294). In Rome during the era of tribes and clans, the principal warriors and clan rulers also acted as priests.

Elias does not ignore the part played by Christianity in shaping the civilized habitus. For example, he notices that 'moderated restraint of the emotions and the disciplined shaping of behaviour' was produced by 'particular tendencies in traditional ecclesiastical behaviour' (Elias 1994a, 83). He also acknowledges that 'in certain sectors of medieval society we find extreme forms of asceticism, self-restraint and renunciation'. However, while Elias argues that these patterns of behaviour are distinct from the 'more dispassionate self-control' found in 'pacified social spaces' (1994a, 451), Foucault is interested in the influence that religious practices exercise upon precisely those forms of routine 'dispassionate' social behaviour.

Elias and Foucault have overlapping research agendas. They both want to investigate the shifting structure of the social pressures and constraints shaping the self. The later Foucault converges with Elias in his understanding of the processual and figurational character of society. However, even the early Foucault and Elias, where they disagree, are often disagreeing about the *particular significance* of mechanisms or processes about whose importance and general character they are in agreement.

For example, take the state of uninhibited behaviour driven by relatively uncontrolled feelings, a condition which interests both writers very much. Foucault and Elias both believed that pre-modern men and women had easier access to this experience than their modern descendants. According to Elias, 'in warrior society, the individual could use physical violence if he was strong and powerful enough; he could openly indulge his inclinations in many directions that have subsequently been closed by social prohibitions. But he paid for this greater opportunity of direct pleasure with a greater chance of direct fear. Medieval conceptions of hell give us an idea of how strong this fear between man and man was. Both joy and pain were discharged more freely. But the individual was their *prisoner*; he was hurled back and forth by his own feelings as by forces of nature. He had less control of his passions; he was more controlled by them' (Elias 1994a, 452; emphasis added).

Foucault would probably have accepted this description with one alteration: what looks to Elias like imprisonment of the self by the passions looks to Foucault like release from the self by those same passions.[22]

To take another example, both scholars make a central distinction between social processes or forces favouring forms of rationality and others favouring forms of unreason. Elias writes: 'But nowhere, except perhaps in the case of madmen, do men in their encounter with each other find themselves face to face with psychological functions in their pristine state, in a state of nature that is not patterned by social learning' (Elias 1994a, 487). Again, Foucault would agree but go on to draw very different conclusions from Elias. For Elias, advances in rationality and control make a humane existence possible. For Foucault the repression of unreason means losing contact with a major source of human creativity.[23]

Earlier, it was suggested that Elias resembles the fisherman who survives the maelstrom while Foucault identifies with the prisoner under observation in the Panopticon. Modernity encompasses both situations. It contains both whirlpools and watchtowers, and human beings are liable to be drawn into the orbit of both. In order to understand modernity we need the resources of both Michel Foucault and Norbert Elias. We also need the insights of Zygmunt Bauman, who is the subject of the next chapter.

Notes

1 This incident occurred on 7th April when Houdini jumped from the top of the Morgue near the pont de l'Archevèche in Paris.

2 See Elias 1994b, 6–8.

3 Foucault's criticism of Sartre is reminiscent of Elias's implied objection to Husserl: that despite his wish to 'bracket' out everything but consciousness of pure existence, he was unable to 'unthink' the culturally embedded categories that 'distort' perception of the true relationship between people within the world.

4 During the 1970s Foucault was an active campaigner for prison reform and other causes that exposed the oppressive practices of the state, as he saw it.

5 Foucault identified himself enthusiastically with writers such as Georges Bataille, Maurice Blanchot, Jean Barraqui, Antonin Artaud, Raymond Roussel and the Marquis de Sade who believed that shocking and risky behaviour can put us in touch with powerful forces beyond language and culture, hidden from our waking consciousness. In their view, we should seek out transgressive limit-experiences. These may be violent, death-defying, erotic or sado-masochistic; or they may be mentally confusing and emotionally shattering, as in Roussel's poems or Artaud's plays.

6 In Smith forthcoming, b.

7 See pages 34–5.

8 To oversimplify, Freudians interpret dreams by deciphering significant words and images contained within them. The analyst has a list of 'significant' indicators which he or she is taught to look for in all cases. These supposedly give clues as to which particular desires are being fulfilled in the realm of fantasy.

9 For example, the dream-experience has epic, lyrical and tragic dimensions. It evokes the epic drama of departure and return, the interplay of near and far. Like lyrical poetry, dreaming takes us through nature's cycles of light and darkness: day and night, summer and winter, and so on. As in tragedy, the fundamental rhythm of rise and fall, ascent and decline, runs through the dream.

10 The idea of self-submergence excited Foucault. It fuelled his suicidal inclinations: 'every suicidal desire is filled by that world in which I would no longer be present here, or there, but everywhere, in every sector; a world transparent to me and signifying its indebtedness to my absolute presence. Suicide is not a way of cancelling the world or myself, or the two together, but a way of rediscovering the original moment in which I make myself world' (Foucault 1993, 69). Fortunately for Foucault's subsequent career, his desire for personal influence and recognition overcame his desire for personal extinction.

11 Georges Canguilhem was another strong influence. Bachelard and Canguilhem were successors to Jean Cavaillès and Alexander Koyré (with whom Elias had contact in Paris during the 1930s). Elias 1994b, 50.

12 Structuralists include thinkers in fields such as sociolinguistics, psychology, social anthropology and philosophy including, for example, Jacques Lacan, Claude Lévi-Strauss, Roland Barthes, Gilles Deleuze. Very briefly, structuralists argue that below surface appearances lie hidden structures. These structures are the creative source which produce the phenomena we recognize as speech acts, mental images, social myths, cultural signs and so on. Phenomena of this kind are dynamic, changeable, like the shifting pattern of colours on traffic lights, or the rapid-fire imagery of television advertising. However, these transformations are orderly and understandable, operating within limits and along pathways determined by the structure's elemental properties, its law-like regularities. This account of structuralism obviously begs a lot of questions. For example: where are structures located? Are they in the mind, in the culture, or in the nature of 'being'? In what sense do these structures 'exist'?

13 As has been seen, Foucault believed that this structuring process is revealed in dream-like states of consciousness and is creatively represented in art forms where Dionysian and Apollonian impulses merge.

14 The title of his post at the Sorbonne should be taken seriously: Professor of the History of Systems of Thought.

15 'What we lack, let us be clear about it, are conceptual models and, beyond them, a total vision with the aid of which our ideas of human beings as individuals and as societies can be better harmonized' (Elias 1991c, 75).

16 For example, if we want understand the history of our visual sense or of the institution of punishment, then we should realize that 'the eye was not always intended for contemplation, and punishment has had other purposes than setting an example. These developments . . . are merely the current episodes in a series of subjugations: the eye initially responded to the requirements of hunting; and punishment has been subjected, throughout its history, to a variety of needs – revenge, excluding an aggressor, compensating a victim, creating fear' (Foucault 1984, 83).

17 The rest of this chapter draws in part upon ideas initially developed in Smith 1999a and Smith forthcoming, a.

18 Foucault 1978, pp. 10–13.

19 He added: 'Furthermore, a certain doctrinal disqualification seems to bear on the love of boys' (Foucault 1988a, 235).

20 In other words, 'the threshold of repugnance' (in Elias's analysis) or the degree of 'austerity' (in Foucault's analysis).

21 At this point in his career he quietly abandoned his previous mode of historical analysis (e.g. in *The Order of Things*) which imposed sharp and absolute breaks between epochs.

22 For Foucault's discussions of pre-modern visions of Hell, the Apocalypse and related scenes, see Foucault 1967, 15–22.

23 See Foucault 1967.

6

BAUMAN AND ELIAS

Postmodernity: for Better or Worse?

Bauman and Elias share their Jewish origins. They were born in cities that are a mere 150 kilometres apart. However, they come from different social classes, different nations and different generations.[1] These differences help explain why, as a young man, Elias wanted to be a German university professor of philosophy, contributing to the tradition of German Kultur while Bauman wanted to be a Marxist revolutionary fighting for socialism.

The early careers of both men were destroyed by anti-Semitism. However, neither responded primarily as a Jew. Elias responded as a German intellectual, Bauman as a Marxist intellectual. Each man attempted to reconstruct the intellectual tradition that let him down. Elias attempted to replace Kantian philosphy with Eliasian sociology. Bauman began by attempting to produce a more modern Marxism and went on to explore the possibilities of a postmodern ethics. Before comparing Bauman and Elias in more detail, it would be as well to explore a little more the 'postmodern turn' of Zygmunt Bauman.

Zygmunt Bauman made his 'turn to postmodernity' in the mid-1980s.[2] For over a decade since then he has explored the nature of the postmodern habitat in which, he argues, we are destined to live. In Bauman's view, this habitat is occupied by rootless strangers disoriented by an overload of ambivalence.

These wanderers try to find comfort, security and order as best they can. One way is to purchase the props for a desirable life-style in the shopping malls. Another is to buy reassurance from 'experts' in health, beauty, career choices, personal relationships and so on. Some find their place by joining one of the many competing neo-tribes, ranging from Hari Krishna-type sects to football supporters' clubs. Each of them totes its own symbols or proclaims its own brand of 'truth'.

Bauman reminds his readers that, postmodern or not, the world remains divided between the rich and the poor, the fortunate and the needy. His message to postmodern men and women is: accept responsibility for making your own choices in life with no other guidance but your own judgement and your own sense of what is 'right'. This is coupled with a challenge: dare to look inside yourself and become aware of your inborn inclination to be-for-the-Other, to respond to the Other's mute demand for care.

Bauman argues we have an innate tendency to express moral concern and identify with the Other's wants but this is stifled in modernity by positivistic science and dogmatic bureaucracy. If the Other does not 'fit in' to modernity's approved classifications, it is liable to be extinguished. Postmodernity is the state of mind that comes when people stop having faith in those classifications and the dogmas that justify them. That is when people discover three things: they have the freedom to make their own life choices, unconstrained by external ideological authority; they cannot avoid those choices; and choosing is painful and difficult.

Before Bauman made his 'turn to postmodernity', for over a quarter of a century his efforts had been focused on the prospects for 'improving' modernity. He developed a strategy for making modernity democratic and socialist: freer, more equal, more just. This strategy, which drew on Marx, Gramsci and Habermas, gave a leading role to intellectuals, especially sociologists. Their task, as Bauman saw it, was to encourage open and informed dialogue among social groups leading towards the identification of shared interests. Dialogue would be one aspect of creative praxis leading in the direction of a socialist utopia.

In other words, Bauman did not always have the extremely pessimistic view of modernity's potential for producing good outcomes that he has recently developed. Furthermore, many of the elements of Bauman's sociology of postmodernity were already present in the work he carried out in his earlier career when he did not look beyond modernity but, instead, sought his utopia within its bounds.[3]

Hope and Disappointment

Some biography is relevant. Zygmunt Bauman came from a background of poverty. He was born in Poznan, fought as a Polish officer with the Red Army during World War II, and served as a high-ranking political officer in the Polish Army during the late 1940s and early 1950s. He was dismissed from this latter position during an anti-Jewish purge in 1953, and subsequently became a revisionist intellectual during the late 1950s and 1960s. Bauman decided to emigrate to the West in 1968 following another anti-Jewish campaign orchestrated by the regime, during which he was castigated as a public enemy.[4]

During the 1960s in Poland Bauman explored the dynamics of the triangular relationships among the state bureaucracy, the people and the intellectuals. He hoped that, under the influence of intellectuals such as himself, bureaucratic planners would become enlightened teachers. They would help raise the people's level of education and understanding.

However, the social contract between the peasantry and the bureaucracy was so strong and so central to Polish society that Bauman and those who shared his aspirations were unable to act as an effective third force. Neither the peasantry nor the bureaucrats felt any enthusiasm for progressive intellectuals who spoke about freedom and seemed to relish uncertainty.

When he emigrated to the West, Bauman retained his commitment to the goal of socialism. Along with this commitment went a strategy and a critique, both initially developed in Poland. The strategy was to continue exploring the 'opportunities involved "objectively"' in unfolding historical situations, East and West, in the hope that a progressive analysis might be heard at the right time. This analysis would include a positive vision of the better society offered by socialism, a vision to inspire praxis.

The critique was initially directed against the socio-political order created in Poland during the 1960s by an unenlightened bureaucracy and a highly conformist population. Bauman pointed out that state socialism had failed to confront three challenges. One was the need to instill a strong sense of personal moral responsibility among citizens and officials. Another was to prepare people, especially the young, for the task of coping with a confusing mix of messages about life-styles and values they would encounter in complex urban-industrial settings. Linking both these challenges was the need to avoid the easy solution of simply obeying without question the instructions handed down by one's immediate superior.

Bauman was committed to the ideal of a social existence in which rational and emancipated human beings exercised their freedom in a creative fashion. As a means of achieving this ideal, and as part of the ideal itself, he wanted to encourage a process of dialogue within civil society. The task for intellectuals was to encourage ordinary people to take an informed, rational and active part in making society freer, more equal and more just.

By the early 1980s, major social changes were underway in both East and West. The successes of Polish Solidarity in 1980 seemed to Bauman to be evidence that the working class could undergo 'True collective learning' in the course of 'collective action' (Bauman 1981, 50). At that time the British political system was being placed under intense strain by the radical reform programme of Margaret Thatcher's Conservative government. Riots occurred in many British cities during 1981.

During the early 1980s Bauman believed that 'a time of transition' had arrived within capitalist societies: 'the whole system of social production and satisfaction of needs seems to be in an acute crisis'. In his view, solving the crisis depended on 're-negotiation of the problems of unfreedom and emancipation' (198). The time was ripe, it seemed, for bringing into being a thoroughly democratic society in which citizens played a much more active part in running their own affairs.

Bauman's writings from this period were optimistic. However, there was a catch. His hopes for encouraging creative dialogue and action depended on a reconstruction of the political sphere. If people took citizenship more seriously they would become actively interested in making more decisions collectively in their localities. Their everyday lives would become more 'political'. As society became more democratic, the central state would take less responsibility for regulating the details of social life.

However, only part of this hoped-for process of reconstruction occurred. The 1980s were certainly a 'time of transition'. However, the beneficiary was not local democracy but global capitalism. National governments certainly became less ambitious. They abandoned the more ambitious strategies of corporatist management within the Keynesian welfare state. The national state went into semi-retirement, and intervened less frequently in the daily lives of citizens.

However, the space vacated by the 'nanny state' was filled not by the citizen but by the consumer. Active citizenship and participatory democracy were easily swamped by consumerism and the power of global capitalism. Governments had less control than before over their own national economies and, as a result, less capacity to control unemployment levels, prices levels and so on.

By the late 1980s it was clear that democratic socialism was not a viable option, at least not in the near future. In these circumstances Bauman reworked his critique of modernity and revised his conclusions. In the 1960s Bauman had argued that the deficiencies of state socialism, especially its failure to meet the challenges of moral responsibility and social complexity, were practical matters that could be dealt with as long as the correct strategies were adopted by leaders who were competent and clear-sighted.

However, during the late 1980s and early 1990s Bauman took a more absolutist line. His revised view was that the prevelance of moral anaesthesia made modernity unacceptable. Furthermore, subcultural heterogenity contributed to a climate of ambivalence that fatally undermined belief in modernity. Finally, the challenge of assuming personal moral responsibility was too daunting for modern men and women to confront as a matter of course. These issues were not practical matters that could be handled within the context of socialist modernity. Instead, they were fundamental flaws that made modernity unacceptable.

The Journey to Postmodernity

Bauman has made an intellectual voyage from the pursuit of the progressive within modernity to the search for humane survival within postmodernity. His analysis of postmodernity employs an intellectual apparatus that took shape at a time when he was committed to the methods and objectives of 'modern Marxism'. However, Bauman acknowledges that the objective conditions have become highly unfavourable to his earlier strategy of achieving social progress through dialogue and collective praxis.

As Bauman sees it, this change in objective conditions has produced the postmodern habitat in which he and the rest of us are forced to dwell. My interpretation is that since he is forced to live in this habitat, Bauman is willing to join in the postmodern game of experimenting with new forms and meanings, especially in the realm of art and literature.[5] However, that does not mean he has totally abandoned his previous standards of judgement or his wish for an improvement in the human situation. In fact, his recent work can be interpreted, in part, as an expression of the belief that the first move in improving our situation is to understand it as clearly and honestly as possible.

Bauman has narrowed his ambitions, not abandoned them. He has directed his old weapons at a more delimited target. Gone is the strategy of encouraging social groups to engage in open communication with each other leading to creative action bringing a 'good' society nearer. One reason for this is that, as Bauman sees it, the postmodern public sphere is in no fit state to support such an enterprise. Another reason is that Bauman has become deeply suspicious of 'manufactured' forms of group solidarity.

Instead, Bauman has turned his attention to the new but rapidly increasing postmodern consituency of isolated strangers. At this point the continuity with his old strategy, the strategy of encouraging open communication and creative action, becomes clear. The difference is that now it is being promoted in terms of interaction between individuals, not between groups. Individual action is creative in the sense that when 'I' enact care for the 'Other', I strengthen the tissue of interpersonal solidarity in which ethical behaviour resides. One way of looking at this, although Bauman does not make the point directly, is that if interpersonal solidarity is rebuilt it may eventually make possible active citizenship within a reconstructed public sphere.

Bauman has made a long and difficult journey from his native 'modern habitat' in communist Poland to an increasingly 'postmodern habitat', one initially located in the West but gradually becoming global in extent. There is a connection between Zygmunt Bauman's life experiences and the development of his theoretical approach.

As I have argued elsewhere, there is a parallel between Bauman and Alexis de Tocqueville, who made a similar journey: in his case from the aristocratic tradition in which he was reared as a child to the more democratic social order with which he was forced to come to terms as an adult. Tocqueville visited the United States in the 1830s in order to see how democracy, which he took to be the pattern of the future, actually worked. In a similar vein to Bauman on postmodernity, Tocqueville regarded democracy as being inevitable rather than welcome. He investigated its culture, values, morality, politics and psychology, the same dimensions that Bauman has analysed in his studies of postmodernity.

Bauman has become one of postmodernity's pioneers. However, his ways of thinking, feeling and behaving, were formed in the 'old world' of modernity. For example, Bauman has retained from the 'old world' his intense hatred of poverty and belief in freedom. He also continues to believe that that culture is the key arena in which the structure of society is determined. Equally long-standing is his conviction that intellectuals, especially sociologists, should stay close to ordinary men and women, injecting a critical perspective on the deeply conservative and potentially oppressive conventions of 'common sense'.

Furthermore, Bauman's contempt for the authoritarian imposition of rules by central political authority assisted by legislating intellectuals is reproduced in his deep hostility to communitarian enterprises which, in his view, are likely to follow a similar strategy of authoritarianism, again backed up by compliant intellectuals.

Zygmunt Bauman remains committed to 'western, Enlightenment values' (Bauman 1992a, 225). These are expressed in the standards of individual responsibility, equality and justice defined by modernity. However, Bauman argues that practical attempts to put those values into practice were frustrated and crushed by modernity itself. As Bauman sees it, the onset of postmodernity removes the obstacles modernity placed in the way of achieving a just, free and equal society but this fact does not ensure that those values will be realized. On the contrary, this task has become harder, mainly because global capitalism appears to be impossible to influence or control.

Exceptions and Prototypes

In Elias's case, the key historical experience which challenged him, both intellectually and in other ways, was the failure of German imperialism in the shape of the *Kaiserreich* which came crashing down in 1918 and, subsequently, the disastrous career of Hitler's Third Reich which promised to recreate and go beyond the glories of the first and second German empires. In Bauman's case, the central event has been the rise and fall of the Soviet empire in the USSR and Eastern Europe, successor to the Czarist empire that was dismembered at Brest-Litovsk in 1917.

Elias treated the German case as *exceptional*, one that stood apart from and expressed different tendencies from the rest of Europe. For his part, Bauman treated the Soviet case as *prototypical*, one that exemplified processes that were destined to occur throughout Europe. Both make strong arguments, but I want to suggest another point of view. I am going to suggest that in some important respects *the German case is prototypical* and that, similarly, in important respects *the Soviet case is exceptional*.

This argument will be developed as part of the larger object of this chapter, which is to explore some convergences and divergences between Zygmunt Bauman's approach to modernity and postmodernity and Norbert Elias's treatment of civilizing and decivilizing processes.

In the next part of this chapter, Elias's analysis of European social development in *The Civilizing Process* is considered once more, paying particular attention to the fact that it was written in the late 1930s. In particular, his assumptions about the role of colonialism will be noted. This will lead to a discussion, in the following part, of the implications of the decline of the European empires for our understanding of decivilizing processes. Subsequently, the argument will return to the comparison with Bauman.

The Civilizing Process as a View from the Late 1930s

There is a passage towards the end of *The Civilizing Process* where Norbert Elias makes the argument that the rationalization of thought and conduct is part of a 'transformation affecting the *whole* personality', including our 'drives and affects'. He adds that rationalization depends upon 'a rise in the standard of living and in security'. This brings protection from 'the uncontrollable fears which erupt far more powerfully and frequently into the lives of individuals in societies with less stable monopolies of force and lower divisions of functions'.

Elias then adds the following words, one of his earliest implicit references to decivilizing processes.[6] He writes:

> At present we are so accustomed to the existence of these more stable monopolies of force and the greater predictability of violence resulting from them, that we scarcely see their importance for the structure of our conduct and our personality. We scarcely realize how quickly what we call our 'reason', this relatively far-sighted and differentiated steering of our conduct, with its high degree of affect-control, would crumble and collapse if the anxiety-inducing tensions within and around us changed, if the fears affecting our lives suddenly became much stronger or much weaker. (Elias 1994a, 519)[7]

Considering that *The Civilizing Process* was first published in 1939, it is not difficult to make connections between this warning about the possible resurgence of irrationality and Elias's experience of Germany during the late 1920s and early 1930s. However, the overall tone of *The Civilizing Process* is not pessimistic. It could be described as realistic, but I would prefer to say that it is on the optimistic side of realistic.[8] There is some evidence that Elias had a broadly optimistic frame of mind in the 1930s.[9]

It is important to recollect the broader context in which *The Civilizing Process* was written – or, rather, the broader context as seen by Elias. Three countries were of special importance to Elias in his youth and early career. These were Germany, France and, belatedly, Britain (although he had a distinct preference for France over Britain as a young man).[10] According to the index of *The Civilizing Process* there are references to France on seventy pages, to Germany on thirty-six pages and to England on thirty-three pages. Russia is not listed, America only twice. No other country has more than five page references.

The Civilizing Process is a book of its time, and at the time it evidently seemed to Elias that the German experience of decivilization and disintegration was not typical of the overall thrust and direction of things. He believed the turbulence of the early twentieth century was part of 'the dynamics of increasing interdependence' leading towards the formation of 'monopolies of physical force over larger areas of the earth' and eventually the emergence of 'a single central political institution' bringing about 'the pacification of the earth'. Within this structure, smaller units or '"states"' would be able to 'grow together in balanced unity'. Human beings faced the challenge of making this pacified world society and its antecedents more civilized (more capable of producing 'happiness' and 'freedom') by mastering and moderating the tensions within and between themselves (Elias 1994a, 523–4).

Elias wrote: 'Only one thing is certain: the direction in which the integration of the modern world is veering'. He believed he could see 'the first outlines of a worldwide system of tensions composed by alliances and supra-state units of various kinds', a necessary precursor to the more 'civilized' world he hoped for. Elias listed these supra-state units as including 'united states, empires (and) leagues of nations' (515). The inclusion of empires is significant. In the 1930s the British and French empires were still in existence, sustaining the self-image of those societies as leading world powers. Furthermore, Elias was greatly impressed by the way the civilizing process had unfolded in these societies, especially in France.[11] As far as Elias was concerned, Britain and France were the big players.

As is well known, as Elias saw it, at Versailles a distinctive form of court rationality had developed along with a civilized personality embodying restraint, foresight and calculation. Subsequently, the standards, rules of conduct, psychological tendencies and habitus of the court were transmitted, in a subtly modified way, to the French bourgeoisie and, later still, to the rest of the population.

Elias treats the relationship between the colonizing and colonized societies as one item in a sequence of established/outsider relationships,[12] following in line behind the relationship between the aristocracy and the bourgeoisie and that between the bourgeoisie and the working class. In each of these relationships, Elias asserts, 'we see a clear tendency for standards of living and conduct to be equalized and levelled out. In each of the waves of expansion which occur when the mode of conduct of a small circle spreads to larger rising classes, two phases can be clearly distinguished: a phase of colonization or assimilation in which the lower and larger outsider class is still clearly inferior and governed by the example of the established upper group which, intentionally or unintentionally, permeates it with its own pattern of conduct, and a second phase of repulsion, differentiation or emancipation, in which the rising group gains perceptibly in social power and self-confidence' (507).[13]

In Elias's view, colonization was part of 'the expansion of Western civilization'. As Western styles of conduct and institutions were spread to the colonies this would lead to 'a reduction in the differences both of social power and of conduct between the colonists and the colonized' (463). Elias clearly saw this as an important way forward towards a future condition of 'balanced unity' between independent states (ex-colonies and ex-colonizers) within a pacified world.

However, Germany had followed a different path. It had no equivalent of Versailles; no assertive bourgeoisie; no colonial responsibilities. It was, according to Elias, atypical.

The Loss of Empire and Decivilizing Processes

Over half a century after *The Civilizing Process* was first published we can see a different picture. Civilization through colonization has been taken off the agenda. The dynamics of the established/outsider relationships between the European overseas empires and their colonies were brutally cut short by the intervention of a third party, the United States, after 1945. American hegemony was a major factor ensuring that the decolonization process occurred very rapidly. It was largely over by the early 1960s, leaving Britain, France and their European neighbours to come to terms with the loss of empire.

The loss of empire was not a small matter. The rhetoric and institutions surrounding the idea of 'empire' had been central to European self-understanding for half a millennium. One meaning of the term 'empire' is a large, complex and centralized political structure in which the centre forcefully dominates, and exacts taxes or tribute from, a collection of populations with a wide range of ethnic and cultural characteristics. However, there is a broader use of the word 'empire'. It refers to the exercise of total command, of supreme and extensive dominion.

In this broader sense, empire has a close relationship to the idea of sovereignty, the absolute control asserted by secular monarchs over their subjects and, later, by the state within the polity. The term 'empire' also refers to the total command over nature envisaged by Europe's philosophers of science from Francis Bacon onward. As Bacon puts it in *New Atlantis*, his plan for a scientific college, 'The end of our foundation is the knowledge of causes and secret motions of things, and the enlarging of the bounds of human empire, to the effecting of all things possible'.

The idea of human empire was a major ideal and legitimizing concept in modern Europe, especially as religious authority declined and belief in divine guidance began to fade. Scientific exploration, service to the state and the conquest of other peoples were mutually supportive activities, all expressing the belief in 'empire'. It is therefore not surprising that the disintegration of Europe's empires, a fact inescapable even to the most reluctant observer by the last quarter of the twentieth century, has coincided with two other phenomena. These are: an upsurge of doubt about the reliability and user-friendliness of scientific knowledge and a loss of confidence in the capacity of the state to produce a civilized society for its citizens. To oversimplify: in Europe, confidence in empire, science and the state have risen and fallen together.[14]

If this analysis is correct, it suggests that the decivilizing tendencies briefly envisaged in the last few pages of *The Civilizing Process* and then explored in much more detail and at much greater length in *The Germans* (Elias 1996) may be much more widespread in Europe than Elias implies. In *The Germans* Elias argues that in 1918 the German empire was stopped in its tracks and felled 'like a runner colliding at full pace with a wall' (183). The shock of this defeat intensified the Germans' endemic feeling that they were living in 'the shadow of their greater past' (4). This was expressed in pervasive unhappiness, self-pity and a wish for revenge against their enemies.

In this book, Elias makes the point that 'Currently, Europe as a whole is losing the monopoly of world leadership claimed by its member states since about the seventeenth century', adding 'How the Europeans will cope with it remains to be seen' (4). He does not develop this point, but it is a major one. Europe's loss of world leadership is closely related to the loss of empire, both the land-locked empires of east, central and south-eastern Europe and the overseas empires in Asia, Africa and the Middle East. The case of the German empire is not *a*typical. Rather it is *proto*typical.

By this is meant that the collapse of the German empire occurred early in the process of imperial disintegration that has been a central feature of the twentieth century. The German empire was obviously not the first of the world's empires, nor the first of Europe's empires, to experience a profound setback.[15] The Spanish empire, for example, had lost most of its European and American territories by the early nineteenth century.

However, the nations 'released' from Spanish dominion either established themselves as colonial powers in their own right (Belgium, the Netherlands) or became enmeshed in the colonial systems of the leading European powers.[16] The British and French both lost overseas territories in the late eighteenth and early nineteenth centuries but they rebuilt their colonial empires later in the nineteenth century. The British empire increased in size at the end of World War I.

Before the twentieth century, the shifts in fortune experienced by the European empires were, in most cases, an aspect of changing power balances within the imperial framework and did not indicate a significant weakening of imperial rule as a set of economic and political arrangements. One major and highly significant exception to this point is the successful attempt by the American colonists to assert their independence from the British state in 1776.

It is well known that by the end of the nineteenth century the United States had established itself as a rapidly expanding capitalist society with a strong ideological commitment to market freedoms and private property. There were some basic similarities with the European societies from which most of America's population had originally derived. For example, there were enormous privileges associated with being white and male both sides of the Atlantic.

However, it is easy to forget in the early twenty-first century how different the United States was from the rest of the world, including Europe, at the end of the nineteenth century. The United States was aggressively democratic[17] while, in Europe, France was the only major power which had an elected president rather than a king, queen, czar or emperor. Europe's politics, culture and economic order were thoroughly embedded in the practices and assumptions of imperialism. By contrast, the United States trumpeted itself as the enemy of empire everywhere. Not all its targets were difficult ones. In 1898 American ships blew the Spanish navy out of the water, allowing the American government to claim a decisive victory over a European imperial power.

During the twentieth century, capitalism – and especially American capitalism – discovered how to turn a high proportion of citizens into contented consumers. Mass production made possible, and required, mass consumption. Keynesian economics and the welfare state helped to keep money in the pockets of ordinary people and to give them an increased sense of security. One effect of these changes was that most of the population acquired a stake in capitalism as property owners, however small. In these circumstances, citizenship was a less dangerous commodity than it had been in the hands of the discontented poor. The polling booth was less likely to breed revolution.

To use shorthand, in the course of the twentieth century capitalism disentangled itself from European imperialism and strengthened its alliance with democracy. It is true that by the end of the century some of the institutional arrangements and cultural understandings that cemented the capitalism–democracy linkage were under strain. For example, the corporatist and Keynesian welfare state had been dismantled to some extent and capitalism was increasingly operating, freer than before from control by national governments.[18] However, by that time the European empires were gone.

The German empire was in the first wave in 1918, along with the Austro-Hungarian, Ottoman and Russian empires. The British and French empires, along with the Dutch and Belgian colonies and the last remnants of the Spanish and Portuguese empires, all went down in the second wave after 1945. Their colonies were either lost or in revolt by the early 1960s. During the 1930s and 1940s, the German and Russian empires made a comeback, under Hitler and Stalin respectively.[19] However, this was relatively short-lived. The break-up of the Soviet empire after 1989 was the last great decolonization movement of this century.

The break up of the European empires is an important instance of the undermining of previously stable power monopolies. The German case after 1918 and again after 1945 comprises two extreme examples of this process: extreme, that is, in rapidity and extent. The Russian case in 1917 and again after 1989 is comparable in terms of the severity of the effects, although the particular structural consequences have been different.

In the rest of Europe the effects of decline upon the populations concerned have been less extreme but they share certain characteristics with those Elias identified in the German case. For example, in Britain and France after 1945 it is certainly possible to see signs of sadness and resentment at the loss of former imperial strength. Two ways in which this has been expressed are anti-Americanism and racist hostility to migrants from the Third World.

In Britain, the loss of the empire undermined the authority of the political establishment and weakened its will to exercise control over the society. This may help to explain the unravelling of the Keynesian welfare state from the mid-1970s onwards and, perhaps, the fading resistance of central government to devolution in Scotland, Northern Ireland and Wales. It is true that in France, the dominance of Paris and the ingrained strength of the central state apparatus have not been seriously challenged. Elias's book *The Civilizing Process* provides us with a major part of the explanation for this. In France, state-formation processes and the formation of a distinctive civilized habitus occurred in a remarkably consistent and cumulative fashion over several centuries.

At first sight the French case seems to challenge the argument that decivilizing processes have been Europe-wide. However, another possibility is that France, the major example used by Elias, is an exceptional case, perhaps more exceptional than Germany. Exceptional, that is, in the strength, consistency and unbroken character of 'the civilizing process' occurring within that society and hence, perhaps, the relative weakness of decivilizing tendencies. If the tendency towards devolution is one sign of decivilizing processes, then France's neighbours Italy, Spain and Belgium have all been more susceptible to those processes than France itself.

Another aspect of decivilizing processes is worth mentioning. Writing about interwar Germany, Elias summed up the dominant code of values as follows: 'Adult life is a constant war of all against all. One has to be a tough customer to win through in this struggle. The untamed warrior ethos comes to life here once again in a bourgeoisified version . . . The harshness of human relationships which finds expression in the use of physical violence, in people being wounded or if need be killed by other people, spreads like an infection even to those areas where physical fights do not occur at all' (108–9). Later, he adds: 'Underlying both the training provided within the student fighting fraternities and the life as a member of the imperial upper classes at which it was aimed is an implicit picture of human social life as a struggle of all against all which was almost Hobbesian in character' (112).

There is some evidence that a modified version of this bourgeoisified warrior ethos emerged in Western Europe during the late 1970s, became dominant and respectable during the 1980s and migrated to central, eastern and southeastern Europe during the 1990s. Its best-known representative was Margaret Thatcher who emphasized the need, as she saw it, to give 'market forces' as much freedom as possible. This was on the grounds that the competitive struggle unleashed within the market would destroy wasteful and inefficient practices, institutions and groups and encourage strong and healthy elements to become more powerful. From another point of view, it was the ethos of a 'decivilizing' society.

In Western Europe the decivilizing process has largely been 'contained' by allowing the market to bear a greater structural weight within societies. It is as if one set of structures, the centralized state apparatus, has been weakened but the interwoven struts formed by the networks of trading links and the activities of buyers and sellers have remained firm. This shift in the structural balance away from the central state has been accompanied by a propaganda campaign giving supercharged legitimacy to the market. Adam Smith has been deified, Hayek glamorized, Thatcher sanctified.

In fact, there was as much of Nietzsche as of Adam Smith in Thatcherism.[20] Its warlike dimension was on display in the Falklands and during the Gulf War and may be echoed in Tony Blair's recent enthusiasm for engagement in a ground war in Kosovo. The danger of a drift towards less well-regulated violence was shown during Britain's urban riots of 1981. The mix of Smith and Nietzsche made Thatcherism a highly importable commodity in Eastern and Central Europe after 1989 where state structures were extensively undermined, losing prestige and credibility. In the successor states of the old Soviet empire the market was already in existence, operating to a great extent on the fringes of the law, or beyond it, cheek by jowl with gangsterism.

Paradoxically, Thatcherism was less 'civilized' than the Keynesian regime that preceded it in Britain but more 'civilized' than the widespread chaos that followed the collapse of the socialist regimes in Eastern and Central Europe. The economics and social philosophy of Thatcherism offered a strategy for lifting the subterranean trading system of the ex-Soviet bloc into respectability and strengthening its institutional base. In other words, it offered a means of containing decivilizing processes and the drift towards violence. This was not always effective, as cases such as Albania show.

Another aspect of the decivilizing process associated with the decline of the European empires has been an increase in the significance of the market as a regulator of trans-national social processes. During the late nineteenth century, the imperial administrators in Paris, London, Moscow, Berlin, Vienna, Brussels, Madrid, Lisbon and elsewhere provided a rough-and-ready framework of law and order over much of the globe and made pragmatic accommodations with the capitalist investors and adventurers who traded throughout the empires. As the empires gradually disintegrated capitalism's freedom of manoeuvre increased – although two world wars and the four decades of Cold War certainly made this process more complicated.[21]

During the 1990s the dynamics of 'decivilized' post-imperial global society are becoming more starkly evident. Large business corporations are much less embedded in national economies than they were under the earlier regime of Keynesian welfarism and corporatist capitalism. They operate transnationally, profiting from the existence of an increasing number of relatively weak states and the absence of other stable transnational power monopolies.[22] Of course, the European Union is an exception to this generalization, one to be discussed shortly.

Decivilizing Processes and Postmodernity in Europe

At this point, Zygmunt Bauman re-enters the argument, especially his recent book *Globalization. The Human Consequences* (Bauman 1998b).[23] In this book Bauman provides an account of the postmodern world as he sees it. It is a world in which the state had gone into semi-retirement and has abdicated responsibility for managing the national economy or shaping the national culture. The market has taken over. Capital moves round the globe with great ease. Powerful businesses make decisions somewhere in global cyberspace. Throughout every continent, global companies compete with each other in bitter dogfights. Governments cannot hold them in check and have let them off the chain.

In Bauman's view, the market rules both locally and globally. The result is a condition of semi-disorder in which '*no one seems now to be in control*', a world that 'does not look like a totality anymore; it looks like a field of scattered and disparate forces, congealing in places difficult to predict and gathering momentum which no one really knows how to arrest' (58; emphasis in original).

Locally, the world is full of sellers and buyers, advocates and clients, pushers and users. As has been seen, the postmodern habitat is filled with competing 'experts', prophets and neo-tribes, each promoting its ideology or its ethnicity or its cure for the world's ills or its style of clothing or its fast-food outlets or its better brand of soft drinks. Within this postmodern habitat, the blandishments of the market where lifestyles are for sale are interwoven with the threat of violence and oppression. Warring tribes aggressively compete for space and attention and do harm to anyone under their control who does not fit in with their ideas.

This is a plausible model, one that can be made to fit a wide range of situations from the shopping malls of Birmingham to the concentration camps of Bosnia – as well as the streets of Berlin in the early 1930s. It converges with an Eliasian approach in some respects. This postmodern world of Bauman's is one in which the civilizing process has faltered.

To recap, a central mechanism of the civilizing process as described by Elias in his classic work is the tension-filled mutual engagement between established and outsider groups within a dense web of interdependence under the aegis of a stable power monopoly. Within this dynamic figuration the civilized habitus of the established group is acquired, typically in a slightly altered form, by the outsider group which in the same process ceases to be 'outside' to the same extent.

However, Bauman describes a world in which the web of interdependence has been torn to shreds, one in which old power monopolies have been destabilized and dispersed, a world without secure establishments, one populated entirely by strangers and outsiders. Looked at in this way, *postmodernity is decivilized modernity*.

Bauman and Elias share enough common assumptions to make it possible to synthesize some of their insights. Bauman certainly uses Eliasian-sounding language at times, for example in his *Thinking Sociologically* where he describes sociology as 'the habit of viewing human actions as *elements of wider figurations*: that is, of a non-random assembly of actors locked together in a web of *mutual dependency*' (Bauman 1990, 7).[24]

There are some differences between the two sociologists. For example, they see European history in dissimilar ways. Bauman's narrative of European development begins with 'hermetically sealed' (Bauman 1973, 134) communities in the Middle Ages. It is when these communities begin to break up and populations merge that the urge to classify and control the masses takes hold within social elites.

By contrast, Elias anchors his account in a more Hobbesian medieval world where power balances are radically unstable, allegiances shift constantly, violence perpetually threatens and the boundaries between one lord's territory and another are forever changing. The ambiguity and flux of this existence were life-threatening but posed no threat to people's sense of reality. The mental and emotional character of participants in this form of life were well adjusted to it. Only later, when stable power monopolies were established at the royal court and elsewhere, were courtiers constrained gradually to abandon their old habitus and adapt to new forms of control.

Secondly, these two writers have very different approaches to the socialization of human beings. Elias argues that we acquire our sense of who we are and the appropriate way to behave as social beings in the course of early experience within the figurations (families, social class, ethnic groups, nations and so on) into which we are born.

Elias assumes, by implication, that there is an innate desire to survive but the new person learns how to do this and, more generally, how to 'go on', from the group to which she belongs. It is through her membership of the group, her participation in the figuration, that the person acquires appropriate dispositions, a distinctive habitus. Different figurations shape their members in very different ways. The French, the Germans, the Dutch, the Italians have different national habituses, differences that are shaped by their history and, in turn, help to shape it.

Bauman has other concerns. For him, the key process is not the shaping of each person's habitus and persona by their participation in figurations from the moment of their birth. Instead, as far as he is concerned, the key process is the imposition of rules of conduct 'from above' by bureaucrats, experts and other agents of oppressive modernity.

Bauman argues that we are all born with innate moral dispositions, including an aversion to causing suffering in others and a desire to exercise care for them. He treats socialization not so much as the 'filling out' or creation of a person as the 'smothering' of their essential humanity. Bauman believes that in modernity people are systematically deprived of the chance to exercise their capacity to act morally, to make ethical choices. Instead, they are forced to follow rules about how to behave which are imposed from 'above' by bureaucrats.[25] In his view, bureaucracies are driven by a fierce urge to classify, pin down, and tidy up the world. Furthermore, they condition people to obey their rules, to accept those rules as guides for conduct. Bureaucracies prepare men and women for this way of life by anaesthetizing their innate disposition to care for others.

This is related to a third point which is that in *Modernity and the Holocaust*, Bauman presents an interpretation of the civilizing process, a term he borrows from Elias, which is quite different from the latter's approach.[26] Unlike Elias, Bauman believes that the practice of etiquette and *civilité* at the royal court was of very little relevance to the 'civilizing process'. This process was, as he sees it, a campaign mounted by the *philosophes* and their successors to civilize the masses, to bring them civilization. In other words, it was 'a conscious proselytizing crusade waged by men of knowledge and aimed at extirpating the vestiges of wild cultures – local, tradition-bound ways of life and patterns of cohabitation'. The trend was towards functional centralization. The experts would be in charge. It was to be 'a knowledge-led management . . . aimed above all at the administration of individual minds and bodies' (93).

Despite these differences of emphasis, some degree of synthesis is possible. Take the first difference mentioned, their diverging pictures of medieval society. In practice, highly mobile feudal warriors require highly *im*mobile serfs to plough their fields while they are away fighting. Servile villagers might well spend all their lives within a few square miles in a community which, if not 'hermetically sealed', has few contacts with others. Secondly, the models of socialization presented by Elias and Bauman are not incompatible. The processes described by the two writers almost certainly both take place and exist in tension with each other. Investigating this is a practical matter.[27]

Thirdly, the world of the court and the bureaucratic expert not only co-existed in late eighteenth-century France, they *both* had influence on the rest of society. Philosophizing courtiers and courtly *philosophes* belonged to overlapping social circles.[28] They exchanged jokes, compliments and insults. There is little doubt that attempts were made to impose panoptical discipline in post-revolutionary France, as elsewhere. However, at the same time as these attempts were being made, *civilité* was being absorbed by the bourgeoisie and, later, their employees. No doubt many a prison governor went home to a carefully laid dinner table and practised his etiquette over the soup. As Bauman put it on one occasion, 'Aristocratic society could not help encouraging imitation' (Bauman 1978, 200).[29] This remained true even after the guillotine had done its work.

Men of their Times

Both writers contribute major insights, and it would be shortsighted to neglect one at the expense of the other. However, the way each sees the world is to some extent influenced by the social and cultural context in which he became a thinker and, more specifically, a sociologist. It has already been mentioned that Bauman and Elias came from different classes, generation and nations, were educated in different traditions, and had different aspirations in their early careers, careers that were disastrously interrupted by the effects of anti-Semitism.

Although both Elias and Bauman discussed Jewishness and anti-Semitism in their later work, neither made it a central issue in his life's work. As far as Elias is concerned, the problem posed by the Nazis was not that Jews were victimized but that the Nazis could have taken root, acquired power and behaved in such a barbaric way *in Germany with the complicity of his own class, the German bourgeoisie*. In a similar way, as far as Bauman was concerned, the problem posed by his own early biography was not that anti-Semitism existed but that it was exploited *in a state socialist society with the complicity of leading members of the Communist party to which he belonged.*

It has already been suggested that Elias exaggerated the extent to which the German case was exceptional. The main reason that Elias came to this conclusion seems to be that he was greatly influenced by the particular circumstances of the 1930s when the British and French empires were impressively intact and Germany had undergone a period of extreme socio-political disintegration. It is argued here that, in fact, the Germans did not follow a peculiar route, different from their European neighbours. Instead, they were prototypical victims of the pan-European malaise produced by the loss of imperial hegemony.

For his part, Bauman has been greatly influenced by the particular circumstances of the 1940s and early 1950s. During those years he took a very active role in the military and political campaigns to defend Russia against Hitler's armies and, subsequently, install state socialist regimes in Eastern Europe, including his native Poland. Bauman believed that Europe's socialist republics were in the vanguard of modernity. In other words, in his view, they represented the most determined and systematic attempt to bring a more perfect society into being through the skills of state bureaucracy aided by scientific rationality.

During the 1970s, Bauman had many fundamental criticisms of communist bureaucracy but he credited the state socialist societies of Eastern Europe with providing an important demonstration of the extent to which equality and social justice could be promoted in the public sphere. As already noticed, as late as the early 1980s, especially during the early months of Polish Solidarity, Bauman continued to hope that creative dialogue within the public sphere, fostered by enlightened intellectuals, might enable significant progress to be made in the direction of the socialist utopia.

When the Berlin Wall came down in 1989 and the state socialist regimes were replaced, Bauman came to the conclusion that if the Soviet experiment, which had encompassed the most advanced forms of modernity, could not succeed in fulfilling its promise then modernity itself was bound to fail. However, this conclusion was wrong or, at the very least, premature. The most important piece of counter-evidence is the European Union, a modern project in the Enlightenment tradition.

In fact, as is argued in the next chapter, the European Union is a good example of the civilizing process in operation.[30] In its sociogenesis it reproduced at a higher societal level some of the mechanisms Elias showed at work in seventeenth-century France. For example, the American government used its position of overwhelming power and authority at the end of World War II to insist that the French and Germans in particular, but also the Italians, Dutch and Belgians should cooperate with each other, especially in economic policy. The European states were pacified by the American 'monarch' just as the French kings pacified their warring nobility.

Since the 1960s the polity now known as the European Union has imposed new standards of decency over an increasing number of areas from pollution levels to the conduct of trade and industry. National states have been subjected to new disciplines from above just as, in previous centuries, noble families had to acquire self-restraint and obey rules imposed by the sovereign.

A notable fact about the European Union is that its leading members consist of the old 'headquarter societies' of the European empires, now almost completely shorn of their colonies. As already noticed, the EU has provided a new home, a new political centre, for the political establishments of Paris, London, Bonn (and, more recently, Berlin), Vienna, Brussels, the Hague, Madrid and Lisbon. All the old imperial capitals of Europe are represented there except for Moscow. Russia was the last of the great nations of Europe to realize that the great game of empire was over. The shock that Germany experienced in 1918 did not hit Russia until 1989. Far from being in the vanguard, Russia is the laggard. Germany is at the heart of the European Union. Russia is the exception, in danger of being left behind.

This leads towards the third part of this book in which theoretical and empirical concerns are drawn closer together. The next chapter discusses the development of the European Union at more length, drawing upon the ideas of Parsons, Arendt and Elias.

Notes

1 To recap, Bauman was born in 1925.

2 For a more extended discussion see Smith 1999b.

3 Bauman incorporates the process of envisioning a possible future into his intellectual strategy. See Bauman 1976a for his treatment of the socialist utopia. Later, he constructed his picture of postmodernity by systematizing his intuitions or 'intimations'. See Bauman 1992a.

4 Biographical details are taken from J. Bauman 1988 and Morawski 1998.

5 See, for example, his chapters on postmodern art, fiction and the 'consumer cooperative' in *Postmodernity and its Discontents* (Bauman 1997, 95–140).

6 Elias does not use the term 'decivilizing' in *The Civilizing Process*.

7 The quotation continues as follows: 'or, as in many simpler societies, both at once, now stronger, now weaker'. Elias makes a number of references to the fact, as he sees it, that civilizing tendencies may be reversed. For example, there may be 'counter-spurts' or phases of 'recession'. However, taking European history as a whole since early medieval times, he believed there was an overall tendency towards increased political centralization and increased personal self-control. See, for example, Elias 1994a, 153, 459–60.

8 Elias had been very happy writing the book and later commented that he had felt

'completely at home' in the British Museum while he was working on it in the late 1930s. It was written before Elias was hit by the tragic events of the early 1940s, both public and private, including the death of his parents. Elias's mother was killed in Auschwitz. In a letter to Elias she told him of the death of his father at home in Breslau. See Elias 1994b, 53, 55.

   9 Only an optimist would set up a toy factory in Paris in the mid-1930s run by a sculptor, a novelist and a philosopher-turned-sociologist. The writer was Ludwig Turek. The sculptor, a communist like Turek, is unnamed by Elias. See Elias 1994b, 46, 49–50.

   10 See Elias 1994b, 19.

   11 Asked about his feelings as a young man for Russia, Elias replied 'Nothing, absolutely nothing. The Tsar and the Cossacks, barbarous. The barbarous east – that was all beyond the pale' (Elias 1994b, 20).

   12 Elias did not develop this terminology till after *The Civilizing Process* was written. See 1994a, 510.

   13 The quotation continues as follows: 'and in which the upper group is forced into increased restraint and isolation, and the contrasts and tensions in society are increased'.

   14 For a discussion, see Bauman 1987.

   15 On imperial disintegration and related themes, see, for example, Tainter 1988; Thompson 1998.

   16 Argentina, for example, could be described in 1914 as an 'honorary dominion'. See Cain and Hopkins 1993, 315.

   17 While also being a society in which dissent that appeared to damage the interests of private property – for example, trade union agitation – was punished vigorously by the police.

   18 See Bauman 1998b.

   19 Both were profoundly anti-capitalist.

   20 On the Nietzschean dimension of German culture, see Elias 1996 115–19.

   21 The Cold War meant that a number of markets were denied to Western capitalists, or at least they were only allowed restricted access to them under controlled conditions. However, the large American market and expanding opportunities abroad in the 'free world' gave an incentive for companies, especially in the United States, to develop techniques of mass production, advertising and systems of strategic control. The large transnational corporations increasingly acquired many of the functions and capacities of small states, enabling them to survive and prosper in an environment of weak government.

   22 There are some similarities between this situation and the situation of merchants in early modern Europe.

   23 See also Bauman 1988 and Bauman 1992a.

   24 The quotation continues: 'Sociologists would ask what consequences this being locked together would have for the possible and actual behaviour of human actors. Such interests shape the object of sociological inquiry: figurations, webs of mutual dependence, reciprocal conditioning of action and expansion or confinement of actors' freedom are the prominent preoccupations of sociology. Single actors, like you or me, come into the view of sociological study in their capacity as units, members or partners in a network of interdependence. The central question of sociology, one could say, is: in what sense does it matter that in whatever they do or may do people are dependent on other people' (Bauman 1990, 7–8).

   25 Bauman does not pay much attention to variations between societies in the content of bureaucratic rules. Nor does he explore the sociogenesis of such variations. German, Polish, Russian, British, American bureaucracies are basically the same, he believes, in those respects he is most concerned with. In fact, it is possible to envisage the existence of cultures with very different patterns of socialization that share certain assumptions about how one 'should' behave. As a proposition it is worth taking seriously, as Barrington Moore does in his book entitled *Injustice* (Moore 1978). Moore argues that human nature gives moral codes a particular 'direction and impulse'. His basic argument is as follows: 'As a working hypothesis, I propose a conception of innate human nature, innate in the sense of being *prior* to any social influence but not necessarily immune to them . . . To the extent such a concept is valid it implies the existence of a "natural morality" in the sense that *some* moral preferences,

particularly negative ones, are not merely the consequence of social training and conditioning' (7; emphasis in original).

26 Bauman argues that Elias's view of the civilizing process supports an 'etiological myth deeply entrenched in the self-consciousness of our western society', in other words, 'the morally elevating story of humanity emerging from pre-social barbarity' (Bauman 1989, 12).

27 The question is related to the issue raised by Habermas in his discussion of the relationship between 'systems' and 'lifeworlds'. See Habermas 1987.

28 It is ironic that Bauman, who began his career as a professional soldier, should have emphasized the situation of the *philosophe*-turned-bureaucrat while Elias, who began as a philosopher, should focus upon the warrior-turned-courtier.

29 Furthermore, Bauman certainly acknowledged the importance of habits of rational self-control in his early writings. He realized that when acquired by the working class they were a potential force for emancipation. These habits could help, indirectly at least, to tip power balances in their favour. Bauman recognized this factor in his book *Between Class and Elite* (Bauman 1972) when he praises the ascetic self-discipline of the pioneer labour leadership in Britain.

30 See also Smith 1999c.

PART 3

TOWARDS GLOBAL MODERNITY

7

EUROPE

Americans in Paris

Elias did not write directly about the sociogenesis of the European move-ment.[1] However, *The Court Society* provides us with some important clues to understanding that process. In *The Court Society*, Elias argues that the structure and organization of key political institutions are shaped by the struggles that bring them into existence. The victors use these institutions to try and stabilize their supremacy and keep the upper hand. As Elias puts it, 'Every form of rule is the precipitate of a social conflict – it consolidates the distribution of power corresponding to its outcome' (Elias 1983, 146). As we have seen already, Elias develops this argument in the case of France in the seventeenth and eighteenth centuries.

During the interminable religious wars of the sixteenth century, French society had been deeply divided. The monarchy was weak. The most important survival unit for people at that time was the family. During the wars, soldiers owed loyalty to specific dynasties and fought under the standard of a Guise, a Condé, a Montmorency or a Coligny. Fundamental issues of religion were at issue also but, broadly speaking, the 'makers and shakers' were the leading warriors of the great French families. The honour of each dynasty was at stake.

At the end of the wars, however, the French crown managed to impose its authority upon the fractious noble families. For some decades, this victory was insecure. For example, half a century after the Edict of Nantes (1598)[2] at the end of the French religious wars, some French nobles were still prepared to challenge the crown during the Fronde rebellion. However, in the course of the early seventeenth century the crown dis-armed the aristocracy. The leading nobles were forced to keep households near the king and attend his royal court where he could keep a close eye on them.

In effect, the king won and imposed his rules on the losers. The crown was helped in this objective by the pervasive war-weariness in French society. As one historian has written, 'The rural population of France was weary of ceaseless war. Starvation and plague were threatening, and in a devastated Britanny great packs of wolves were on the prowl . . . It was to the idealized figure of a patriarchal king, the upholder of justice, the champion of order, that . . . (the peasantry) now instinctively turned . . . It was an extraordinary spontaneous movement, compounded of hatred of anarchy and social oppression, and a mass rallying of the people of France to their anointed king . . . It was as if the country were purging itself of the religious hatreds of half a century. "We all promise and swear before God to love and cherish each other". There would be "no more war among them, nor reproach for diversity of religion, and each would be free to live as he desired"' (Elliott 1968, 356).

It is interesting to reflect that Thomas Hobbes, author of *Leviathan* (Hobbes 1962), made a number of visits to France during the early seventeenth century when the monarchy was gradually winning the battle to impose its authority. The social atmosphere and intellectual climate he encountered must have shaped his thinking to a significant extent. It seems likely that behind the expressions of human tolerance just quoted there was a willingness to accept strong regulation from above, an almost Hobbesian willingness to be ruled. As has been seen, this moment of submission was balanced by a countervailing moment of resistance, for example in the Fronde. However, the Fronde was decisively defeated.

During the early seventeenth century, the balance of power and the locus of authority shifted decisively 'upwards'. By the middle of the seventeenth century, states rather than families were the most prominent survival units in Europe. To put it another way, in each polity a leading dynasty (the royal family) was pursuing its interests by 'riding' the state just as a cavalryman might ride a horse. However, in the process the institutions, practices and discourses of the state were taking shape. The horse eventually unseated its rider.

The state's resources were often mobilized to serve the ambitions of royal dynasties in France, Austria, Russia and elsewhere throughout the eighteenth century. However, royal heads rolled throughout Europe between the French and Russian revolutions. In most European polities members of the propertied class were reluctant to abandon the idea of royalty, perhaps because it helped keep the peasantry loyal and hardworking.

However, by the early nineteenth century Europe's kings and queens largely held their positions on suffrance, on condition that they served the interests of the society's leading interests. By the early twentieth century these interests included large urban-industrial populations who, increasingly, had the vote and were demanding that the state pay attention to their needs.

There was a great clearout of royal families after World War I. The new states created out of the wreckage of the German, Russian, Austro-

Hungarian and Ottoman empires had a penchant for presidents rather than monarchs. By the early twentieth century, the violent struggles that shaped European politics were not between dynasties but between national armies.

During the twentieth century the balance of power between 'levels' in Europe shifted decisively 'upwards' once again. During the two world wars, the inter-state competition became not merely European but global (as indeed the name now given to those wars implies: they were 'world' wars). By the end of World War II, the United States had emerged as a clear victor in this global competition.

During the late 1940s and 1950s the leading position of the United States was virtually unchallenged although, to anticipate the argument, Britain and France engaged in a Fronde-like rebellion against American authority in 1956 over Suez. In the late 1940s the US government was a victorious super-state. It behaved like a monarch that had subdued an unruly nobility.

Marshall Aid

Like the French king in the early seventeenth century, the American government set about imposing rules and protocols that would encourage peaceful cooperation and impose limits on disruptive forms of competition and conflict. The leading expression of this approach was the establishment of the United Nations, founded in 1945. The fact that it was sited in New York reflected the unchallenged global dominance of the United States.[3] In 1946 the US Government committed itself to defending the principles of the UN Charter 'in the interest of world peace'. In practice, this entailed a strategy of 'containing' the Soviet Union.[4]

American anxieties about Europe focused on its economic and military weakness in the face of potential Soviet aggression. They were also concerned about the advance of left-wing organizations in western Europe, especially in Italy and France. From the American point of view, the defence situation was improved by the establishment of the North Atlantic Treaty Organization in 1949 based in Brussels.[5] In 1950 an integrated force for the defence of Western Europe was established under a Supreme Headquarters Allied Powers Europe (SHAPE). Its first chief was General Eisenhower, later to be American President. Eisenhower was the man who had commanded the Allied forces during the final victory over Germany a few years before.

In the late 1940s the economic condition of Europe was very bad. Farms had been ruined and industry shattered by bomb damage. Trade was at a low level, the population was in decline and inflation was widespread. The war had used up a great deal of capital and, as a result, many European governments were short of assets and heavily in debt.[6] The American response was set out in a speech at Harvard University in 1947 by Secretary of State George C Marshall. Discussing 'the rehabilitation of the economic structure of Europe', Marshall declared that 'Europe's requirements for the next three or four years . . . – principally from America – are so much greater than her present ability to pay that she must have substantial additional help or face economic, social and political deterioration of a very grave character'.[7] This was the founding logic behind the Marshall Plan.

Very soon after that speech was made the French and British governments, with strong American behind-the-scenes encouragement, invited over twenty European countries to a conference in Paris. The object of the conference was to draw up a plan which would set out what help the Europeans wanted from the Americans. The American government was not officially represented at the Paris conference. However, Americans officials made it quite clear, unofficially, that: 'Participating countries should take effective steps to create internal monetary and financial stability . . . Steps should be taken to diminish trade barriers, with the eventual goal of complete uniformity with the International Trade Organization . . . [and] . . . A permanent organization should be created'.[8]

Marshall Aid under the Economic Recovery Plan (ERP) was channelled through the Organization for European Economic Cooperation (OEEC), a body that represented the sixteen European nations benefiting from Marshall Aid.[9] The money was not given without strings attached. The Americans insisted that OEEC should produce a pan-European plan aimed at encouraging free trade and reducing protectionism.[10] Furthermore, under the rules of the programme the Americans had to give their agreement before funds could be spent on specific projects. For example, approval was not given for contracts with firms recognizing communist trade unions.[11]

At the end of the French religious wars, Henri IV of France supposedly said that he wanted to put a chicken in the pot of every French household. This offer applied to Protestants and Catholics alike.[12] In a similar way, the Americans offered Marshall Aid to ex-enemies and friends alike – although they were less charitable to 'new' enemies such as European communist parties they suspected of having links with the Soviet Union.

For example, there was a massive propaganda campaign in support of Marshall Aid, especially in countries such as Italy which were thought to be in danger of 'going communist'. As David Ellwood has shown, the Marshall Plan was presented to Italians (and other Europeans) as the gateway to American standards of material life. During the 1948 general election in Italy the State department made it clear 'that Communist voters would be banned from emigration to the US, and Marshall himself declared that should the Left win, the country would be excluded from the benefits of the ERP' (Ellwood 1998, 34).

The ERP injected nearly $12.5 billion into Europe between 1948 and 1952. During the decade after 1945 the total amount of American support for Europe added up to nearly $25 billion. The UK received $6.9 billion, France $5.5 billion, the Federal Republic of Germany $3.9 billion and Italy $2.9 billion.[13] This freed up domestic funds for capital formation.

In 1947 George Kennan argued that the Europeans had no shared sense of direction and that the US State Department would have to 'decide unilaterally' what was in Europe's best interests.[14] For a few years in the late 1940s this is what they tried to do although with slightly more subtlety than Kennan's words imply. There were vocal enthusiasts for pan-European institutions in most European nations and had been for decades.[15] However, it was the Americans who, in the late 1940s, pushed the West European states into cooperating with each other.

Marshall Aid was administered on the American side by the Economic Cooperation Agency (ECA). Its chief administrator, Paul Hoffman, was a moderate Republican who had previously worked in the automobile business. In 1953 he described his approach to dealing with his European counterparts:

> I had learned from experience that if you want enthusiastic cooperation, you have to get those concerned to do the planning, or at least to participate in the development of the planning. If, for example, in Studebaker, I believed that our body department was not as efficient as, say, that of Oldsmobile, I wouldn't go to the Oldsmobile company, study what they are doing and then give an order to the head of our body department. Instead, I would talk to our man, saying that they seem to be doing some interesting things in connection with bodywork at Oldsmobile, and I would suggest that he go and take a look.

> He comes back, and if he is any good, he will have ideas. He will say that Studebaker has developed this or that which is desirable, but of course it needs modification and improvement – for which he takes the initiative in suggesting improvements, and he accepts the responsibility. In a larger way, we were successful in getting this done in Europe. There was development by each country of its own plans and proposals. It was their initiative and enthusiasm, and they took responsibility for the plans.[16]

This vignette of a 'good' relationship between a company boss and a managerial subordinate nicely sums up the relationship with Europe that the Americans were looking for in the late 1940s and early 1950s. It is the equivalent, in a more commercialized and bureaucratic world, of the relationship between the absolute monarch who commands the key military and economic resources and the court noble who is available for loyal service and eager for preferment. In this case the 'monarch' had some definite ideas about what was wrong with the European realm but was less clear about how to remedy matters.

One of Hoffman's chief aides, Richard Bissell, later commented that 'Before the Marshall plan began, there was a clear intention to try in a four year period to bring about some structural changes in Europe. It was recognized that the things that were wrong were deep-seated and that, therefore, deep-seated efforts would be needed to cope with them'. In his view, the 'structural change' of 'European unification' received 'a good deal of intelligent attention all through' but not enough was done to 'really come to grips with . . . the problem of the relatively decadent managerial class and weak labour especially in France and Italy (not in North Europe, Germany etc. generally).' Bissell regretted that the Americans had not managed to do 'something important on that front'.[17]

By October 1949, American frustration at the slow pace of structural change in Europe led to a more forceful and direct approach. Paul Hoffman made a major speech at a conference of the OEEC insisting that the price for continued dollar aid was 'integration,' a word he used repeatedly. By integration he meant 'the formation of a single large market in which quantitative restrictions on the movement of goods, monetary barriers to the flow of payments and, eventually, all tariffs are permanently swept away.'[18] As a step in this direction, the Americans supplied the Europeans with a plan for a European Payments Union (EPU), in other words a system for handling debts between European states so that national currencies could become fully convertible.[19] The EPU began operating in September 1950.

Life at Court

The Americans did not always get their way any more than Henri IV or Louis XIV did. However, they gave a powerful shove in the direction of pan-European institution building. They wanted a regime of increasingly rational, increasingly rule-bound behaviour and they got it. Their capacity to control this regime gradually diminished. After 1950 the outbreak of the Korean War shifted American attention to the Pacific, and the European economies began to revive rapidly.

The weakening capacity of the Americans to force their views about institution building on their European allies was made clear in 1953 when they gave their support to federalists such as Jean Monnet who were arguing for the creation of a European Defence Community (EDC). The EDC would control a new European Army including a German contingent. Crucially, French opinion was hostile. The American government made military aid under the Mutual Security Program of 1953–4 contingent on the EDC being created; if it was not created half the planned aid would be withdrawn. This strategy of winning policy victories by the carrot of aid had been reasonably successful in the days of Marshall Aid but by 1954 it no longer worked. The French National Assembly refused to ratify the EDC and the plan collapsed.[20]

However, during the 1950s it became clear also that there would be no return to the 'old days' of direct military confrontation between West European states. This did not mean that national interests were forgotten, any more than court aristocrats stopped caring about the size of their hereditary estates. Just as French nobles learned to pursue their dynastic interests by intrigue at Versailles, worming their way into and up the networks of influence, so Europe's politicians tried to shape the institution-building process to serve their own national ambitions.

Take the case of the Schuman Plan which led to the setting up of the European Coal and Steel Community launched in 1950. In retrospect, this is sometimes presented as one of the building blocks for a new pan-European institutional order moving beyond petty national rivalries. However, one motive for establishing the ECSC was that it gave the French a means of exerting influence over German reindustrialization, making sure their own interests were protected. The crucial difference from the 'old days' is that by the early 1950s peaceful and 'civilized' strategies were used to pursue national interests.

This approach was significantly different from the approach adopted by the French government a quarter of a century earlier. In 1923, it sent in troops to occupy the German district of the Ruhr in order to neutralize the threat posed by its industrial capacity. This was equivalent, at a higher level of social integration, to the French aristocracy conducting its disputes by laying seige to each others' castles. By ceasing to behave in this way European governments were, in Elias's terms, giving evidence of a significant advance in the civilizing process.

Just as the court nobility were permitted to keep their swords, as long as they did not use them, so the leading West European states have maintained their 'independent' nuclear arsenals. Instead of jousting, there are NATO exercises. Western Europe was not disarmed and pacified to the same extent as Eastern Europe under Soviet control but military expenditure certainly dropped as a share of national budgets.[21] Between 1953 and 1970 defence spending fell from 11 per cent of GNP in Britain to 5 per cent. In France the drop was from 11 per cent to 4 per cent, in Italy and West Germany from 5 per cent to 3 per cent. This reduction would not have been possible without an immense American military presence on European soil.

According to Michel Jobert, French foreign minister in 1973–4, west Europe in the immediate post-war decades was 'Lined up in one camp, under strict US control, taking orders and reporting for duty'. Jobert added: 'Europe was reassured but at a cost of irresponsibility'.[22] Jobert's comments may be exaggerated but they show how it felt to be subject to the constraints of a new power monopoly.

The disciplinary power of the Americans was certainly shown during the Suez adventure of 1956 when Britain and France were punished for acting like 'over-mighty subjects'. The secretly organized attack by Britain, France and Israel on Egypt was an act straight out of the old closed book of imperialism. As Colin Cross put it, John Foster Dulles, the American secretary of state 'did not equate the containment of Communism with the maintenance of British authority in the Middle East' (Cross 1970, 327).

Caught in the glare of American disapproval, the British and French faced utter condemnation at the United Nations where they secured only five votes of support in General Assembly; sixty-four members voted against them. The British Prime Minister, Anthony Eden, did not lose his head as he might have done had he been similarly disobedient at Louis XIV's court. However, he lost his job, his health and his reputation.

Rule-bound Interdependence

There are some similarities between the sociogenesis of the European Union and the sociogenesis of European states. The two processes have a similar structure although they occurred at different levels of integration. Following World War II, American economic, political and military power in

Europe enabled them to impose higher standards of restraint in the use of violence. The Americans also encouraged a regime of increasingly rule-bound interdependence between West European states, a regime that bound together their major economic enterprises such as coal, steel, nuclear energy and agriculture.

This regime has continued even though American influence has more recently been exercised in a less direct way and the disparities in economic strength between the United States and the European Union have been significantly reduced. The European Union after the Maastricht Treaty is the latest expression of this regime. Most of Western Europe now has a major stake in this highly developed figuration. The continuing European dependence upon American military capacity was shown during the Balkan War in 1999.

At the centre of Europe-formation is a shift from national states that mainly *impose* discipline on those subject to their domination, to national states which are themselves to a very considerable extent *subject* to continuing discipline from 'above'. The lives of citizens in all member states are affected by laws made in Brussels. In 1994 the British government calculated that a third of all British law was, in effect, written in Brussels. In 1988 Jacques Delors, President of the European Commission, suggested that at some time in the future 80 per cent of economic legislation affecting national states would be enacted in Brussels.[23]

These laws range from employment legislation to the environment. A notable aspect of these laws is that they impose standards, for example in water purity, hours of work, and so on. They express new thresholds of decency. In the late twentieth century there was a medium-term tendency for the standards imposed to be gradually raised, a process in some ways similar to the increase in the level of sensitivity to infringements of 'decency' that Elias traced through the centuries in *The Civilizing Process*.

One of the main attributes of the state, according to Elias, is its capacity to 'individualize' – in other words, to disembed people from their family, tribe or other 'pre-state forms of integration' (Elias 1991b, 181) and treat them according to the state's own rules and categories. This has the effect of weakening the hold on people of these older forms of integration. People become less constrained by their attachments to specific dynasties, clans or tribes and more attached to the national state.

The penetrative powers of the European Union have some resemblance to those previously exercised by the national state.[24] For example, the EU is giving special recognition to the regions (Emilio-Romagna, Rhône-Alps, Baden-Würtemberg, Catalonia, Scotland and so on),[25] providing them with an alternative source of funding and legitimacy, an alternative, that is, to relying on the national state. In this way, the European regions are gradually being disembedded from their national states.[26]

Another interest that has been affected in a similar way is the large business corporations. EU regulations can have a direct impact on profit levels. It is worth while for these companies to have lobbyists working for them in Brussels. Through mechanisms such as these, the European Union is contributing to the disembedding of large business corporations from the national state, a process that has clearly been considerably advanced as a result of the development of multinational and transnational forms of business organization.

Brussels, home of the European Union and NATO, has become a modern Versailles. The players in this environment are engaged in a long game where persistence of effort over many years counts at least as much as the size of your team at any point in time. According to a recent study of the 'informal politics' of the European Union, the influence of firms 'ought not to be measured only by the number of experts implanted or lobbyists employed. The firm's long-term influence may be directed towards creating an attitude of mind among officials, a predisposition towards a particular technology, or fuel, or standard, or even a recognition of one firm's status *vis-à-vis* another' (Middlemas 1995, 461).

In the passage just quoted, Middlemas is, in effect, describing the strategy of psychological manipulation that Elias traces back to the royal court,[27] to La Bruyère and Saint-Simon. Middlemas compares companies' lobbying strategies to trench warfare involving 'periods of low-key surveillance and monitoring followed by intensely fought battles, resulting in what are usually marginal gains' (456). This is reminiscent of La Bruyère's comment that 'Life at court is a serious, melancholy game, which requires us to arrange our pieces and our batteries, have a plan, follow it, foil that of the adversary, sometimes take risks and act on impulse. And after all our measures and meditations we are in check, sometimes checkmate' (Elias 1994a, 475).[28] This careful, realistic, calculating attitude of mind is deeply developed among those lobbyists, diplomats and officials who spend long months and years at Brussels.

As Middlemas puts it, 'Entry to the European game imposes a sense of interdependence. Where information exchange transactions with Commission officials (which comprise the largest single part of firms' activities) are concerned, even commercial firms have to accept an element of shared interest, which makes them much acceptable in officials' eyes' (Middlemas 1995, 458). In the medium term, simply by joining in the lobbying game, business, professional and regional interests strengthen Europe-wide exchange networks and develop a commitment to those very networks.

Over the long term, the disembedding processes just mentioned may combine with the integrative processes just described to create a psychological and political 'space' for the development of a new European identity. It is possible to identify two possible growth points for a European 'we-image'. One is in the newly liberated regions. The other is among the professional classes within national states that have been 'outsiders' within Europe.

Much German enthusiasm for Europe stems from the opportunity the European movement gives to escape from the stigmatizing effects of history. For the Irish, Europe provides an affirmation of Ireland's emancipation from its old colonial subjection to British rule. For the Spanish, the Portuguese and the Greeks, membership of the European Union is a sign of acceptance within the European establishment.[29]

Returning briefly to the opening theme of this chapter, it seems likely that a successful integration of the utilitarian and idealistic traditions within the European Union will be easier to achieve if and when a richer and more meaningful 'we-identity' develops within Europe. The development of such an identity is likely to be fostered by a growth in the active participation of citizens within distinctively European institutions.

The very low turn-out in the elections for the European Parliament in 1999 suggests that this development, if it is occurring, is happening quite slowly. Nevertheless, it is worth noticing that social processes identified by Elias, especially a gradual shift within the 'we' identities of Europeans, are closely related to the intellectual trends investigated by Parsons and the fears and aspirations reported by Arendt.

The layers of identity entrenched within the social personalities of European men and women are being slowly and sometimes painfully 'loosened up' and reshuffled. At the same time, as European interest groups have become more tightly bound together across national boundaries, the European Commission and the European Court of Justice have spun an increasingly dense web of rules and regulations, setting standards and defining rights. Meanwhile, the boundaries of the Union have gradually extended outwards, turning many who were previously outsiders into committed members of the European professional establishment.

There is, however, another side to the coin. This is what Elias describes as 'the drag effect' (Elias 1991b, 211) of the habitus or social personality created by the national states. As far as survival is concerned, the crucial level of integration is, to an increasing extent, located above the level of the national state. However, generations of experience have made us think of ourselves in Europe as primarily 'English', 'French, 'Swedish' and so on.

In Elias's view, losing this sense of national identity or at least treating it as secondary is experienced by the people involved as a fundamental loss of meaning, a kind of 'death'. This feeling may become so intense that it overwhelms the dictates of utilitarian rationality.[30] To return to the parallel with the French court, it was because the Duke of Montmorency was not prepared to accept that dynasties such as his own no longer held the whip-hand in France that he rebelled against the king, met the king's army in battle, engaged in a heroic but totally ill-judged cavalry charge, was defeated, and faced execution in the courtyard of the town hall at Toulouse.[31]

If Montmorency had received more support, if the French state had been less well organized, if its centralized power monopoly had been less stable, and if its leading functionaries, such as Cardinal Richelieu, had been less skilful, the rebellion might have contributed to a renewed disintegration of the unified French polity. In a similar way, the European Union might be at risk if it suffers a combination of ineffective central management and sustained, widespread 'revolt from below'.

At the turn of the millennium this fragmentary outlook seems unlikely. However, Europhiles should not make this a reason for feeling complacent. A great deal depends upon the further development of the rule-bound interdependence that has been described.

Elias, Parsons, Arendt and Europe

In the meantime, the European Union seems to embody the hopes of not just Elias but also Parsons and Arendt. It institutionalizes the inter-dependence of France and Germany, the two societies whose estrangement was an important element in determining the way Elias wrote *The Civilizing Process*. The EU also provides a practical illustration of the attempt to synthesize the utilitarian and idealistic social theories analysed by Parsons in *The Structure of Social Action*.

Europe's 'utilitarians' want to maximize the scope for individuals and businesses to make their own rational decisions unimpeded by 'irrational' barriers to the movement of people, capital or other economic factors. Europe's 'idealists' have an idea in their heads: the idea of a unitary Europe with a strong and stable central executive, legislature and judiciary respon-sible to a coherent and highly involved *demos*, the citizens of Europe. They want to see that idea take shape in the empirical world.

The utilitarians are concerned with sweeping away inconvenient institu-tional and cultural barriers to free trade. The idealists want to build up new institutions and a new culture. The challenge of integrating these potentially conflicting approaches occurs when regulations are proposed imposing uniformity across national boundaries, either in the form of common restrictions or common rights. What is 'raising our standards' from one point of view is 'tying us up in red tape' from another.

If Parsons gives one possible guide to some aspects of the ideological conflicts within the European Union, Hannah Arendt has asserted what is at stake, politically and morally. As has been seen, two institutions sum up the standard by which she judges modernity and her fears as to where it might lead. They are, in turn, the Athenian *agora*, where citizens in classical Greece debated and decided policy, and the concentration camp. Each one reverses the values and conditions of the other.

During the 1990s, Europe has had intimations of both these poten-tialities. In ex-Yugoslavia, ethnic tribalism took ferocious forms, including the systematic use of torture in detention camps such as Tuzla and Trebinje in Bosnia. On the other side of the coin, in March 1999 the European Parliament took a bold and unexpected initiative. Its members confronted the European Commission with proof of widespread corruption and created a situation in which the Commission resigned en bloc. It was an unexpected eruption of assertive parliamentary democracy.

Tuzla was not Auschwitz. Furthermore, Europe's MEPs[32] do not rival Pericles in either their inspirational qualities or their effectiveness. However, the alternative possibilities signalled by Arendt alert us to what is at stake. It is impossible to predict whether the European Union will survive if it does not acquire the same degree of commitment and involvement from the European citizenry as national states receive from their own electorates. That degree of commitment has not yet been achieved. A further strengthening of democratic institutions is necessary.[33]

Being large and lasting fifty years do not in themselves constitute a guarantee for longevity. The German Empire looked powerful in 1914, and the Soviet Union seemed invincible in 1968. Neither made their centenary.[34]

Notes

1 Although he comments in *The Society of Individuals* that 'It would make rational sense and possibly bring benefits if the European nation states combined into the United States of Europe'. He adds immediately: 'the difficulty lies in the fact that intellectual awareness of the logic of integration meets the tenacious resistance of emotive ideas which give the integration the character of ruin, a loss that one cannot cease mourning' (Elias 1991a, 225). Elias is referring to the feeling that Europe-making processes entail a loss of national identity. Elias had a strong sense of his own German-ness but at the same time he was able to identify strongly with the wider entity of Europe. When in his late eighties he was asked what nationality he identified with. He replied: 'Basically, I am a European' (Elias 1994b, 74). Elsewhere he described himself as 'a person who feels deeply bound to the European tradition' (Elias 1996, 428).

2 As is well known, the Edict of Nantes gave Protestants equal political rights with Catholics and also allowed Protestants a certain amount of religious freedom. Henry IV also worked with his minister Sully on a 'grand design' to establish a universal Christian polity in Europe comprising six hereditary monarchies (France, England, Spain, Denmark, Sweden, Lombardy), five elective monarchies (the empire, the papacy, Hungary, Poland and Bohemia) and four republics (Switzerland, Italy, Venice and Belgium). In practice, for all its pan-European rhetoric, this scheme was in effect a proposed alliance against the Hapsburgs.

3 Another example is the General Agreement on Tariff and Trade (1947), a watered-down version of the American plan for an international trade organization that would coordinate different nations' counter-cyclical policies.

4 Secretary of State Byrne announced this intention at the Overseas Press Club in New York on 28 February 1946 (van der Beugel 1966, 20). This approach was enshrined as the Truman Doctrine. The thinking behind it was set out in George F. Kennan's article in *Foreign Affairs* setting out the American administration's intention to engage in 'firm and vigilant containment of Russian expansive tendencies' (Kennan 1947, 581).

5 The original treaty powers were Belgium, Canada, Denmark, France, Iceland, Italy, Luxembourg, the Netherlands, Norway, Portugal, the UK and the USA. Greece and Turkey joined in 1951, the Federal Republic of Germany in 1955.

6 Europe's need for imports and consequent chronic trade deficit left the continent short of dollars at a time when the dollar was on the way to becoming the global currency. As *The Economist* put it on 31 May 1947, 'the whole of European life is being overshadowed by the Great Dollar shortage' (833).

7 Quoted in van der Beugel 1966, 50–1.

8 Quoted in van der Beugel 1966, 80.

9 In 1961 the OEEC became the Organization for Economic Cooperation and Development (OECD), expanding its membership to include advanced industrial countries (such as USA and Canada) outside of Europe.

10 See Griffiths 1995, 8–15.

11 Griffiths 1995, 8–9.

12 Henry IV was a Protestant and, of course, most of his French subjects were Catholic.

13 Judt 1997, 37. Between 1945 and 1971 US aid to Europe (military and civilian) amounted to $53 billion gross and $43 billion net, of which $39 billion was in the form of grants (Maddison 1976, 475). It is worth mentioning that Elias wrote about the position of the French Protestants in an essay published in 1935 (Elias 1935).

14 Quoted in Judt 1997, 17.

15 A United States of Europe was advocated by *Le Moniteur*, a French newspaper, in 1848. An international steel cartel had linked Germany, France and several other European producers between 1926 and 1929. Aristide Briande and Gustav Stresemann had worked for greater Franco-German cooperation leading to a united Europe with its own single European currency, during the 1920s. During the 1930s organizations such as *Jeune Europe* provided a forum for enthusiasts such as the Belgian Socialist Paul-Henri Spaak. See Judt 1997, 6–9, 14. Other enthusiasts for a united Europe have included Alterio Spinelli, Luigi Einaudi, Giovanni Agnelli, Andrea Cabiati, Maurice Renoult, Bertrand de Jouvenel, Roger Manuel, Herman Kranold, Sobei Mgoi, Edo Fimmen, to name but a few.

16 Taken from an interview with Paul Hoffman conducted by 'HBP' on 28 January 1953. Located in the Truman Presidential Library Digital Archives. This may be located through the Internet at the following address: www.whistlestop.org/study_collections/marshall/large/folder7

17 Taken from an interview with Richard M Bissell Jr conducted by Sam Van Hyning, Harvey Mansfield, Guy Horsley and 'HBP' on 19 September 1952. For location see previous note.

18 Quoted in Griffiths 1995, 10.

19 This plan was drawn up by Richard Bissel. Griffiths 1995, 10.

20 Judt 1997, 17–18; Congressional Record, 83rd congress, Ist session, p. 8683; van der Beugel 1966, 287.

21 It would be interesting to compare the west European and east European versions of the civilizing process after World War II at greater length than is possible here. Just one question: from an Eliasian perspective, does the breakup of the Soviet Union after 1989 represent a decivilizing process of equivalent dimensions to the collapse of the German Empire in 1918? The USSR was in existence just two decades longer than the *Kaiserreich*.

22 *Le Monde*, August 10, 1991; Judt 1997, 29, n 7. Elias 1994a, 512–3.

23 *The Economist* 3 January 1998, 28.

24 These comments apply also to the EU's previous incarnation, the European Community.

25 See Middlemas 1995, 383–434.

26 The extent to which the EU has penetrated the boundaries of its member states and influenced their internal workings is astonishing. This is now so much taken for granted by most people within the EU that it is surprising to discover how unusual it is. In a recent issue, *The Economist* commented that while most of the world, including the United States, Japan, China, and most of Asia, Latin America and Africa hold on to 'traditional ideas about the husbanding of state power', in Europe the situation was very different. In their words, 'In no other part of the world is the idea of a diminution of national sovereignty anywhere near so readily accepted'. Compare, for example, the Association of South-East Asian Nations (ASEAN) whose 'cardinal principle . . . is a mutual pledge of non-interference in internal affairs' (*The Economist* 3 January 1998, 28).

27 Although it was, no doubt, also to be found in the monastery and the cathedral chapter house.

28 The quotation is from La Bruyère 1922, 237.

29 Jáuregui 1999.

30 Exaggerating to make his point vividly, Elias suggests that the situation of the national state merging within a European super-state is comparable to that of a native American tribe having to give up its hunter-gatherer existence and find a future in the big city. In Elias's view, 'it usually takes at least three generations for these process-conflicts to die down' (214). If Elias is right, Europe is about half to two-thirds of the way through its period of adjustment.

31 These details are taken from Elias 1983, 195.
32 Members of the European Parliament.
33 See Smith and Wright 1999b.
34 This chapter draws in part upon Smith 1999c.

8

SHAME AND HUMILIATION

Introduction

So far in this book I have suggested that Elias exaggerated the extent to which Germany was an exceptional case and misread the French case as being typical. I have argued that the response of German society to the collapse of the German empire was mirrored in important respects by the rest of Western Europe during the middle and late twentieth century. This entailed important decivilizing tendencies such as Thatcherism and devolution, tendencies to which France was unusually resistant because civilizing processes (such as political centralization, the penetration of regulation from the centre, and the development of a dominant national 'we' identity) had advanced much further there than in other European societies.

On the other side, I have suggested that the formation of the European Union is a good example of the operation of what Elias called the monopoly mechanism. In other words, it was a result of the eradication of violence between conflicting parties by the development of a stable power monopoly, in this case the United States, which imposed a structure of civilized behaviour upon former combatants. There is even a parallel between the way the nobility acquired control over French court procedure in the eighteenth century and the way the Europeans themselves, from the 1950s onward, regained control from the Americans over the institution-building processes.

Now, however, I want to make the further argument that there is very little reason for accepting Elias's belief that the early modern aristocracy made a particularly significant contribution to the development of the civilized habitus, although I do accept that they gave it a certain amount of prestige.

This conclusion is an outcome of two proposals I make in this chapter. One is that humiliation must be given a much more prominent place in our understanding of social development and the shaping of modernity than Elias gives it. The second is that alongside the civilized habitus and inter-woven with it is the humiliated habitus whose origins are at least as ancient. There are strong reasons for believing that both were highly developed at a very early point in the human experience.

My analysis in this chapter has been greatly influenced by the innovative work of Evelin Lindner, a cross-cultural social psychologist with whom I am collaborating to develop further the ideas presented here. It was through becoming familiar with her work that I came to realize how important the theme of humiliation is not only in analyzing the modern human condition but also in developing strategies for ameliorating it.[1]

Civilization, Christianity and Shame

Although the main focus of this chapter is upon humiliation, it is convenient to begin with its half-sister, shame. According to Elias, the roots of civilization are firmly rooted in the soil of shame. As 'civilized' people get more self-disciplined and self-aware, their 'threshold of repugnance' shifts. They become more disgusted by their bodies. They clothe and screen their animal selves. Higher levels of delicacy and restraint are demanded. Natural functions become more and more distasteful. Sexuality and aggression are increasingly inhibited.[2]

To continue Elias's argument, while civilization is rooted in shame, shame is, in turn, rooted in the body. The human metabolism is always liable to run out of control (blushing, trembling, sweating, breaking wind and so on). This makes the person who occupies the body vulnerable. When the body plays its tricks, he or she will get the blame for transgressing the rules of 'correct' behaviour. Ironically, the feeling of shame triggers many of the same bodily reactions (blushing, trembling, sweating . . .) that cause shame in the first place. Such bodily reactions are proper and, indeed, functional in fight-or-flight situations: on the battlefield, for example. But they are 'out of place' in social settings which demand physical restraint.

For Elias, shame is a complex mixture. It includes self-disgust, inhibition, a feeling of isolation and, above all, fear. Civilized men and women fear the fact that emotions can disrupt rationality and undermine control. The more they depend on rationality, the more they fear that it will be disrupted. Rationality breeds fear of emotion; emotion undermines rationality; fear is an emotion; hence, rationality indirectly undermines rationality. This paradox makes it difficult for people to achieve detachment when thinking about the human personality and social relationships. These are the troubles of civilization.

Shame is produced by any kind of transgression against the rules of the group to which one belongs or with which one identifies. However, according to Elias, a very high proportion of the shame feelings civilized people experience is produced by specific embarrassment about the body. In Elias's view, the reason for this is that the exercise of great restraint over the body became a functional requirement for physical survival and social advancement within civilized societies. In other words, people put their own bodies under lock and key and became nervous jailers, looking out for escape attempts.

Foucault tells a different story, just as plausible. In *The History of Sexuality* (Foucault 1978; originally published in 1976), Foucault's thesis is that medieval priests and, subsequently, modern scientists, therapists and government bureaucrats have deliberately encouraged people to get anxious about their own bodies.[3] They have done this by creating an obsessive interest in sexuality in the minds of ordinary people. They have got them to think and speak about their sexuality, made them put a spotlight on it. The master technique is the confession or, later, the therapeutic encounter. This is used to elicit or, perhaps, to create the 'truth' about people's sex lives. Medieval priests did this. So do modern psychoanalysts.

Foucault's main point is that by making people become preoccupied with their sexuality, those with power can generate a climate of anxiety. Once fear has been deliberately created, the authorities can manipulate it. The priest tells his communicants how to save their souls. The psychoanalyst gives guidance about how to cure the personality. This 'caring guidance' is domination in disguise. It is a way of creating sets of understandings and emotional responses that can be manipulated by the authorities in order to influence the behaviour of the population at large.

The arguments of Elias and Foucault may both be drawn upon to provide an account of the origins of modern shame. Both writers provide good reasons why medieval and, later, modern men and women had an anxious preoccupation with the body. In both of their analyses, the body is perceived as a threat because if it gets out of control it can pull people down or stop them rising up. In Foucault's argument the 'up' leads to Heaven, the 'down' to Hell. In Elias's argument the 'up' leads to social success, the 'down' leads to social failure.

One way to bring Elias and Foucault closer together is to see that Foucault, like Elias, is aware of the way structures of inter-personal control and self-control are shaped by the dynamics of specific social settings. Elias pays particular attention to the setting of the royal court. Foucault draws upon two other settings that brought human beings together in environments where individuals risk failure yet hope for success. One is the monastic cloister in which Christian brothers shivered before the power of the Almighty and the gaze of their colleagues. The other is the urban market-place where traders sold their wares.[4]

All three settings – the court, the cloister and the market – required acute observation and self-control to ensure that one was not 'caught out'. To do well in the court, the monastery or the market you needed to monitor yourself and others very carefully. Foucault pays special attention to the way these pressures worked themselves out in the practices of monks, priests and the laity who came in from the market-place to confess their sins.

Like Elias, Foucault shows that where the monitor-and-control habitus is in operation among a particular population, the individual's sense of identity is susceptible of being controlled by others. Elias and Foucault both know that one of the main means of social control is to make people feel ashamed of what they have done or of who they are. They both know that this control capacity can be mobilized by the group (e.g. fellow courtiers, fellow monks, business partners) and by hierarchical authority (the monarch, God, the priest, the therapist).

Despite some reservations about the unhealthy repression of inner drives that comes from fear of embarrassment, Elias evidently thought that shame feelings had, on balance, made a positive contribution to human society over the very long time period covered by the civilizing process. The clear message and tone of *The Civilizing Process* is that the progressive permeation of controls through society and the personality in the course of modernity has raised people up. The book is largely free from evaluations but it is clear that Elias regarded the 'civilized' character of European society in general (as he saw it) as being far superior to its previous condition of disorder of which inter-war Germany was a frightening reminder.

However, as far as Foucault is concerned, during the medieval and modern epochs people in authority have taken every opportunity to aggravate and exploit the human propensity to feel shame in order to improve their own power position at the expense of the majority of the population. In his view, modern civilization has not raised people up but, on the contrary, it has diminished them, held them down, and made them far less than they could have been. To put it another way, although Foucault does not emphasize the concept of humiliation, his argument is that modern men and women have been humiliated by their culture and institutions.

One way to state the difference between Elias and Foucault is as follows: Elias brings out, with some reservations, the positive contribution made by shame; Foucault brings out, without reservations, the negative contribution made by humiliation. This begs the question of the difference between shame and humiliation. The best place to explore that question is in the Garden of Eden.

Adam, Eve and God

The Civilizing Process carries a covert message, perhaps hidden even from Elias. It is that becoming civilized is, in one sense at least, like leaving the Garden of Eden. Just like Adam and Eve, men and women acquire knowledge but also become ashamed. Control over the emotions has a plus side: it brings scientific objectivity, rational calculation and the technological and organizational achievements that go with those things. However, there is a minus side, too: civilized people become ashamed of their bodies and emotions, frightened to reveal them.

The 'Garden of Eden' makes its fleeting, almost subliminal appearance in the short section entitled 'Scenes from the life of a knight' (Elias 1994a, 168–78). In these pages, Elias describes a sequence of drawings that portray the world of the secular upper-class in the Middle Ages. This is Europe at a very early phase of the civilizing process. In the drawings, life and death, pain and pleasure are all portrayed in a very matter of fact way. Fields are ploughed, men go hunting, peasants are hanged, naked lovers embrace.

Elias argues that modern observers would find the scenes disgusting if they saw them in real life. However, the medieval knight, the local master, would find 'nothing shameful or embarrassing' in the inequality, violence, suffering and lust portrayed (171). The knight's view would be: 'So God made the world: some are rulers, the others bondsmen. There is nothing embarrassing about this' (174).

Two paragraphs later, Elias describes a drawing of 'a little garden. Trees form a kind of bower, beneath which is an oval bathtub' and the in tub are a young man and woman, naked. In such scenes, Elias comments, 'Nakedness is not yet associated with shame' (175). The image lurking in the language is the happy state of Adam and Eve.[5]

This interesting passage is not just about shame or the absence of shame. It is also – although Elias does not emphasize this – about humiliation. Notice the phrase that Elias puts in the knight's mouth: 'So God made the world: some are rulers, the others bondsmen. There is nothing embarrassing about this.'

Those few words encapsulate a creation myth whose central figures were God and Adam (in other words, 'Man'). This myth will be explored shortly but its main elements are as follows:

- Adam and Eve enjoyed an existence of pristine equality as hunter-gatherers in the Garden of Eden, under the lordship of God;
- Adam, aided and abetted by Eve, tried to assert his equality with God;
- for this Adam was punished by being demoted in the cosmic order;
- Adam was expelled from Paradise and bound to the soil as a farmer;
- Eve was punished by being put under Adam's authority;
- according to God's forcefully expressed will, human society was structured on the basis of inequality and hierarchy (God over humankind; man over woman; ruler over bondsman); and
- despite Adam's initial revolt, humankind came to accept this hierarchical order as proper and appropriate. In other words, it was not regarded as shameful to be in a position of subordination.

This myth contains a central 'anthropological' truth. This is that the creation of inequality and hierarchy is a social process that involves humiliating weaker individuals and groups. This occurs when hunter-gatherers are forced into farming, when farmers are made to give up part of their surplus to a feudal lord or a royal tax-collector, when tribal elders are required to bow down before a chiefdom, when chiefs have to pay tribute to colonial rulers, and when imperial powers (like Japan, Britain and France after 1945) have to swallow their pride and take orders from a new global superpower, the United States.

The myth also captures the essence of a social process that frequently recurs in these situations. There is, initially, considerable resistance and revolt against the loss of relative autonomy that comes when a power that one has regarded as being no 'better' than oneself (perhaps 'worse') forces one to bow down before it. This is frequently followed by a psychological acceptance that the new superior has a 'right' to be in authority and that the new hierarchical order is appropriate and legitimate.

However, the fact that the new hierarchical order becomes 'acceptable' to its underlings should not disguise from view the moment of resistance to humiliation that precedes this acceptance. The possibility of revolt may persist. This potential is illustrated by a case such as French society under German domination in the early 1940s. The Vichy government which kowtowed to the Nazis coexisted with a resistance movement that wished to overthrow the new overlords. If the outcome of World War II had been different, the resistance movement would have been forgotten.

However, our primary task at the moment is to distinguish humiliation from shame. Let us return to the Garden of Eden. By taking the apple from the Tree of Knowledge (or, to give it its full name, the Tree of Knowledge of Good and Evil) the primal pair learned that they were naked and that such a state was shameful, a transgression. To put it another way, they acquired 'civilized' standards and discovered at the same time that they were failing to meet them. By their own actions they 'switched on' the faculty of shame. This is the capacity (a) to recognize when one is failing to follow a rule one accepts and (b) to feel diminished by that fact.

However, the rules that Adam and Eve chose for themselves were not the rules God wanted them to follow. Adam decided to supply himself with his own moral guidebook. He stole God's own knowledge of good and evil with the intention of making his own judgements.

For His part, God wanted the primal pair to subordinate their judgement to His commands. In order to teach Adam the rule that he should obey God's rules (and not his own), God humiliated Adam. In other words, He imposed subordination where it did not exist before. This was appropriate because subordination is precisely the precondition for making people obey rules given from above. Once subordination is established, (a) the ruling power (in this case, God) can dictate the rules (b) everyone is required to obey the rules appropriate to their position in the rank order, and (c) those who break the rules will feel shame.

By biting the apple, Adam had tried to become as good as God. As God remarked at the time, 'Behold, the man is become as one of us' (*Genesis* 3, 22). The angry and sarcastic tone of the Almighty, as reported in *The Bible*, is pretty clear. The first humans had to learn the hard way whose rules they should be ashamed of disobeying.

God was furious with three offenders against His will and command: Adam, Eve and the serpent. God humiliated them all. The serpent was made the most cursed of all beasts and forced to go about on its belly: 'dust shalt thou eat all the days of thy life' (*Genesis* 3, 14). Eve was forced to accept obedience to her husband: 'and he shall rule over thee' (*Genesis* 3, 16). She went with Adam as he was ejected from Paradise. By this act, humankind was removed permanently to a lower plane. Adam had enjoyed an easy hunter-gatherer existence in God's well-stocked heavenly fields. After expulsion he was forced to accept the back-breaking toil of the farmer's life. Along with Eve, he was 'sent . . . forth from the Garden of Eden to till the ground from whence he was taken' (*Genesis* 3, 23).

Transgression, Correction and Destruction

Shame and humiliation are not the same. It is quite possible to be made to feel ashamed without at the same time being subjected to humiliation. For example, children and motorists may both be kept in line with some fairly gentle shaming: 'really, is that the way to behave?' The flashing sign that tells everyone the registration number of the speeding vehicle mobilizes a sense of embarrassment in order to keep the traffic under control. This kind of shaming is a discomforting but non-humiliating strategy to draw the offender back into the 'law-abiding' community. It is a form of correction.

There is a crossover point at which shaming turns into humiliation. If shaming is taken too far it may have destructive rather than positive results. Almost every social group has a 'shaming machine', a sort of microwave into which it puts those who are caught breaking the rules. Shaming machines have tremendous power and if someone is left inside for too long they are liable to be burnt to a crisp, ruined. They end up not shamed but humiliated. The ticking-off that is taken too far turns into a show trial.

It is possible to be humiliated without feeling shame. Suppose an invading army makes an example of a village which has resisted fiercely. Suppose its soldiers hang the leading villagers in the main square, rape the village women and use the village church or mosque as a urinal. It is not to be expected that the surviving inhabitants will feel ashamed at having resisted their aggressors. They are much more likely to feel anger and hatred. They will strike back or flee when they can.

Shame and humiliation are parallel in the following respect: they both entail an emotion and a social mechanism. The emotion of shame cannot be separated from the mechanism of shaming by which a person or group is made to feel ashamed. A person can impose shame upon herself even if no-one else is present. Suppose you know you 'should' wash your hands before eating but one day at home alone you decide to neglect this requirement. No one else can discover your offense but you may well still feel ashamed. In this case, the actors involved in the process of shaming all exist 'within' the shamed person: the person who has committed the offense is confronted 'internally' by the person who believes in the values against which the offense was committed.

In the case of both humiliation and shame, the victim is pronounced to be inadequate by the standards of the group or society to which he or she belongs. However, beyond that point shame and humiliation differ. Shaming, when not carried to extremes, may be a strategy for reforming the victim and reintegrating her within the group. A group may use its 'shaming machine' to enforce conformity upon its 'backsliding' members. This is not a pleasant experience for the victim and there is a real possibility that the controllers of the shaming machine may take pleasure in their work. However, the main point is that if the shaming is effective, those who transgress are brought back into line and, the offenders become conformists.

As has been seen, when the shaming machine is turned up too high, it becomes a humiliation machine. In fact, when humiliation is the game, the victim is not only fried in the microwave but also battered with a mallet and, in extreme cases, thrown into the dustbin.

Unlike shaming, humiliation does not pull its victims back into their proper place. Instead, it pushes them out of their old place; it displaces them.[6] Instead of trying to reform the victim, humiliation deliberately weakens and damages her. The humiliated victim is not reintegrated into the group but cut off from it.

Humiliation pushes its victims 'down' or 'out', imposing upon them an identity that is 'spoiled' from the rejecting group's point of view. Once this has happened, the victim cannot be re-established as a 'normal' member of the rejecting group.[7] In extreme cases, the humiliated victim may be destroyed physically and/or psychologically. Such victims cease to 'exist'. One does not 'know' them and they do not have to be 'taken into account'.

To return briefly to shame and shaming, these create an uncomfortable sense of culpable unfitness in an 'offending' person or group. This is due to the offenders' failure to adhere to norms prevailing in the wider collectivity to which they feel they belong. They have fallen below the mark. Humiliation, too, gives its victims a sense of becoming 'lower' than before. But the difference between them is that whereas shame produces a feeling that *one's own* efforts have been inadequate, humiliation instills the perception that one has been violently pushed down or kicked out *by others*.

The victims of humiliation undergo forced deprivation of benefits to which they feel they have a legitimate claim. Humiliation is not produced by the constraining power of norms in which one believes. Unlike those who feel ashamed, the humiliated do not feel a strong urge to 'do better'. Instead, they feel outraged, violated and bereaved.

Although shame and humiliation are different, it is possible to envisage cases where they overlap to a very high degree: for example, the case of someone who passionately adheres to a group's values, is a thoroughly committed and integrated member of the group, and yet finds himself in a position of offending against the group's values. Take the case of the German Jews during the nineteenth and early twentieth century as described by Bauman. He shows that they lived their lives according to the same standards as good respectable Germans. Their intellectual leaders rationalized Jewish cultural lore. There was a strong movement to acquire 'refined and respectable manners, new standards of cleanliness, sexual etiquette . . . [and] public demeanour' (129).

However, the Jewish bourgeoisie were caught between two standards, two sets of rules. On the one hand, they conducted themselves according to the same standards as their non-Jewish German neighbours. On the other hand, German non-Jews judged them as belonging to a category that did not meet those standards. From the non-Jewish point of view, all Jews were regarded as having the 'embarrassing' characteristics of lower class Jewish immigrants from Eastern Europe who were thought of as noisy, over-demonstrative and unclean.

The German Jews felt *shame* as Germans at having 'dirty' Jews in their midst. As Jews they felt *humiliated* at being uncompromisingly rejected by the German society to which they thought they belonged. Some German Jews admitted to having 'The evil wish . . . that in some painless way the world might be rid of these disagreeable objects' with their 'laziness, their filth, their perpetual readiness to cheat'.[8] Many responded to this uncomfortable situation by adopting the hostile attitude of mainstream German society towards the less 'civilized' Jews of Eastern Europe. Arguably, this made the Holocaust more likely and did nothing to save the German Jews from sharing the fate of their Polish counterparts.[9]

According to Bauman, the German Jews felt rejected and put down without any possibility of appeal against their tormentors: the essence of humiliation. Their response was to attempt to transfer the burden to another group, the Jews of Eastern Europe. The structure of this argument is very similar to the case made by Elias in *The Germans* (Elias 1996). The difference is that Elias is referring to the whole German nation. He argues that after World War I Germans felt humiliated by their defeat and wished to transfer the burden to another group. They chose the German Jews.

Abasement, Humbling and Humiliation

It does not take much reflection to conclude that the humiliation of the European Jews by the Nazis is a process that differs in certain fundamental respects from the humiliation of Adam and Eve (humankind) by God. The two examples also have similarities. In both cases, the perpetrator of the humiliation (God, Hitler) had no visible doubts about the rightness of the action being taken. In both cases, the victims felt extreme hurt, sorrow and anger.

The difference between the two cases relates to the outcomes of the two acts of humiliation. To take the Biblical example, Adam and Eve tried to assert equality with God and had to be taught a nasty lesson. They were expelled from their privileged relationship with God. The humiliation of humankind was a profound shock which acted forcefully upon the basic attitudes of men and women. It restructured the relationship between God and humankind and reshaped the habitus of the latter. After the Fall, human beings knew it was their place to obey God's commands.

Humankind 'learned the hard way' that it had a lowly place at the foot of God. Only then was it in a fit state to receive the law of God. Adam's successors were reintegrated into a new relationship to their divine master. The bane of suffering imposed by God upon Adam for his transgression was still there but another strand was added into the relationship between humankind and God: the Ten Commandments. The law of God provided a new bond between the Almighty and his human subjects. It brought God down into the world, so to speak.

Adam, it will be recalled, had brought the faculty of shame down to earth with him after his disastrous adventure in Paradise. All the main elements were thus present for a cosmic order regulated by a body of law promulgated by God for His earthly subjects. Henceforth, those who offended against the law felt shame before their fellow human beings and before God.

Theologians and other keen Bible readers may quarrel with many aspects of this interpretation but it suggests that extreme humiliation may be one stage in a process of restructuring and re-education within social relationships. The victims may judge the eventual outcome of their humiliation in such cases to be beneficial. Looking back, they may talk about a 'beneficial humbling'. There is an initial experience of humiliation that involves a painful displacement and severance; the victims are 'cut out' from their established niches and ejected from their old haunts. However, this is the prelude to welcoming the victims back to a legitimate place where they may 'belong' on a different basis.

The example of the Holocaust is very different. The Jews were deprived of their property, their dignity was taken away, and they were murdered. This humiliation was not intended to benefit the victims. Nazi ideology envisaged that the 'final solution' would be part of a larger strategy of restructuring German society and re-educating its people. However, the Jews were not intended to share the 'benefits'. The humiliated ones were marked out for destruction, not re-education.

	Perception of the agent of abasement	Perception of the victim of abasement
Humiliation	Agent perceives herself to be inflicting humiliation (agent feels shame)	Victim perceives herself to be undergoing humiliation (victim feels anger)
Humbling	Agent perceives herself to be inflicting a process of necessary humbling (agent feels anger)	Victim perceives herself to be subject to necessary humbling (victim feels shame)

Figure 8.1   *The dynamics of abasement*

How is the obvious difference between the two cases to be set within a broader framework of analysis that takes account of the fact that in the Biblical case the process of abasement was eventually accepted as appropriate and beneficial by its victims? Two factors are relevant. One relevant factor is the way that the agent and the victim of abasement, respectively, perceive the victim's 'proper' place in the world.

Those who see that the place actually occupied by the victim is 'too high' and therefore in need of rectification are liable to accept the process of abasement (or 'bringing down') as a necessary and legitimate 'humbling' of the victim.[10] Those who believe that the victim occupied her 'proper' place in the social order before abasement took place will be liable to regard abasement as an unnecessary and illegitimate 'humiliation' of the victim.

Another relevant factor is the way in which agents and victims of abasement respond emotionally to that process. In this respect, two assumptions will be made. The first is that if someone is perceived to have arrogantly claimed a social position to which she does not have a right, the normal response of others to this offense will be anger.[11] The second assumption is that if someone offends against a set of norms in which she believes, including the norms expressed in the social order to which she belongs, the normal response of that person will be shame.

Consider the case where a person is seen by others to be 'too high' within a social hierarchy, raised above her 'proper' position. In that case, inflicting abasement upon her is perceived by those who carry it out as being a necessary process of *humbling* (not humiliating) her. Abasement brings her back down to the position she 'ought' to be in. It restores the proper order. In the course of the abasement, the agent is liable to express a sense of justified anger against the victim.

If the victim herself believes that her claim to a higher position is legitimate, she is likely to feel anger at being put down. From her point of view, the process of abasement will be experienced as *humiliation* (not humbling) and she is liable to feel anger. This anger will be justified by the perception that humiliation displaces her from the position she 'ought' to be in. It disrupts the proper order. In such a case, the victim feels anger at the offensive presumption of the agent. If the agent later comes to perceive the situation in a similar way, then she will as a result feel shame on account of her past offensive conduct against the victim.

In the case of God and the primal pair, God grew angry with Adam and Eve. He decided that their proper place was no longer in Paradise. Consequently, He humbled them, reducing them to the earthly realm. That, at least, was how it looked to God. From Adam's point of view, it was a humiliation. Adam clearly thought not only that he should be in Paradise but also that he should have even more power there than God had granted him. So for him ejection from the Garden of Eden was a displacement, upsetting the proper order as he understood it.

Adam's anger could not be expressed openly and was, no doubt, recycled as sorrow and suffering. However, over time, humankind learned that its abasement at the hand of God was a necessary humbling. As a result, men and women felt shame at their past conduct which had led to God's punishment of them.

The story of the Holocaust and its aftermath follows a different pattern although it begins at the same place. The Nazis, supported by a large part of the German population, believed they were carrying out the 'necessary' task of humbling the Jews who were angrily blamed for the misery of the Germans. As far as the Nazis were concerned, the 'proper' place for the Jews was, ultimately, the gas chamber.

For the Jews this was a disastrous humiliation although only the survivors have had the opportunity to express their justified anger. This case differs from the Biblical story because over time a large part of the German population who saw the treatment of the Jews as a necessary humbling have come to see that it was an unacceptable humiliation which justifies feelings of deep shame among its agents.

To summarize, in the Biblical case, the perception of the victims (or, more precisely, their descendants) shifted and the emerging consensus stabilized around the idea of 'humbling'.[12] In the second case, the perception of the agents (or, more precisely, their descendants) shifted and the emerging consensus has stabilized around the idea of 'humiliation' (see Figure 8.2).

	Initial situation	Subsequent situation
The Biblical myth	God perceives process as necessary humbling Adam perceives process as humiliation	God perceives process as necessary humbling Humankind perceives process as necessary humbling
The Holocaust	Nazis perceive process as necessary humbling Jews perceive process as humiliation	Germans perceive process as humiliation Jews perceive process as humiliation

Figure 8.2 *Humiliation and humbling*

Humiliation in Elias's writings

It would be wrong to suggest that Elias is unaware of the nature of humiliation. He shows on more than one occasion how the victims of humiliation cope with their plight by acquiescing in the value system of their oppressor. By doing this they accept that their own subordination is legitimate. By making this concession, they soften the blow of humiliation. They redefine it as a necessary humbling which they would be wrong to resist.

One example of this is to be found in *The Established and the Outsiders* (Elias and Scotson 1994). In this book, Elias and Scotson analysed Winston Parva, a local community on the fringes of Leicester (UK). They found that there were three main groups of residents. One group consisted of established village families who had been in Winston Parva for several generations. They were predominantly working class. A second group consisted of middle-class families who had moved into the village recently to occupy newly built housing. A third group of newcomers in a different part of the village had a working-class background, like the established village families.

Elias and Scotson discovered that the established working-class families were successful at maintaining a reputation for being 'respectable'. They were happy to associate with the new middle-class families in the village to a certain extent. However, they stigmatized the working-class newcomers by the use of 'blame gossip'. The established families, who controlled the gossip networks, imposed 'group disgrace' (104) upon these 'outsiders' who had no effective way of answering back. The authors comment that the latter 'seemed to accept with a kind of puzzled resignation, that they belonged to a group of less virtue and respectability' (8). They acquiesced in the way they were labeled and accepted that they were unworthy. Here is an example of humiliation being culturally recycled by the victims as justified humbling.

Elias tackles humiliation more directly in *The Germans* (Elias 1996). As was seen in an earlier chapter, in this book he shows that Germans experienced their history as a long process of decline from medieval greatness. Germany was seen as undergoing a long and undeserved process of abasement within Europe. The response of the Germans was sorrow, anger and an intense desire for revenge. This was intensified by the shocking defeat experienced in 1918 after half a century during which the German Empire had become very powerful.

The experience of humiliation shaped the German national habitus, in Elias's view. Hitler had the political skills as a propagandist and speechmaker to built up the resentment of ordinary Germans during inter-war years. He had two sources of resentment to work on. One was the fact that German men and women had suffered constant humiliation at the hands of the militaristic aristocracy that had been the dominant class in the Kaiser's empire. The other was the fact that Germany had been very severely treated by the Allies after World War I. They made Germany a pariah nation and heaped suffering upon its people. Elias traces the way that as Germany grew stronger in the 1930s and early 1940s the energy brewed by humiliation was released against Germany's neighbours and against the Jews. As a German Jew, Elias knew these processes from the inside. The result is a classic text.

However, we do not know Elias as the sociologist of the humiliation process but as the author of *The Civilizing Process*. It is deeply ironic that the humiliation processes which were so important in shaping Elias's own life were largely effaced by his concentration upon the 'civilizing' theme. Again and again in *The Germans*, Elias stresses that Germany is a 'peculiar' case, one that differs from the general pattern of social development in Europe. In fact, he categorizes the German case with reference to this (in his view) dominant European trend. He treats it as an instance of what he came to call 'decivilizing' processes.

How do humiliation processes interweave with the civilizing process, as seen by Elias?

Let us return to Elias's paradigm example, the court at Versailles. The first thing to notice is that humiliation has a taken-for-granted status in the argument. Elias clearly recognizes that the establishment of a powerful and stable royal court in France was only possible because the monarch humiliated his main aristocratic rivals. Elias does not choose to use the word 'humiliation' but he shows that court society was only able to serve as the seedbed of *civilité* because the warrior nobility had been forcibly deprived of their defining function as fighters and made to bow their heads before the throne. They were turned into subjects. The courtiers were a conquered population. Those who continued to resist departed or died.

Elias focuses his attention on courtly culture, especially the system of etiquette that ritualized the complex system of rank and precedence. This culture told everybody where they 'ought' to be and how they 'ought' to behave. It made a virtue out of the condition of royal service that all courtiers were required to accept, a condition that they or their forefathers had violently resisted. This is the second example (Winston Parva was the first) of humiliation being culturally recycled by the victims as justified humbling. The courtiers were like Adam's descendants who embraced their own subordination and felt shame if they broke the rules that prevailed in their overlord's domain.

Humility before the monarch was perfectly compatible with arrogance towards underlings and rivals. European aristocracies are not well known for their self-effacement. Nevertheless the culture was a humbled one which accepted monarchical authority and drew reflected glory from it. Elias traces the growth of *civilité*, seen as a major advance in the development of the civilized habitus, from out of this humbled culture of aristocratic etiquette.

There is no need to repeat once more the main outlines of Elias's argument. Instead, it is time to explore an alternative way of relating humiliation and the development of the civilized habitus.[13]

The Civilized Habitus and the Humiliated Habitus

This chapter began by noting Elias's assumption that the civilized habitus is rooted in the soil of shame. The analysis subsequently developed suggests that in many instances the civilized habitus is interwoven with a humiliated habitus grounded in anger. Even where humiliation has been culturally recycled as justified humbling, underneath there still remains a molten core of continuing resentment.[14]

If we are alert to the widespread existence of the humiliated habitus, then we may become more sensitive to its role in everyday life. According to Elias, civilized men and women direct a lot of pressure inwards, trying to contain their 'shameful' inner demons. However, these civilized people are in many cases also wrestling with the passions stimulated by the humiliated habitus which directs its animus outwards against a real or, possibly, imagined aggressor.

Elias sees the development of the civilized habitus as occurring over a very long period of historical time with no discernible beginning point. As has been seen, a key role is played by the development of shame feelings which are in turn stimulated by sensitivity to how other members of one's social group judge one's social performance. When the judgements of others within a social network are crucial to one's success or failure, then the shaping power of that figuration upon the psyche or social personality is very high.

The figuration that Elias emphasizes is court society, especially the royal court where the stakes are the highest available. The impact of court society upon its participants is particularly dramatic and visible because they are in the course of making an extreme transition from being uninhibited feudal warriors to highly disciplined courtiers.

Elias successfully demonstrates the great distance that the aristocracy have to travel, emotionally and psychologically, in adapting to court society – in other words, the significance *for them* of the enormous change in their lifestyle. What he does not do is demonstrate that the experience of court society produced any fundamental innovation in the civilized habitus. It is true that the styles of Versailles reverberated throughout subsequent history but did court society produce any profound shift in the habitus that produced those styles?

The main point about court society from Elias's perspective is that a group who suffered defeat and humiliation adapted and survived by acquiring and developing the civilized habitus. This is an unobjectionable analysis but it misses out a crucial fact and so misinterprets the whole story. The real point, which Elias misses, is that *in undergoing the experience just described the aristocracy were not prototypical. On the contrary, they were social laggards.*

Long before humiliation was heaped on the head of Europe's aristocracy, this emotion and social process were regularly experienced by those much nearer the bottom of the heap. Peasants forced into bondage on great landed estates and lesser knights made to pay homage to more powerful feudal masters knew how to 'eat dirt'. When the rage of humiliation made them want to strike out, it was fortunate that the countervailing force of the civilized habitus was applying pressure in the other direction, helping them to keep violent feelings inside.

There are strong reasons for believing that the central features of what Elias calls the civilized habitus are nearly as old as humankind. Anyone who hunts animals either alone or as part of a team needs to exercise great control in order to outwit the prey. There is an obvious advantage to hunters in monitoring their own performance and coordinating tactics with each other.

Societies which lived in conditions of rough equality such as hunter-gatherer bands could only survive if they contained many members with a well-developed habitus of self-control and mutual monitoring of performance. It was in the interests of every member of the group to praise successful hunters, especially given the normal practice of sharing kills among the whole band. A hunter who is motivated by praise is also susceptible to shame if his performance falls below expectations.

The conclusion of the reasoning just developed is that the main elements of the civilized habitus were in existence and played a central role in human affairs long before court society took shape. It is also possible that simple band societies were familiar with some limited aspects of humiliation, for example, casting 'undesirables' out of the band. However, these societies were so internally interdependent that it was essential to avoid the build-up of resentments.

Elias places a great deal of emphasis upon the European aristocracy as a group that – in his view – played a major role in defining what it is to be a modern person. Weber made a similar claim when drawing attention to the specific experience of protestant business people. Both Elias and Weber tell a story of the master's habits being transmitted downward through the social order.

However, it is quite possible, and indeed very likely, that a very long history of disciplined practices amongst the 'lower orders' may exist which is being overlooked because they have left no written records. Protestant merchants left their ledgers and their diaries. Courtiers left their books of manners. It is far too easy to assume that they were the first to develop the habitus that lies behind the practices that are recorded there and that lesser beings followed behind later.

In fact, it is reasonable to suppose that long before royal courts and double-entry bookkeeping were major features of social life, underlings were thoroughly familiar with the survival value of self-discipline in the face of powerful authority. Many protestants who cowered before God came from families that had beaten their servants for generations. Some of the aristocratic dynasties that were coming to terms with the disciplines of life at the royal court in the seventeenth century had bound their peasants to the soil for half a millennium.

In the medieval period, fighting was an expensive activity that could only be afforded by someone with sufficient time and resources. To put a man on horseback and in armour it was necessary to keep many other men working in the fields and stables. Feudal warfare was backed up by the efforts of many craft-workers and traders who, like farmers planting their crops, needed to think ahead and balance many input and output factors. The civilized habitus was part of the medieval worker's stock-in-trade. While underlings were going about their regular business, their masters were, on Elias's account, releasing their violent feelings in the heat of combat.

Elias emphasizes the functional value of letting your instincts guide you on the battlefield. A ferocious charge full of sound and fury might sway a battle. These were restless men. Active medieval knights had a wandering life and many found a nomadic existence appealing. Buckling down to a sedentary court life must have been tough. Elias is right about all that. However, the aristocracy was almost the last major group within medieval and early modern society to be confronted with the challenge of being tied down to a particular place and being forced to do what they were told by an overlord. *They were late-comers to that modern game.*

The court aristocracy had to serve the king. The monarch's demands had to take priority over the pursuit of dynastic ambitions back home in the provinces. For centuries feudal aristocrats had made their bondsmen sweat on the lord's demesne before they were released to tend their family plots. The peasantry had long been tied to the manorial soil; now their masters were bondsmen to the monarch.

The nobility, at long last, got a taste of its own medicine. It had to learn the practices of 'civilized' self-discipline. There was something else as well. Since the nobility had no choice but to acquire these disciplined ways – for centuries consigned to lesser, more constrained beings – it had every incentive to dignify this necessary labour and call it a 'privilege'. This is not an aberrant pattern. How many single homeless men forced into the monastic life by indigence found it convenient to think of their daily service in the Lord's vineyard as 'perfect freedom'? The noble confined to the royal court brought an extra social cachet to this ancient condition.

The monitor/control/shame habitus had a yo-yo-like existence, sometimes rising up the social order, sometimes losing ground. Its writ was variable and intermittent, sometimes extending far and wide and deep, sometimes remaining thin and patchy. When it finally made itself at home in the highest circles of the royal court, it acquired additional legitimacy, strengthening its position as a powerful social force. Almost everything the court aristocracy did was, because *they* did it, prestigious. If even the monarch and his attendants were trapped in self-discipline's iron cage, and wore a serene smile, how could any other group escape, and why should they want to?

This chapter has been able to do no more than scratch the surface of the many issues that are raised when the importance of the humiliated habitus and the humiliation process are recognized. There is much more to be done in this direction.

Notes

1 Evelin Lindner's conceptual analysis of humiliation has been formed over several years of research and clinical practice in several countries including Egypt, China and Africa. In 1998–99 she spent several months in Rwanda, Burundi and Somalia interviewing many hundreds of survivors of genocide, war-rape and massacre. We are currently preparing a book on the theme of humiliation and its theoretical and socio-political significance in analyzing and managing human conflict. See Lindner 1999a; Lindner 1999b; Lindner 2000a; Lindner 2000b; Smith forthcoming, a.

2 This oversimplifies the argument since the civilizing process is interwoven with decivilizing tendencies and phases of greater informality.

3 Foucault's argument is a development of the analyses developed in both *Discipline and Punish* (Foucault 1977a) and *The Birth of the Clinic* (Foucault 1973).

4 The importance of these social settings for understanding Foucault's contribution is brought out most clearly in the work of Richard Sennett. Unfortunately, there is no space here to carry out a critique of Sennett who draws upon both Elias and Foucault in his work in a very creative way. Sennett extends the territory patrolled by shame to include not just thoughts and feelings relating to the body but also the whole project of the self as a being whose presence in the world needs justifying. According to Sennett, shame is the punishment we experience whenever we can be made to feel that we are not making enough of ourselves, that we are failing to develop ourselves. It is central to Sennett's argument that vulnerability to shame weighs much more lightly on those at the top of the society than it does on those in the middle and at the bottom. The latter feel not merely ashamed but humiliated. Rationality and control are applied in ways that systematically diminish them. See Sennett 1970; Sennett 1977; Sennett 1980; Sennett 1990; Sennett 1994; Sennett 1998.

5 Elias emphasizes that reversals of the civilizing process are frequent and does not suggest that there are precise starting points from which this process may be dated. Furthermore, in *The Civilizing Process* Elias acknowledges, once and briefly, the possible importance of 'preceding . . . civilizations' (Elias 1994a, 300). However, the work does not devote much attention to the fact that developments in the early Middle Ages could be treated as being, in part at least, the product of a *decivilizing* process related to the dissolution of the Roman Empire.

6 The main exception to this is what I have elsewhere called 'reinforcement humiliation.' This refers to the routine blows, insults and abuses that are inflicted from 'above' (by lords, masters, husbands, parents and so on) upon 'lower' individuals and groups in order to stamp upon any tendency for those underlings to get 'above' themselves and invade the 'higher' social space occupied by their superiors. Reinforcement humiliation is necessary in order to prevent any reversal of past processes of 'conquest humiliation' (whereby hierarchy is imposed) or 'relegation humiliation' (whereby individuals or groups are forced to accept demotion within a hierarchy that has been established). See Smith forthcoming, a.

7 Unless the group changes its character radically, for example by changing its principles, disavowing the practice of humiliation and putting effort into healing the damage done by previous acts of humiliation.

8 Hugo Ganz quoted in Wertheimer 1987, 148. See Bauman 1991, 133.

9 Bauman comments, 'The shame still hurts, now as suppressed memory, in the new and yet more painful form of guilt. It cries out to be exorcised or argued away. As the moment of redemption has been missed, the only way left is to prove that there was nothing to be redeemed in the first place. [In other words] . . . There must have been at least a rudimentary truth in Jewish Germanhood, and so there must have been some truth in the charges the German Jews proffered against their East-European neighbours. If the latter were charged, they had only themselves to blame. Being accused, so it transpires, was their guilt. The guilt has outlasted the accusation' (Bauman 1991, 140–1).

10 There is no space to consider the equally important possibility that the position of a person or group may be regarded as being 'too low' and that what is required is not abasement but elevation. This will be explored in future work with Evelin Lindner.

11 The process of arrogation – in other words, the making of claims (for example, to resources and social respect) that are considered illegitimate in terms of prevailing social norms – is one form of attempted elevation (see previous note). It may be distinguished from the process of making legitimate claims to elevation (or to 'dignification') on the basis of the ideology of human rights. This will be explored in future work with Evelin Lindner.

12 Christian writers often use the word 'humiliation' to describe the abasement of human beings before God but in terms of the analysis presented here they are describing the process and condition here described as 'humbling'.

13 The approach to humiliation taken here has been influenced by a number of thinkers including Evelin Lindner, Thomas Scheff, Avishai Margalit, Richard Sennett, William Ury, Zygmunt Bauman and Norbert Elias. See Lindner 1999a; Lindner 1999b; Lindner 2000a; Lindner 2000b; Scheff 1990; Scheff 1994; Scheff 1997; Margalit 1996; Sennett 1998; Bauman 1989; Bauman 1999; Ury 1999. See also Goffmann 1967, 97–112; Garfinkel 1956; Klein 1991; Klein 1992; Barrett and Brooks 1992; Griffin 1991; Silver et al 1986; Miller 1993; and Gilbert 1997.

14 See Elias 1983, 214–67.

9

A CIVILIZED DEBATE

Convergence and Conflict

In this book Norbert Elias's writings have been compared with the work of two sociologists with philosophical interests (Talcott Parsons and Zygmunt Bauman) and two philosophers with sociological concerns (Hannah Arendt and Michel Foucault). These scholars were chosen mainly on the basis of an intuition that dialogue between them and Elias would be fruitful.

This intuition had to fight its way through some pretty strong negative evidence. For example, Arendt was a student of existentialism and a pupil of Martin Heidegger, whom Elias classified with 'fools and metaphysicians' (Elias 1994b, 92). Furthermore, Foucault opened his *History of Sexuality* (Foucault 1978) by carrying out a hatchet job on Freudianism, one of the bastions of Elias's approach. Add to this the fact that Bauman included a curt dismissal of Elias's *The Civilizing Process* at the heart of his most discussed book, *Modernity and the Holocaust* (Bauman 1989). To cap it all, Talcott Parsons was one of the few scholars that Elias singled out for direct and sustained attack.

Not the most promising material, at first sight. However, think of it another way. Elias and Arendt were both German Jewish intellectuals confronted with the challenge of Hitler. Elias and Parsons both devoted themselves to discovering what made societies orderly and published their main works in the late 1930s.[1] Foucault was a product of the very society, France, that Elias most admired, especially for the high degree of continuity in its civilizing process. Finally, Bauman was, like Elias, a Jewish exile who ended up in Britain. One would expect these people to have something to say to each other.

In fact, what has been uncovered is a pattern of convergence in assumptions, methodologies and themes among these five writers, a pattern that has been obscured by the fog of discord and the mask of indifference. In this case, convergence is not fusion. There are important disagreements and differences of emphasis among these five writers. This is much more conducive to future theoretical development than a synthesis that locks all elements into a tightly closed system. Better to have an open structure and a continuing argument that allows for innovation and new insights.

However, despite the disagreements, many of the concepts and propositions from the different writers are mutually supportive. In Figure 9.1 the main points of agreement are summarized in a single diagram. In the next

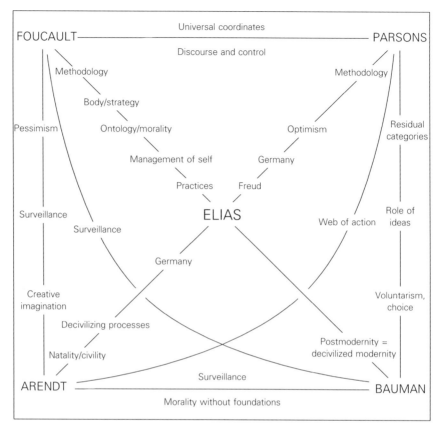

Figure 9.1 *Convergent and complementary themes in the work of Elias, Arendt, Parsons, Foucault and Bauman*

two parts of this chapter, the main points of convergence and difference between Elias and the four others are summarized. In the following part, some additional convergences and differences between Parsons, Arendt, Foucault and Bauman are noted.

The Self

Placing Elias in the midst of this company of sociologists and philosophers exposes a certain one-sidedness in his approach to the development of identity and habitus or psychological make-up. Elias's approach to the shaping of the self by the civilizing process is heavily influenced by his paradigmatic example of the royal court. As will be recalled, Elias argues that the stable power monopoly enjoyed by the monarchy led the courtiers to develop civilized forms of behaviour, a process that was associated with the strengthening of self-control and rationality. The civilized personality was, according to Elias, in large part, an unplanned outcome of the need for courtiers to parry the surveillance of others and penetrate the impassive surfaces presented by their smooth-talking rivals.

However, courtiers were aristocrats, an unusually confident group of human beings whose families were extremely powerful. Although they might well have socialized each other, so to speak, into a civilized habitus, other, weaker social groups acquired modified versions of this habitus either as willing tutees receiving authoritative instruction[2] or as subordinates shaped and conditioned 'from above' within institutional orders (the church, the state, the professions) over which they had very little influence in normal everyday life.

Arendt, Foucault and Bauman all regard this last mode of socialization as the dominant one in the modern era. However, they all refer to other situations which are less oppressive, for example, the Greek city-state (Arendt) the Roman Republic (Foucault) or the public sphere in a just and equal society (Bauman) in which reciprocal interchanges within groups play a much greater part in shaping shared meanings. Seen against the background of these situations, the royal court appears as another unusual or special case, one where substantial freedom within a set of rules was enjoyed by most of the actors, and where power balances were not so centralized nor social relationships so tightly integrated that initiative, imagination and inventiveness were squeezed out of social life.

However, Foucault does not agree with Arendt and Bauman about the detailed way modern organizational hierarchies affect those who are in their power. Foucault thinks they stir up feelings; Bauman disagrees. More specifically, Foucault emphasizes the systematic creation of self-disgust and moral anxiety by Christianity and its secular successors in the modern state. By contrast, Bauman, like Arendt, notices a tendency for bureaucracies to anaesthetize the moral scruples of employees.

Figuration and Process

Despite Foucault's disagreements with Elias about the dynamics of the self and socialization, the two scholars both made use of figurational and processual analysis. In fact, the second and third volumes of Foucault's history of sexuality[3] read like companion volumes to The *Civilizing Process*.

In these works Foucault and Elias both use advice books to get access to standards of behaviour and the workings of the psyche in the past. They are concerned with the links between how people manage their bodily urges and conceptualize the self. In this context, each tries to trace the connections between practices in areas of human conduct involving bodily functions (such as sex, excretion and eating) and the strategies people adopt in pursuit of survival or advancement in society.

They both explore how, historically, men and women have answered the practical question 'how *should* one behave?' and show that underlying that question are ontological issues and questions about the objects of ethical behaviour. They relate long-term changes in standards of behaviour to changes in respect of contemporary ideas about the nature of the self, the strength of the desire to avoid specific bodily functions or activities, the level of anxiety or fear, the extent of political centralization, and the density and complexity of interdependence chains.

This convergence was largely a result of the fact that Foucault changed his analytical style in his last major works, drawing closer to Elias. However, even before this convergence occurred, Foucault and Elias focused on broadly the same mechanisms or processes, for example the conflict between tendencies towards order and disorder, and between rationality and passion.[4] Where they disagreed was on the question of their significance.

For Elias, advances in rationality and control make a humane existence possible. As has been seen, for Foucault the repression of unreason and the elimination of disorder mean losing contact with a major source of human creativity. Elias wants knowledge to give leverage to rationality. Foucault wants freedom from the constraints imposed by rational discourses that place a straitjacket around the self.

There is another case of overlap in methodology and themes when attention is turned to the comparison between Elias and the early Parsons.[5] Both used historical documents (theory texts, manners books)[6] as a means of tracing long-term processes, in the ideas of intellectuals and the habitus of the literate upper class, respectively. In both cases, they drew conclusions about larger groups on the basis of the literary activities of a minority.

Each man optimistically believed he had discovered an important conceptual key – the voluntary theory of action and the civilizing process, respectively – which could, if used properly, unlock the door to greater understanding of societies. Parsons envisaged that concerned but disinterested professionals such as himself would use this special knowledge to influence society's understanding or definition of the situation. Elias hoped that sociologists, equally involved in social problems but also detached, would discover more about the civilizing process and make this knowledge available to all.

At first sight these two ambitions need not be incompatible. After all, there are some resemblances between the *modus operandi* of the civilized personality and the procedures summed up in the voluntaristic theory of action. In both cases, rational calculations are made and acted on subject to the rules of how you should behave that exist in the relevant figuration. Understanding either one should help understand the other.

However, the two analyses are couched, respectively, in two extreme and opposite versions of the Knowledge/Understanding model (see Chapter 4). In fact, as has already been argued, there is no need for the readers of Elias and Parsons to make a choice between these two extremes. Each version conveys part of the process by which people orient themselves within the world and pursue their objectives within it.[7]

Elias and the early Parsons share the same agenda to a great extent. They both want to know the conditions under which social order is achieved. They both tell a story that begins in the Hobbesian world of the Middle Ages. They both focus on the historical opposition between the utilitarian ethos of French and Anglo-Saxon 'civilization' and the idealism of German Kultur.

Furthermore, they produce overlapping analyses of the sociogenesis and psychogenesis of totalitarianism in Germany. They both make a distinction between the subservient, order-seeking tendency and the resentful, romantic element in the German personality structure, as they see it, and point out the effective way in which the Nazis managed to appeal to both.

So far, it has been seen that *The Civilizing Process* converges with certain aspects of *The Structure of Social Action* and Foucault's history of sexuality. In a similar way, Elias's *The Germans* complements Arendt's *The Origins of Totalitarianism*. However, in this case the two works, each with a strong processual aspect, combine to provide a history that has the structure of a genealogy, a form of presentation recommended by Foucault, borrowing from Nietzsche.[8]

Arendt and Elias both made creative intellectual use of the challenge facing German Jews in the 1930s and early 1940s. At one level, their perspectives differ. Elias's object is to obtain knowledge of the blind and unplanned social processes that shape human figurations in order to help prevent the worst evils they might produce. His strategy is to obtain knowledge of those processes by detached observation and reasoning. This will supposedly make it possible to respond to those processes in a realistic way.

Arendt's response is more active and direct. She believes that individuals and groups confronted with a hostile world always have the option of acting so as to help create alternative meanings, standards and realities. In her view, this action is most effective when it takes place within a web of social relationships among people able and willing to share the continuing task of creating and maintaining a common world

Despite Elias's contempt for phenomenology and existentialism, he agrees with Arendt on the importance of pacified, agonistic arenas of discourse and action such as courts and parliaments where passionate but rational debate can take place. These arenas can only exist in figurations that had certain characteristics. They have to be sufficiently centralized and integrated for stable human interaction to be possible. At the same time, it is important that they are not so completely centralized as to deprive people of the chance to express their capacity to speak, debate, argue and act.

Finally, they should not be so completely integrated as to remove the psychological and political space for doing and imagining things differently from the status quo. In arenas that meet these conditions, what might be called 'civilized contestation' can occur. Although neither Arendt nor Elias make the point, such arenas require the convergence of two features. Each writer emphasizes one of them. Elias analyses the characteristics of civility, or 'civilized conduct' (Elias 1994a, 505), the code of restrained and deliberate behaviour associated with civilized personalities. Arendt stresses what she calls 'natality', creative action in the public sphere.

Drawing on the work of both writers, a typology of decivilizing processes has been proposed.[9] In this typology, variations in degree of centralization and degree of integration map four possible directions of 'decivilizing' movement away from the socio-political conditions for civilized contestation. The type of decivilizing process that most concerns Arendt is authoritarian centralization leading to the erosion of any freedom to be or think for oneself. For his part, Elias concentrates upon the decivilizing process associated with decentralization and social disintegration. In the chapter on Bauman and Elias, it was argued that a major example of this variant was the break-up of the European empires, a process that contributed to the condition that Bauman labels 'postmodernity'.

Returning, briefly, to the theme of figurational analysis, it is intriguing to notice that Parsons (in *The Structure of Social Action*) and Arendt (in *The Human Condition*) both use the image of the web. Arendt writes about 'the web of human relationships' (Arendt 1958a, 324) upon which human action impinges. Parsons discusses the '"web" of interwoven strands' (Parsons 1968, 740) created by sequential and interrelated human actions. This image suggests that they both share, along with Elias, a concern with the connectedness of human beings.

At first sight, it appears that Arendt and the early Parsons both pay more attention than does Elias to the dynamic effect of human action in driving social processes. However, this is not the case. All three are interested both in the energizing and the constraining aspects of figurations. Arendt treasures the potential capacity of human action to burst through social constraints. However, she also analysed the tendency for actions within webs of relationships to have unpredictable and unintended consequences that rebound upon actors, restricting their freedom.[10] Elias gave due attention to the part played by competition between individuals and groups, the strength of inner drives, and, not least, the stifling of revolutionary creativity by powerful and conservative figurational influences.[11] For his part, Parsons maintains a balance between the voluntarism of the human agent and the part played by normative controls in creating solidarity and consensus.[12]

Some other Findings

The main focus of this experiment in comparative analysis has been upon Elias but in the course of carrying it out a fascinating pattern has emerged in which Parsons and Arendt each occupy a middle position between Bauman and Foucault. This will be briefly described.

Taking Arendt first, she anticipates the view later taken by both Foucault and Bauman that late modernity is an era of intensified surveillance of the population at large. Arendt makes this case in *The Human Condition* (Arendt 1958a) where she argues that the control techniques employed in totalitarian regimes are used, in modified or disguised form, throughout all modern societies. For his part, *Foucault* analyses the 'disciplinary society' in *Discipline and Punish* (Foucault 1977a).

Arendt's critique is mainly focused on the public sphere. She abhors the dullness of conformist and apathetic politics. For Foucault, the matter is more personal, stemming from a hatred of the controls on emotional expression and sexual behaviour imposed by modern institutions and conventions. Bauman borrows Foucault's use of the Panopticon metaphor but his main preoccupation is, like Arendt, with the disappearance of an active public sphere.

Arendt shares Foucault's belief in the vital importance of the creative imagination and the need to resist and overcome the repressive institutions that stifle it. She also has something of his Nietzschean sense that new things of value can be made by daring exercises of the will.[13] For Foucault much of the benefit from innovative or unexpected personal behaviour comes from the very fact of transgression, the breaking of established taboos. Because of this, he does not try to codify the insights obtained from transgression in terms of a set of ethical rules or a coherent alternative world view that may provide a systematic orientation for behaviour.

Arendt is more concerned than Foucault about the lack of guidance in late modernity about how one should behave as a 'moral' person. She faces up to the late modern (Bauman would say 'postmodern') dilemma of the need to make personal and political choices without knowing what is 'right' or 'true'. This dilemma weighs heavily on Bauman also. However, he does not have Foucault's compensating belief in the intrinsic value of transgression, nor Arendt's commitment to heroic politics.[14]

Parsons also mediates between Foucault and Bauman. For example, Parsons is very interested in techniques for influencing the 'definition of the situation' within societies such as Germany. He explores the way the authority of doctors, priests and other professionals is maintained through their practices and the assumptions embedded within them. Parsons believes that modern social life is thoroughly impregnated by routines that maintain institutional patterns and reinforce cultural traditions.

In Parsons's view, the legitimizing routines of science (the white coats, the titles, the specialized language and so on) reinforce the established order as surely as regular attendance at religious services buttresses belief in God and the authority of the priesthood. This takes him close to Foucault who, at a later date, also takes an interest in the way relatively unconscious automatic control mechanisms work.[15]

Parsons and Foucault are linked by their shared interest in the control functions of discursive practices. They also both hanker after the security of universal categories 'behind' or 'within' the flow of human existence. However, this should not be overplayed. Parsons certainly draws upon his neo-Kantian (and Calvinist) early training. However, Foucault is as much inspired by Nietzsche with his relish for creative disorder and forceful assertion of the will to power and knowledge, as he is by Kant.[16]

Parsons and Bauman are also linked, in this case by a deep interest in intellectual movements during the modern era. However, while Parsons focuses upon transformations in the fortunes of intellectuals systems, Bauman concentrates upon changes in the fortunes of the intellectuals themselves, especially their transformation from 'legislators' to 'interpreters' (Bauman 1987). In fact, although Parsons does not mention the fact, the intellectual trends about which he writes register in the lives of ordinary people mainly because intellectuals as 'legislators' have been a very influential group within government and the education system. Intellectual systems matter most when intellectuals have enough influence to disseminate them to groups with both the desire and the capacity to implement them.

It is fascinating to note that these two analyses – in *The Structure of Social Action* and *Legislators and Interpreters* – are linked by another factor. The dynamism in both flows from the aggressive drive to eliminate residual categories and the frustration caused by the failure to do so. Bauman shows that legislating intellectuals took on the task of ensuring society was so well ordered that all individuals and groups had their proper activities and place. This 'regulatory zeal' was 'all-embracing' (Bauman 1987, 59).

However, when, as a result of repeated failures to achieve this objective, the level of ambiguity and contradiction mounted up to an intolerable level, the legitimacy of the legislating intellectuals was undermined. That is not the whole story. However, it is the point where Bauman's analysis makes closest contact with Parsons's argument. Parsons argues that it was their respective failures to eliminate residual categories that drove utilitarian and idealistic theories into each others' arms.

As a final point, it is more than interesting to note that Bauman's socialist utopia as set out in his work during the 1970s[17] has echoes of the utopia built into Parsons's model of voluntaristic action. In both cases, human actors are envisaged as exercising freedom of choice within the bounds of a normative consensus that expresses the best interests of all people.

To conclude this part of the argument, it can be seen that Norbert Elias deserves his place in the canon. He is part of the debate going on there. His very presence is valuable because it suggests new questions and provides new insights with respect to other theorists of equal stature. Their presence, in turn, allows Elias's work to be seen in a fresh light. Elias is part of an important, continuing, civilized intellectual contest.[18] If it is understood in this context, Elias's work can make an important contribution to our understanding of the figurations and processes of global modernity.

The Blurred Map of Global Modernity

The old maps of modernity (and postmodernity)[19] have become blurred in the era of global modernity. This is partly because the accumulation and ordering of empirical generalizations about globalization is still at an early phase,[20] partly because processes of globalization at the turn of the millennium are not associated with encompassing ideologies in the way that was the case with processes focused at the level of national states. Such ideologies provide a focus for intellectual critique, including empirical investigations to confirm or 'unmask' them.

Globalization is no longer to be accounted for in terms of (for example) the outward thrust of imperialism or the spreading tentacles of the Cold War, both of which could be related back to ideologies rooted in the ambitions of national elites. The dynamics of capitalism provide a partial explanation for globalization processes but it is very difficult to be sure what those dynamics are since capitalism is operating under conditions that are significantly different from those that applied during most of the twentieth century.

In fact, capitalism – or, rather, the free-market version rediscovered during the 1980s – is undergoing a process of delegitimization. By being sold so heavily within the successor states of the Soviet Bloc, neo-liberal forms of marketization have become implicated in the widespread failures of their economies. Another source of delegitimization is the fact that big business is no longer interwoven with national government. It cannot claim to be serving the interests of particular national populations. The question arises: whose interest, then, do capitalists serve apart from their own? The 'global managerial class' will not for long feel comfortable being treated like robbers and bullies. Brute power without a cloak of legitimacy is difficult to institutionalize.

A comparison can be made between transnational corporations and the monarchies that managed to establish themselves during the late medieval epoch. In both cases, as with all 'nouveau' establishments, there is a keen urge to become 'respectable'. The Church was able to provide this respectability through the act of coronation. Several centuries later it is the turn of 'global capitalism' to look for legitimacy. It is turning not to religion (although individual capitalists have done that) but to science, including the social sciences, and, more generally, the universities. Corporate heads like to use the aura of authority, independence and objectivity of these institutions to help sanctify their businesses.[21]

These circumstances give intellectuals a certain amount of leverage. It should not be exaggerated. If big business is feeling the loss of legitimizing support from the national state, so are the universities, in the West at least.[22] One temptation is for academics, individually and collectively, to make a fast buck at whatever rate the market will bear. However, the authority and independence of intellectuals as a group, their capacity to exercise autonomy and influence the terms of their relationship with other groups, might be increased if they were to achieve a higher degree of transnational interconnectedness among themselves and establish a global discourse.

What is needed is a much richer multi-directional conversation between people from many cultural backgrounds, one that enables the insights and perspectives produced by the contrasting historical experiences of different societies to be woven into debates in social theory.[23] This conversation would feed into the larger project of constructing practical responses to the challenges posed to human rights by the humiliating conditions under which globalization is occurring. If intellectuals concerned with social theory wish to have any influence in shaping these responses, they must establish alliances with experts in other disciplines, including professionals working on the frontline, dealing with problems of poverty and suffering.

Elias and Wirth

It is interesting to end with a very brief comparison between Elias and another Jewish sociologist, also born in Germany in 1897. This man was, like Elias, influenced by Mannheim.[24] Like Elias, he emigrated from Germany. However, he left much earlier in life, at the age of fourteen, before World War I, and rather than staying in Europe, he went to the United States and became an American citizen.[25]

The reference is to a leading member of the Chicago School: Louis Wirth, author of *The Ghetto*).[26] In 'Consensus and mass communication' (Wirth 1948) Wirth argued that social scientists and other academics should work towards replicating in a global context the pragmatic consensus that was already, in his view, taking shape in modern cities. There, he argued, 'we have . . . learned to live with people of diverse background and character to a degree sufficient at least to achieve the requirements of a fairly orderly, productive and peaceful society' (13).

Wirth recommended a spirit of tolerance and compromise, regular communication between groups and the cultivation of widespread participation and mutual identification. In those conditions, he believed, people would be more likely to accept group decisions 'unless the matter is fundamentally incompatible with [their] . . . interests and dignity' (10). He anticipated with considerable concern the enormous influence of mass communications, 'a new social force of as yet incalculable magnitude . . . It has the power to build loyalties, to undermine them, and thus by furthering or hindering consensus to affect all other sources of power'. He concluded: 'it is of the first importance, therefore, that we understand its nature, its possibilities, its limits, and the means of harnessing it to human purposes' (12).[27]

Wirth was no naïve optimist. He knew that the market in ideas was 'highly monopolistic' (Wirth 1964c, 153). In his preface to Mannheim's *Ideology and Utopia*, published shortly before *The Civilizing Process* first appeared, Wirth complained about 'the deepening twilight of modern culture' and the need for 'intelligent and resolute measures' to avoid this 'catastrophe' (Wirth 1964b, 141). Wirth called for action. It was no longer reasonable for 'saints to sit in their ivory towers while burly sinners rule the world' (Wirth 1948, 15). As he put it, sarcastically, there is 'no inherent reason why intellectuals should be totally unaware of the facts of life' (Wirth 1964c, 155).[28]

In the early part of the new millennium global conditions are very different from the way they were in the late 1940s when the disparity between American influence and the power capacities of other states was larger than before or since. Nevertheless, there is something to learn from the experience of the Chicago School. Its members had to survive and preserve their independence in a society dominated by big business. They tried to influence a culture that was inclined to be anti-intellectual and hostile to the spirit of free inquiry whenever it questioned or probed behind cherished beliefs. That is the situation facing many intellectuals in the world today.

The Chicagoans broadly divided between those who saw their main task as to generate knowledge without being very involved in its dissemination or application and those who, like Wirth, wanted to exercise moral and political influence within the world by helping to shape the 'definition of the situation'.[29] Both professional tendencies are needed in the context of global modernity.

For example, further work is needed on two themes discussed in earlier chapters. One is the part played by the monopoly mechanism in bringing into being supra-national polities which subject their member states to a degree of discipline 'from above'. The other is the dynamics of humiliation (and, indeed, the sociogenesis of pride) within groups and organizations, within national societies and transnationally.

These are important areas, not least because both relate to the possibilities of regulating globalization processes. It is impossible to go into any detail here but some brief points may be reiterated. One is that the dynamics of humiliation are evident in places such as Kosovo and East Timor.[30] Another is that the conditions under which the European movement developed after World War II are unlikely to occur often, although proposals for south-east Europe developed by the World Bank and the EU in the wake of the Balkan War of 1999 had an uncanny echo of the Marshall Plan about them with the EU playing the role of patron.[31]

Comparative analyses of the development of inter-societal figurations in other areas of the world apart from Europe and the transatlantic area will, it is hoped, improve our knowledge of the range of circumstances that are favourable to a healthy balance between social stability and political freedom.[32] It will be helpful if this is accompanied by the development of a more 'democratic' pattern of intellectual exchange between different global cultures, one in which Western intellectuals spent at least as much time listening to their non-Western colleagues as they do talking. Such a pattern of discussion would help enlarge our understanding of the potentialities for creative social and political organization.

In conclusion, it is not sensible to expect agreement in the near future on a unified political and moral order for global society.[33] However, it is reasonable to hope, and work, for a civilized debate on equal terms among intellectuals, professionals and experts from different traditions and back-grounds within a global context.[34]

Notes

1 As was pointed out in an earlier chapter, Arendt, Parsons and Elias all spent time at Heidelberg University during the late 1920s. Although Elias seems to have known Arendt, at least slightly, he does not mention meeting Parsons. However, all three knew key figures such as the philosopher Karl Jaspers.

2 A scenario mocked by Molière in his play *Le Bourgeois Gentilhomme*.

3 Foucault 1987 and Foucault 1988a.

4 However, the view of historical periods as a sequence of contingently related epistemic orders rather than a long-term developmental processs, as conveyed in *The Order of Things* (Foucault 1974), was not one with which Elias had much sympathy.

5 None of these comments are intended to the later career of Parsons. Shils's remark is interesting: 'Until *The Structure of Social Action* was complete, Talcott Parsons knew where he was going. When it was over he did not stop, but his direction became less clear' (Shils 1981, 191).

6 In *The Structure of Social Action* (Parsons 1968) and *The Civilizing Process* (Elias 1994a), respectively.

7 In other words, on the one hand it can be seen that, to a degree, knowledge shapes perception which presents the challenge of explanation to the understanding. However, on the other hand, it can also be recognized that the understanding provides an explanatory frame-work or conceptual order that shapes our perception and provides the knowledge or 'know-how' that enables society to function.

8 See Figure 3.1. See also Foucault 1977b.

9 See Figure 3.2.

10 See her passages on 'The process character of action', 'Irreversibility and the power to forgive' and 'Unpredictability and the power of promise' in *The Human Condition*. Arendt 1958a, 230–47.

11 See his study of Mozart published posthumously. Elias 1993.

12 For a fascinating analysis of the distinctive positions of Elias, Foucault and Arendt see the work of Keith Tester, especially Tester 1992 and Tester 1995. Tester shrewdly deconstructs Elias's 'debanalization of the mundane' (Tester 1992, 6) and suggests that his accomplishment is that he 'demonstrates how modernity imagined itself as a continual process of civilization' (91). For a helpful discussion of Arendt's way of using the idea of 'process' see Tester 1995, 14–16.

13 On Arendt and Nietzsche, see Villa 1996.

14 Compare Arendt's attitude to the Hungarian revolution and Bauman's interest in Polish Solidarity. For Arendt, the people's councils of the Hungarian Revolution in 1956 were important because they were an example of the people speaking with their own voice and acting creatively. This act of self-expression had value in itself, she believed, even if their efforts were futile in practical political terms. Bauman took a different line. For him, Polish Solidarity was important because it was an example of working class leaders engaging in a process of political learning and then behaving with strategic effectiveness within and upon the existing power structure. See Arendt 1963a; Bauman 1981.

15 See Chapters 4 (on Parsons) and 5 (on Foucault).

16 On these themes see Foucault 1997. Also see Foucault 1993.

17 See Bauman 1976a; Bauman 1976b.

18 It has not been possible here to engage in discussion with a number of important works that have a bearing on the argument developed here. For example, Steven Seidman's *Contested Knowledge* (Seidman 1998) deals with overlapping themes. In *A Sociology of Modernity* (Wagner 1994) Peter Wagner brings together a consideration of social transformation and

social theory in a historical framework. Arpad Szakolczai's forthcoming book on reflexive historical sociology will be highly relevant. Graham Crow's *Comparative Sociology and Social Theory* (Crow 1997) develops some promising lines of analysis. Keith Tester provides penetrating insights on Elias, Foucault and Arendt in *Civil Society* (Tester 1992) and *The Inhuman Condition* (Tester 1995). Nicos Mouzelis's *Sociological Theory. What went wrong?* (Mouzelis 1995) includes an important discussion of Parsons and Elias. This list of relevant literature is certainly incomplete.

19 I am treating 'postmodernity' as a phase intervening between 'old-style' or 'Western' modernity and a new epoch of global modernity which may not, in the long- or even medium-term, be dominated by the West.

20 See, for example, Held et al. 1999.

21 This is obviously not a new phenomenon but the circumstances in which it is occurring are new.

22 I do not feel able at this point to generalize about Japan, China and other parts of Asia. On the dethronement of the 'legislating' intellectual, see Bauman 1987.

23 Some relevant contributors to this debate – not necessarily in agreement with each other – are represented in the following: Albrow 1996; Anderson 1991; Appadurai 1995; Bauman 1998b; Bhabha 1994; Billig 1995; Boulding 1988; Castells 1996–8; Cohen 1997; Featherstone 1990; Featherstone, Lash and Roberston 1995; Furedi 1998; Geertz 1973; Giddens 1991; Gilroy 1993; Golding and Harris 1996; Hall 1991; Held 1995; Huntington 1998; Lash and Urry 1994; Mlinar 1992; Miyoshi and Harootunian 1989; Moore-Gilbert 1997; Robertson 1992b; Rushdie 1991; Said 1993; Spybey 1996; 1999; Tibi 1995; Urry 1995; Werbner and Modood 1997; Young 1995. This list could be considerably extended.

24 Richard Kilminster speculates that in some respects the direction of influence was the reverse, from Elias to Mannheim. See Kilminster 1993.

25 Wirth managed to get all his family out of Germany between 1932 and 1937. See Wirth 1964a, 338.

26 *The Ghetto* makes an argument similar to some aspects of Bauman's analysis in *Modernity and Ambivalence* (Bauman 1991). For example, Wirth argues that Jews who left the ghetto in Chicago were condemned by traditional Jews for their assimilationist tendencies but not allowed by the Gentile world to forget their Jewishness. See Smith 1988, 156.

27 On Wirth, see Smith 1988, 153–66.

28 Manuel Castells once attacked Wirth's 'myth' of 'urbanism' on the grounds that it was an 'ideology of modernism ethnocentrically identified with the crystallization of the social forms of liberal capitalism' (Castells 1976, 60). In fact, Wirth, with his German Jewish background, was deeply aware of the potential for disorienting fragmentation and violent conflict inherent in modern society and wanted to find a way of allowing different social, cultural and intellectual tendencies to co-exist in a creative and non-destructive way. See Smith 1988, 11–12.

29 Wirth was a frequent broadcaster and became very involved in issues related to planning, housing and race. He was, for example, Director of the Illinois Post-war Planning Commission in 1944. Smith 1988, 157.

30 For example, the Serbian and Indonesian governments were accused of shameful behaviour, and the Serbian and Indonesian armies were both concerned with avoiding humiliation. That, at least, is how the conflicts were reported in the British news media. Shaming and humiliation are not identical. See Chapter 8. I am grateful to Evelin Lindner for her comments on this theme.

31 In June 1999 proposals were being discussed for a series of 'donor conferences' to raise funds to provide emergency relief, public works and, eventually, development in the whole region.Tony Blair was reported as 'arguing strongly that south-eastern Europe (as the powder-keg peninsula now prefers to be called) should become like the rest of Europe: a place where rising prosperity, economic interdependence and diverse, tolerant societies make war almost unthinkable' (*The Economist* 19 June 1999, 47).

32 Studies such as Hefner 1998 are important and interesting but the focus on individual cases (such as the Ukraine and Turkey) should be balanced by paying equivalent attention to the inter-societal context in which such societies develop.

33 Although attempts to design democratic constitutions for a global order are extremely useful exercises. See, for example, Held 1995.

34 Among other things, this means confronting and taking seriously the problems surrounding plurilingualism and translation. See, for example, Wright 2000 in Smith and Wright 1999b.

BIBLIOGRAPHY

Albrow, M. (1996) *The Global Age. State and society beyond modernity*, Cambridge: Polity Press

Alexander, J.C. (1984) *Theoretical Logic in Sociology. Volume 4: The modern reconstruction of classical thought: Talcott Parsons*. London: Routledge

Anderson, B. (1991) *Imagined Communities. Reflections on the origin and spread of nationalism*, rev edn. London: Verso

Appadurai, A. (1995) *Modernity at Large. Cultural dimensions of globalization*. Oxford: Oxford University Press

Archer, M.S. (1996) *Culture and Agency. The place of culture in social theory*, rev edn. Cambridge: Cambridge University Press

Arendt, H. (1953) 'A reply', *Review of Politics*, 15 (1): 76–84.

Arendt, H. (1958a) *The Human Condition*. Chicago: Chicago University Press

Arendt, H. (1958b) *Rahel Varnhagen: The Life of a Jewess*. London: East and West Library

Arendt, H. (1963a) *On Revolution*. New York: Viking Press

Arendt, H. (1963b) *Eichmann in Israel. A report on the banality of evil*. New York: Viking Press

Arendt, H. (1970) *On Violence*. London: Allen Lane/Penguin Press

Arendt, H. (1971) 'Martin Heidegger at Eighty', *New York Review of Books*, 21 October, 51.

Arendt, H. (1973) *The Origins of Totalitarianism*. New York: Harcourt, Brace & Co; originally published in 1951

Arendt, H. (1977) *Between Past and Future. Eight exercises in political thought*. Harmondsworth: Penguin; originally published in 1961

Arendt, H. (1978a) *The Life of the Mind. Volume 1: Thinking*. London: Secker and Warburg

Arendt, H. (1978b) *The Life of the Mind. Volume 2: Willing*. London: Secker and Warburg

Arnason, J. (1987) 'Figurational sociology as a counter-paradigm', *Theory, Culture and Society*, 4 (2–3): 429–56

Arnason, J. (1996) 'State formation in Japan and the West', *Theory, Culture and Society*, 13 (3): 53–75

Ash, T.G. (1993) *In Europe's Name. Germany and the divided continent*. London: Cape Bacon, Francis 1627 *New Atlantis*

Barrett, P.J. and Brooks, J.S. (1992) 'Dealing with humiliation individually and collectively', *Journal of Primary Prevention*, 12 (3): 223–41

Bataille, G. (1970) *Oeuvres complètes I: Premiers écrits*, with an introduction by M. Foucault, Paris

Bauman, J. (1988) *A Dream of Belonging. My years in postwar Poland*. London: Virago

Bauman, Z. (1971) 'Twenty years after. The crisis of soviet-type systems', *Problems of Communism*, 20 (6): 45–53.

Bauman, Z. (1972) *Between Class and Elite*. Manchester: Manchester University Press

Bauman, Z. (1973) *Culture as Praxis*. London: Routledge

Bauman, Z. (1976a) *Socialism – the Active Utopia*. London: Allen and Unwin

Bauman, Z. (1976b) *Towards a Critical Sociology. An essay on common sense and emancipation*. London: Routledge

Bauman, Z. (1978) *Hermeneutics and Social Science. Approaches to understanding*. London: Hutchinson

Bauman, Z. (1979) 'The phenomenon of Norbert Elias', *Sociology*, 13 (1): 117–25

Bauman, Z. (1981) 'On the maturation of socialism', *Telos*, 47: 48–54.

Bauman, Z. (1982) *Memories of Class. The pre-history and after-life of class*. London: Routledge

Bauman, Z. (1987) *Legislators and Interpreters*. Cambridge: Polity Press

Bauman, Z. (1988) *Freedom*. Milton Keynes: Open University Press

Bauman, Z. (1989) *Modernity and the Holocaust*. Cambridge: Polity Press

Bauman, Z. (1990) *Thinking Sociologically*. Oxford: Basil Blackwell

Bauman, Z. (1991) *Modernity and Ambivalence*. Cambridge: Polity Press

Bauman, Z. (1992a) *Intimations of Postmodernity*. London: Routledge

Bauman, Z. (1992b) *Mortality, Immortality and Other Life Strategies*. Cambridge: Polity Press

Bauman, Z. (1993) *Postmodern Ethics*. Cambridge: Polity Press

Bauman, Z. (1994) *Alone Again. Ethics after Certainty*. London: Demos

Bauman, Z. (1995) *Life in Fragments*. Cambridge: Polity Press

Bauman, Z. (1997) *Postmodernity and its Discontents*. Cambridge: Polity Press

Bauman, Z. (1998a) *Work, Consumerism and the New Poor*. Buckingham: Open University Press

Bauman, Z. (1998b) *Globalization. The human consequences*. Cambridge: Polity Press

Beetham, D. (1985) *Max Weber and the Theory of Modern Politics*. Cambridge: Polity Press

Bell, C. and Newby, H. (eds) (1974) *The Sociology of Community: A Selection of Readings*. London: Frank Cass.

Bellah, R. (ed.) (1973) *Emile Durkheim on Morality and Society*. Chicago: Chicago University Press

Bellamy, R. (1992) *Liberalism and Modern Society. An historical argument*. Cambridge: Polity Press

Benhabib, S. (1995) 'The pariah and her shadow. Hannah Arendt's biography of Rahel Varnhagen', *Political Theory*, 23 (1, February): 5–24

Benthem van den Bergh, G. van (1971) *The Structure of Development. An invitation to the sociology of Norbert Elias*, Occasional paper 84, The Hague: Institute of Social Studies

Berger, P. (ed.) (1969) *Marxism and Sociology. Views from Eastern Europe*. New York: Appleton-Century Crofts

Berman, M. (1982) *All That is Solid Melts into Air. The experience of modernity*. London: Verso

Bernstein, R.J. (1996) *Hannah Arendt and the Jewish Question*. Cambridge: Polity Press

Beugel, Ernst H. van der (1966) *From Marshall Aid to Atlantic Partnership: European Integration as a Concern of American Foreign Policy*. Amsterdam: Elsevier

Bhabha, H. (1994) *The Location of Culture*. London: Routledge

Billig, M. (1995 *Banal Nationalism*. London: Sage

Blanchot, M. (1982) *The Space of Literature*, translated by Ann Smock, Lincoln, Neb.; originally published in 1955

Bogner, A. (1986) 'The structure of social processes. A commentary on the sociology of Norbert Elias', *Sociology*, 20 (3): 387–411

Bogner A. (1987) 'Elias and the Frankfurt School', *Theory, Culture and Society*, 4 (2–3): 249–85

Bogner, A. (1992) 'The theory of the civilizing process – an ideographic theory of modernization?', *Theory, Culture and Society*, 9 (1): 23–53

Bouchard, D. (1977) *Language, Counter-Memory, Practice*. Oxford: Basil Blackwell

Boulding, E. (1988) *Building a Global Civil Culture*. New York: Syracuse University Press

Breuer, S. (1991) 'The denouements of civilization. Elias and modernity', *International Social Science Journal*, 128: 401–16

Brinkgreve, C. and Korzec, M. (1979 'Feelings, behaviour, morals in the Netherlands, 1938–78: analysis and interpretation of an advice column', *Netherlands Journal of Sociology*, 15 (2): 123–40

Brown, R. (1987) 'Norbert Elias in Leicester. Some recollections', *Theory, Culture and Society*, 4 (2–3): 533–9

Buxton, W. (1985) *Talcott Parsons and the Capitalist Nation-State. Political sociology as a strategic vocation*. Toronto: University of Toronto Press

Cain, P. and Hopkins, A. (1993) *British Imperialism. Innovation and expansion 1688–1914*.
London: Longmans

Camic, C. (1986) 'The matter of habit', *American Journal of Sociology*, 91 (5): 1039–87

Camic, C. (ed.) (1991) *Talcott Parsons: The early essays*. Chicago: University of Chicago Press

Canovan, M. (1992) *Hannah Arendt. A reinterpretation of her political thought*. Cambridge:
Cambridge University Press

Castells, M. (1976) 'Theory and ideology in urban sociology' in Pickvance 1976, 60–84;
originally published in 1969

Castells, M. (1996–8) *The Information Age. Economy, Society and Culture*, 3 volumes, Oxford:
Blackwell

Chartier, R. (1988a) 'Social figuration and habitus: reading Elias' in Chartier 1988b, 71–94

Chartier, R. (1988b) *Cultural History. Between practices and representations*, translated by
Lydia Cochrane, Cambridge: Polity Press

Cipolla, C.M. (ed.) (1976) *The Fontana Economic History of Europe. The Twentieth Century*.
London: Collins/Fontana

Cohen, R. (1997) *Global Diasporas. An introduction*. London: UCL Press

Collini, S. (1979) *Liberalism and Sociology. L.T. Hobhouse and political argument in England
1880–1914*. Cambridge: Cambridge University Press

Connolly, B. (1995) *The Rotten Heart of Europe*. London: Faber and Faber

Coser, L. (1980) 'Review of What is Sociology? and Human Figurations', *American Journal of
Sociology*, 86 (1): 192–4

Cross, C. (1970) *The Fall of the British Empire*. London: Paladin

Crow, G. (1997) *Comparative Sociology and Social Theory. Beyond the three worlds*. London:
Macmillan

Déchaux, J-H (1995) 'Sur le concept de configuration. Quelques failles dans la sociologie de
Norbert Elias', *Cahiers internationaux de Sociologie*, 99: 293–313

Deigh, J. (1995 'Shame and self-esteem: a critique' in Dillon 1995, 133–56

Dillon, R.S. (ed.) (1995) *Dignity, Character and Self-Respect*. London: Routledge

Drost, H. (1995) *What's What and Who's Who in Europe*. London: Cassell

Dunning, E. (ed.) (1971) *The Sociology of Sport*. London: Frank Cass

Dunning, E. (1987) 'Comments on Elias's "Scenes from the life of a knight"', *Theory, Culture
and Society*, 4 (2–3): 366–71

Dunning, E. and Mennell, S. (1998) 'Elias on Germany, Nazism and the Holocaust: on the
balance between "civilizing" and "decivilizing" trends in the social development of Western
Europe', *British Journal of Sociology*, 49 (3): 339–57

Elias, N. (1929) 'Zur Soziologie des deutschen Antisemitismus', *Israelitisches Gemeindeblatt:
Offizielles Organ des israelitischen Mannheim und Ludwigshafen*, 12: 3–6

Elias, N. (1935) 'Der Vertreibung der Hugenotten aus Frankreich', *Der Ausweg*, 1 (12): 369–76

Elias, N. (1950) 'Studies in the genesis of the naval profession', *British Journal of Sociology*,
1 (4): 291–310

Elias, N. (1956) 'Problems on involvement and detachment', *British Journal of Sociology*, 7 (3):
226–52

Elias, N. (1968) 'Introduction to the 1968 Edition' in Elias 1994a, 181–215

Elias, N. (1969) 'Sociology and Psychiatry' in Foulkes and Prince 1969, 117–44

Elias, N. (1970) 'Processes of state formation and nation building', *Transactions of 7th World
Congress of Sociology*, volume 3, 274–84

Elias, N. (1971) 'The sociology of knowledge: new perspectives', *Sociology*, 5 (2): 149–68, 355–
70

Elias, N. (1974a) 'The sciences: towards a theory' in Whitley 1974, 21–42

Elias, N. (1974b) 'Towards a theory of communities', in Bell and Newby 1974, ix–xi

Elias, N. (1978) *What is Sociology?*, translated by Stephen Mennell and Grace Morrissey,
London: Hutchinson; originally published in 1970

Elias, N. (1982) 'Scientific establishments', in Elias, Martins and Whitley 1982, 3–69

Elias, N. (1983) *The Court Society*, translated by Edmund Jephcott, Oxford: Blackwell;
originally published in 1969

Elias, N. (1984) 'On the sociogenesis of sociology', *Sociologisch Tiidchrift*, 11 (1): 1452; originally published in 1962

Elias, N. (1985a) *The Loneliness of the Dying*, translated by Edmund Jephcott, Oxford: Blackwell

Elias, N. (1985b) 'Das Credo eines Metaphysikers: Kommentare zu Poppers *Logik der Forshung*', *Zeitschrift für Soziologie*, 14 (2): 93–114; first presented in 1970

Elias, N. (1986a) 'The genesis of sport as a sociological problem', in Elias and Dunning 1986, Oxford: Blackwell; originally published in 1971

Elias, N. (1986b) 'An essay on sport and violence', in Elias and Dunning 1986, 160–74

Elias, N. (1986c) 'Soziale Prozesse' in Schäfers 1986

Elias N. (1987a) 'The changing balance of power between the sexes – a process-sociological study: the example of the ancient Roman state', *Theory, Culture and Society*, 4: 287–316

Elias, N. (1987b) 'On human beings and their emotions: a process-sociological essay', *Theory, Culture and Society*, 4: 339–61

Elias, N. (1987c) *Involvement and Detachment* [part III originally published in 1983, translated by Edmund Jephcott], Oxford: Blackwell

Elias, N. (1987d) 'The retreat of sociologists into the present', *Theory, Culture and Society*, 4 (2–3): 223–47

Elias, N. (1987e) 'Introduction', in Elias 1987c, vii–lxxii

Elias, N. (1987f) 'Problems of involvement and detachment', in Elias 1987c, 1–41

Elias, N. (1987g) 'The fishermen in the maelstrom', in Elias 1987c, 43–118

Elias, N. (1987h) 'Reflection on the great evolution', in Elias 1987c, 121–78

Elias, N. (1989) 'The symbol theory', *Theory, Culture and Society*, 6, 169–217, 339–383, 499–537

Elias, N. (1991a) *The Society of Individuals*, edited by Michael Schröter, translated by Edmund Jephcott, Oxford: Blackwell; originally published in 1987

Elias, N. (1991b) 'The society of individuals', in Elias 1991a, 1–66.

Elias, N. (1991c) 'Problems of self-consciousness and the image of man', in Elias 1991a, 67–151.

Elias, N. (1991d) 'Changes in the I–we balance', in Elias 1991a, 153–237

Elias, N. (1991e) *The Symbol Theory*. London: Sage

Elias, N (1992) *Time: An Essay*, translated in part by Edmund Jephcott, Oxford: Basil Blackwell

Elias, N. (1993) *Mozart: Portrait of Genius*, edited by Michael Schröter, translated by Edmund Jephcott, Cambridge: Polity Press

Elias, N. (1994a) *The Civilizing Process* (originally in two volumes: volume 1, *The History of Manners*, volume 2, *State Formation and Civilization*), translated by Edmund Jephcott, Oxford: Blackwell; originally published in 1939 as *Über den Prozess der Zivilisation*, Basel: Haus zum Falker

Elias, N. (1994b) *Reflections on a Life*, translated by Edmund Jephcott, Cambridge: Polity Press

Elias, N. (1995) 'Technization and civilization', *Theory, Culture and Society*, 12 (3): 7–42

Elias, N. (1996) *The Germans. Power struggles and the development of habitus in the nineteenth and twentieth centuries*, edited by Michael Schröter, translated with a preface by Eric Dunning and Stephen Mennell, Cambridge: Polity Press

Elias, N. and Dunning, E. (1966) 'Dynamics of sport groups with special reference to football', *British Journal of Sociology*, 17 (4): 388–402

Elias, N. and Dunning, E. (1969) 'The quest for excitement in leisure', *Society and Leisure*, 2: 50–85

Elias, N. and Dunning, E. (1971a) 'Folk football in medieval and early modern Britain', in Dunning 1971, 116–32

Elias, N. and Dunning, E. (1971b) 'Leisure in the spare-time spectrum', in Elias and Dunning 1986, 91–125

Elias, N. and Dunning, E. (1986) *Quest for Excitement. Sport and leisure in the civilizing process*. Oxford: Basil Blackwell

Elias, N. and Scotson, J.L. (1994) *The Established and the Outsiders*. London: Sage

Elias, N., Martins, H. and Whitley, R. (1982) *Scientific Establishments and Hierarchies. Sociology of the Sciences Volume IV*. Dortrecht, Netherlands: D. Reidel

Elliott, J.H. (1968) *Europe Divided 1559–1598*. London: Fontana

Ellwood, D.W. (1992) *Rebuilding Europe. America and West European Reconstruction*. London: Longmans

Ellwood, D.W. (1998) '"You too can be like us": Selling the Marshall Plan', *History Today*, 48 (10): 33–39

Engels, F. (1969) *The Condition of the Working Class in England*, with an introduction by Eric Hobsbawm. London: Granada

Eribon, D (1991) *Michel Foucault*. Cambridge, MA: Harvard University Press

Ettinger, E. (1995) *Hannah Arendt – Martin Heidegger*. New Haven: Yale University Press

Eyerman, R. (1995) 'Review of Elias', *Acta Sociologica*, 38 (2): 113–214

Featherstone, M. (1987) 'Norbert Elias and figurational sociology: some prefatory remarks', *Theory, Culture and Society*, 4 (2–3): 197–211

Featherstone, M. (ed.) (1990) *Global Culture. Nationalism, globalization and modernity*. London: Sage

Featherstone, M., Lash, S. and Roberston, R. (eds) (1995) *Global Modernities*. London: Sage

Fitzhenry, R. (1986) 'Parsons, Schutz and the problem of verstehen' in Holton and Turner 1986, 143–78

Fletcher, J. (1997) *Violence and Civilization. An introduction to the work of Norbert Elias*. Cambridge: Polity Press

Fontaine, S. (1978) '*The Civilizing Process* revisited: Interview with Norbert Elias', *Theory, Culture and Society*, 5 (1): 243–53

Foucault, M. (1967) *Madness and Civilization. A history of insanity in the Age of Reason*, translated by Richard Howard, London: Tavistock; originally published in 1961

Foucault, M. (1973) *The Birth of the Clinic*, translated by A.M. Sheridan, London: Tavistock; originally published in 1963

Foucault, M. (1974) *The Order of Things. An archaeology of the human sciences*. London: Tavistock/Routledge; originally published in 1966

Foucault, M. (1977a) *Discipline and Punish. The birth of the prison*, translated by Alan Sheridan, Harmondsworth: Penguin; originally published in 1975

Foucault M. (1977b) 'Nietzsche, genealogy, history' in Bouchard 1977, 139–64

Foucault, M. (1978) *The History of Sexuality, Volume I: An Introduction*, translated by Robert Hurley, Harmondsworth: Penguin; originally published as *La volunté de savoir* in 1976

Foucault, M. (1984) 'Nietzsche, genealogy, history', in Rabinow 1986, 76–100

Foucault, M. (1986) 'What is an author?', in Rabinow 1986, 101–20; originally published in 1969

Foucault, M. (1987) *The Use of Pleasure. The History of Sexuality, Volume 2*, translated by Robert Hurley, Harmondsworth: Penguin; originally published in 1984

Foucault, M. (1988a) *The Care of the Self. The History of Sexuality, Volume 3*, translated by Robert Hurley, Harmondsworth: Penguin; originally published in 1984

Foucault, M. (1988b) 'The minimalist self' in Foucault 1988c

Foucault, M. (1988c) *Politics, Philosophy, Culture. Interviews and other writings 1977–1984*, edited by Lawrence D. Kritzman, New York: Routledge

Foucault, M. (1991) *Remarks on Marx. Conversations with Duccio Trombadori*, translated by R. James Goldstein and James Cascaito, New York: Semiotext[e]; originally published in 1981

Foucault, M. (1993) 'Dream, imagination and existence' in Foucault and Binswanger 1993, 31–78

Foucault, M. (1996) *Foucault Live (Interviews, 1961–84)*, edited by Sylvère Lotringer, translated by Lysa Hochroth and John Johnston, New York: Semiotext(e)

Foucault, M. (1997) *The Politics of Truth*, edited by Sylvère Lotringer and Lysa Hochroth, New York: Semiotext(e)

Foucault, M. and Binswanger, L. (1993) *Dream and Existence*, edited by Keith Hoeller, New Jersey: Humanities Press

Foulkes, S.H. (1990) *Selected Papers. Psychoanalysis and Group Analysis*, edited by Elizabeth Foulkes, London: Karnac Books

Foulkes, S.H. and Steward Prince, G. (eds) (1969) *Psychiatry in a Changing Society*. London: Tavistock

Freud, S. (1994) *Civilization and its Discontents*. New York: Dover Publications; originally published in 1930

Fulbrook, M. (1990) *A Concise History of Germany*. Cambridge: Cambridge University Press

Furedi, F. (1998) *The Silent War. Imperialism and the changing perception of race*. London: Pluto Press

Garfinkel, H. (1956) 'Conditions of successful degradation ceremonies', *American Journal of Sociology*, 61 (March): 420–24

Gastelaars, M. and de Ruitjer, A. (eds) (1988) *A United Europe. The quest for a multifaceted identity*. Maastricht: Shaker Publishing

Gaus, G. (1964) *Zur Person*. Munich: Feder

Geertz, C. (1973) *The Interpretation of Cultures*. New York: Basic Books

Giddens, A. (1971) *Capitalism and Modern Social Theory*. Cambridge: Cambridge University Press

Giddens, A. (1991) *Modernity and Self-Identity. Self and society in the late modern age*. Cambridge: Polity Press

Gilbert, P. (1997) 'The evolution of social attractiveness and its role in shame, humiliation, guilt and therapy', *British Journal of Medical Psychology*, 70: 113–47

Gilroy, P. (1993) *The Black Atlantic*. London: Verso

Gleichmann, P., Goudsblom, J. and Korte, H. (eds) (1977) *Human Figurations. Essays for Norbert Elias*. Amsterdam: Amsterdams Sociologisch Tijdschrift

Gleichmann, P., Goudsblom, J. and Korte, H. (eds) (1984) *Macht und Zivilisation. Materialen zu Norbert Elias' Zivilisationstheorie 2*. Frankfurt: Suhrkamp

Goffman, E. (1967) *Interaction Rituals. Essays on face-to-face behaviour*. New York: Pantheon Books

Goldhagen, D. (1996) *Hitler's Willing Executioners. Ordinary Germans and the Holocaust*. New York: Albert A. Knopf

Golding, P. and Harris, P. (eds) (1996) *Beyond Cultural Imperialism. Globalization, communication and the new international order*. London: Sage

Goudsblom, J. (1987) 'The sociology of Norbert Elias. Its resonance and significance', *Theory, Culture and Society*, 4 (2–3): 323–37

Goudsblom, J. (1992) *Fire and Civilization*. London: Allen Lane/Penguin Press

Goudsblom, J. (1995) 'Elias and Cassirer, sociology and philosophy', *Theory, Culture and Society*, 12 (1): 121–6

Goudsblom, J. and Mennell, S. (eds) (1998) *The Norbert Elias Reader*. Oxford: Blackwell

Grathoff, R. (ed.) (1978) *The Theory of Social Action*. Bloomington: Indiana University Press

Griffin, J.T. (1991) 'Racism and humiliation in the African-American community', *Journal of Primary Prevention*, 12 (2): 149–67

Griffiths, R.T. (1995) 'The European integration experience', in Middlemas 1995, 1–70

Habermas, J. (1987) *The Theory of Communicative Competence, Volume 2: The Critique of Functionalist Reason*, translated by Thomas McCarthy, Cambridge: Polity Press

Habermas, J. (1991) *Communication and the Evolution of Society*, translated with an introduction by Thomas McCarthy, Cambridge: Polity Press; originally published in 1976

Habermas, J. (1996) *Between Facts and Norms*, translated by William Rehg, Cambridge: Polity Press; originally published in 1992

Haferkamp, H. (1987) 'From the intra-state to the inter-state civilizing process?', *Theory, Culture and Society*, 4 (2–3): 545–57

Hackeschmidt, J. (1995) 'Norbert Elias – Zionist and "bündisch" activist', *Figurations*, 3, June, 4–5

Hackeschmidt, J. (1997) '"Die Kulturkraft des Kreises": Norbert Elias und die zionistische

Jugendbewegung 1918–1925', paper presented at the *Norbert Elias Centenary Conference*, Zentrum für interdisziplinäre Forschung, University of Bielefeld, Germany, 20–22 June 1997

Hall, S. (1991) 'The local and the global. Globalization and its ethnicities' in King 1991, 19–30

Hama, N. (1996) *Disintegrating Europe. The twilight of the European construction*. London: Adamantine Press

Hamilton, P. (1983) *Talcott Parsons*. London: Tavistock Publications

Hatt, P. and Reiss, A. (1957) *Cities and Society. The revised reader in urban sociology*. Glencoe, IL: Free Press

Hawthorn, G. (1976) *Enlightenment and Despair. A history of sociology*. Cambridge: Cambridge University Press

Hefner, R. (ed.) (1998) *Democratic Civility. The history and cross-cultural possibility of a modern political ideal*. London: Transaction Publishers

Heinich, N. (1997) *La sociologie de Norbert Elias*. Paris: Editions de Découverte

Held, D. (1995) *Democracy and the Global Order*. Cambridge: Polity Press

Held, D., McGrew, A., Goldblatt, D. and Perraton, J. (1999) *Global Transformations*. Cambridge: Polity Press

Hetherington, K. (1994) 'The contemporary significance of Schmalenbach's concept of the Bund', *Sociological Review*, 42 (1): 1–25

Hirschman, A. (1970) *Exit, Voice and Loyalty. Responses to decline in firms, organizations, and states*. Cambridge: Harvard University Press

Hobbes, T. (1962) *Leviathan*. London: Fontana

Holton, R. and Turner, B. (1986) *On Economy and Society*. London: Routledge

Huntington, S.R. (1998) *The Clash of Civilizations and the Remaking of the World Order*. London: Touchstone Books

Jáuregui, P. (1999) 'National pride and the meaning of Europe: a comparative study of Britain and Spain' in Smith and Wright 1999b, 257–87

Jay, M. (1996) *The Dialectical Imagination. A History of the Frankfurt School and the Institute of Social Research 1923–1950*. London: University of California Press; originally published in 1973

Johnson, C. (1996) *In With the Euro, Out With the Pound*. Harmondsworth: Penguin

Judt, T. (1997) *A Grand Illusion. An essay on Europe*. Harmondsworth: Penguin

Keane, J. (eds) (1988) *Civil Society and the State. New European Perspectives*. London: Verso

Kennan, G.F. (writing under the pseudonym of 'X') (1947) 'The sources of Soviet conduct', *Foreign Affairs*, 25, July

Kilminster, R. (1987) 'Introduction to Elias', *Theory, Culture and Society*, 4: 213–22

Kilminster, R. (1993) 'Norbert Elias and Karl Mannheim: closeness and distance', *Theory, Culture and Society*, 10 (1): 81–114

Kilminster, R. (1998) *The Sociological Revolution. From the Enlightenment to the global age*. London: Routledge

Kilminster, R. and Varcoe, I. (eds) (1996) *Culture, Modernity and Revolution. Essays in honour of Zygmunt Bauman*. London: Routledge

Kilminster, R. and Wouters, C. (1995) 'From philosophy to sociology: Elias and the neo-Kantians (a reply to Benjo Maso)', *Theory, Culture and Society*, 12 (1): 81–120

King, A.D. (1991) *Culture, Globalization and the World System*. London: Macmillan

Klein, D.C. (1991) 'The humiliation dynamic: an overview', *Journal of Primary Prevention*, 2 (2): 93–121

Klein, D.C. (1992) 'Managing humiliation', *Journal of Primary Prevention*, 12 (3): 255–68

Knox, D. (1991) '*Disciplina*. The monastic and clerical origins of European civility' in Monfasani and Musto 1991, 107–35

Koestler, A. (1964) *The Act of Creation*. London: Hutchinson

Krieken, R. van (1989) 'Violence, self-discipline and modernity: beyond the "civilizing process"', *Sociological Review*, 37 (2): 193–218

Krieken, R. van (1990) 'The organisation of the soul: Elias and Foucault on discipline and the self', *Archives européennes de sociologie*, 31 (2): 353–71

Krieken, R. van (1998) *Norbert Elias*. London: Routledge

Kuzmics, H. (1987) 'Civilization, state and bourgeois society. The theoretical contribution of Norbert Elias', *Theory, Culture and Society*, 4 (2–3): 515–31

Kuzmics, H. (1988) 'The civilizing process' in Keane 198, 149–76

Kuzmics, H. (1991) 'Embarrassment and civilization: on some similarities and differences in the work of Goffman and Elias', *Theory, Culture and Society*, 8 (1): 1–30

La Bruyère, J. de (1922) *Caractères*. Paris: Hachette; originally published in 1688

Lasch, C. (1985) 'Historical sociology and the myth of maturity. Norbert Elias's "very simple formula"', *Theory and Society*, 14: 705

Lash, S. and Urry, J. (1994) *Economies of Signs and Space*. London: Sage

Layder, D. (1986) 'Social reality as figuration: a critique of Elias's conception of sociological analysis', *Sociology*, 20 (2): 376–7

Lazare, B. (1949) *Job's Dungheap*, edited by Hannah Arendt. New York: Schocken Press

Lindner, E. (1999a) *Humiliation Dynamics and Humiliation Entrepreneurship – the Dyad of Slave and Master*. Bujumbrara, Burundi: Ministière de l'Education Nationale

Lindner, E. (1999b) 'Love, Holocaust and Humiliation. The German Holocaust and the Genocides in Rwanda and Somalia', in *Medlemsbladet for Norske Leger Mot Atomkrig, Med Bidrag Fra Psykologer for Fred*, 1 (November): 28–29

Lindner, E. (2000a) 'Hitler, Shame and Humiliation: the Intricate Web of Feelings Among the German Population Towards Hitler', in *Medlemsbladet for Norske Leger Mot Atomvåpen, Med Bidrag Fra Psykologer for Fred*, 1 (February): 28–30

Lindner, E. (2000b) 'Humiliation and the Human Condition: Mapping a Minefield', in *Human Rights Review*

Lyotard, J.-F. (1984) *The Postmodern Condition. A report on knowledge*. Manchester: Manchester University Press

Macey, D. (1993) *The Lives of Michel Foucault*. London: Hutchinson

Maddison, A. (1976) 'Economic policy and performance in Europe 1913–1970' in Cipolla 1976, 442–508

Mannheim, K. (1936) *Ideology and Utopia*, translated with an introduction by Louis Wirth, London: Routledge

Margalit, A. (1996) *The Decent Society*. Cambridge, MA: Harvard University Press

Maso, B. (1995a) 'Elias and the neo-Kantians. Intellectual backgrounds of *The Civilizing Process*', *Theory, Culture and Society*, 12 (1): 43–79

Maso, B. (1995b) 'The different theoretical layers of *The Civilizing Process*: a response to Goudsblom and Kilminster & Wouters', *Theory, Culture and Society*, 12 (1): 127–45

McLellan, D. (1977) *Engels*. London: Fontana

Mastenbroek, W. (1993) *Conflict Management and Organization Development*. London: Wiley

Mennell, S. (1985) *All Manner of Food. Eating and tasting in England and France from the Middle Ages to the present*. Oxford: Basil Blackwell

Mennell, S. (1989) *Norbert Elias*. Oxford: Blackwell

Mennell, S. (1990) 'The globalization of human society as a very long-term social process: Elias's theory' in Featherstone 1990

Mennell, S. (1996 'Foreword' in Russell 1996, vi–viii

Mennell, S. (1998) *Norbert Elias*. Dublin: University College Dublin Press

Mennell, S. and Goudsblom, J. (eds) (1998) *Norbert Elias on Civilization, Power and Knowledge*. Chicago: Chicago University Press

Mestrovic, S. (1993) *Emile Durkheim and the Reformation of Sociology*. Lanham, MA: Rowman and Littlefield

Middlemas, K. (1995) *Orchestrating Europe. The informal politics of European union 1973–95*. London: Fontana

Miller, J. (1993) *The Passion of Michel Foucault*. London: HarperCollins

Miller, R.S. (1996) *Embarrassment, Poise and Peril in Everyday Life*. New York: The Guilford Press

Miller, W.I. (1993) *Humiliation and Other Essays on Honor, Social Discomfort and Violence*. Ithaca, NY: Cornell University Press

Mills, C.W. (1959) *The Sociological Imagination*. Harmondsworth: Penguin

Milward, A.S. (1992) *The European Rescue of the Nation State*. London: Routledge

Miyoshi, M. and Harootunian, H. (eds) (1989) *Postmodernism and Japan*. Durham, NC: Duke University Press

Mlinar, Z. (1992) *Globalization and Territorial Identities*. Aldershot: Avebury

Mommsen, W. and Osterhammel, J. (eds) (1987) *Max Weber and his Contemporaries*. London: Unwin Hyman

Monfasani, J. and Musto, R. (1991) *Renaissance Society and Culture. Essays in honor of Eugene F. Rice Jr*. New York: Italica Press

Mongardini, C. (1995) 'L'idée de société chez Georg Simmel et Norbert Elias', *Cahiers internationaux de Sociologie*, 99: 265–78

Moore, B. (1978) *Injustice. The social bases of obedience and revolt*. White Plains, NY: Sharpe

Moore-Gilbert, B. (1997) *Postcolonial theory. Contexts, practices, policies*. London: Verso

Morawski, S. (1998) 'Bauman's way of seeing the world', *Theory, Culture and Society*, 15 (1): 29–38

Mouzelis, N. (1993) 'On figurational sociology', *Theory, Culture and Society*, 1: 239–53

Mouzelis, N. (1995) *Sociological Theory. What went wrong? Diagnosis and remedies*. London: Routledge

Myrdal, G. (1962) *An American Dilemma. The Negro problem and modern democracy, volume 1*. New Brunswick: Transaction Publishers; originally published in 1944

Naphy, W. and Roberts, P. (ed.) (1997) *Fear in Early Modern Society*. Manchester: Manchester University Press

Nathanson, D.L. (1992) *Shame And Pride. Affect, sex and the birth of the self*. New York: Norton

Newton, T. (1999) 'Power, subjectivity and British industrial and organizational sociology: The relevance of the work of Norbert Elias', *Sociology*, 33 (2): 411–40

Nielsen, J. (1991) 'The political orientation of Talcott Parsons. The Second World War and its aftermath' in Robertson and Turner 1991

Parsons, T. (1942a) 'Propaganda and social control', *Psychiatry*, 5 (4): 551–72

Parsons, T. (1942b) 'Some sociological aspects of the fascist movements', *Social Forces*, 21 (2): 138–43

Parsons, T. (1945) 'The problem of controlled institutional change', *Psychiatry*, 8 (1): 79–101

Parsons, T. (1968) *The Structure of Social Action*, 2 volumes, New York: Free Press; originally published in 1937

Parsons, T. (1970a) 'On building social systems theory: a personal history', *Daedalus*, 99 (3): 826–81

Parsons, T. (1970b) '"The intellectual": a social role category' in Rieff 1970, 3–26

Pickvance, C. (1976) *Urban Sociology. Critical essays*. London: Tavistock

Rabinow, P. (ed.) (1986) *The Foucault Reader*. Harmondsworth: Penguin

Reiss, A. (1964) 'Introduction' in Wirth 1964a, ix–xxx

Rieff, P. (ed.) (1970) *On Intellectuals*. New York: Doubleday

Ringer, F. (1969) *The Decline of the German Mandarins*. Cambridge, MA: Harvard University Press

Robertson, R. (1992a) '"Civilization" and the civilizing process: Elias, globalization and analytic synthesis', *Theory, Culture and Society*, 9 (1): 211–27

Robertson, R. (1992b) *Globalization: Social theory and global culture*. London: Sage

Robertson, R. and Turner, B. (eds) (1991) *Talcott Parsons: Theorist of Modernity*. London: Sage

Rojek, C. (1986) 'Problems of involvement and detachment in the writings of Norbert Elias', *British Journal of Sociology*, 37 (4): 584–96

Rosenwein, B. (1998) *Anger's Past. The social uses of an emotion in the Middle Ages*. Ithaca, NY: Cornell University Press

Rushdie, S. (1991) *Imaginary Homelands*. London: Granta

Russell, S. (1996) *Jewish Identity and Civilizing Processes*. London: Macmillan

Said, E. (1993) *Culture and Imperialism*. London: Vintage

Salomon, E. von (1931) *Die Geächteten* [The Outlaws]. Berlin: Ullstein

Scaff, L. (1989) *Fleeing the Iron Cage. Culture, politics and modernity in the thought of Max Weber*. Berkeley: University of California Press

Schäfers, B. (ed.) (1986) *Grundbegriffe der Soziologie*. Opladen: Leske en Budrich

Scheff, T.J. (1990) *Microsociology. Discourse, emotion and social structure*. Chicago: Chicago University Press

Scheff, T.J. (1994) *Bloody Revenge: Emotions, Nationalism, and War*. Boulder, CO: Westview Press

Scheff, T.J. (1997) *Emotions, the Social Bond and Human Reality. Part/Whole Analysis*. Cambridge: Cambridge University Press

Schnädelbach, H. (1984) *Philosophy in Germany 1831–1933*. Cambridge: Cambridge University Press

Schumpeter, J. (1986) *History of Economic Analysis*, edited by Elizabeth Boody Schumpeter, London: Allen and Unwin; originally published in 1954

Seidman, S. (1998) *Contested Knowledge. Social theory in the postmodern era*, 2nd edition, Oxford: Blackwell

Sennett, R. (1970) *The Uses of Disorder. Personal identity and city life*. London: Allen Lane

Sennett, R. (1977) *The Fall of Public Man*. London: Faber and Faber

Sennett, R. (1980) *Authority*. London: Secker and Warburg

Sennett, R. (1990) *The Conscience of the Eye. The design and social life of cities*. London: Faber and Faber

Sennett, R. (1994) *Flesh and Stone. The body and the city in Western civilization*. London: Faber and Faber

Sennett, R. (1998) *The Corrosion of Character. The Personal Consequences of Work in the New Capitalism*. New York: Norton

Sennett, R. and Cobb, R. (1972) *The Hidden Injuries of Class*. Cambridge: Cambridge University Press

Shils, E. (1981) 'Some academics, mainly in Chicago', *American Scholar*, 50 (2): 179–96

Silver, M., Conte, R., Miceli, M. and Poggi, I. (1986) 'Humiliation – Feeling, Social Control and the Construction of Identity', *Journal for the Theory of Social Behaviour*, 16 (3): 269–283

Skocpol, T. (1984) *Vision and Method in Historical Sociology*. Cambridge: Cambridge University Press

Smith, D. (1982) *Conflict and Compromise. Class formation in English society 1830–1914*. London: Routledge

Smith, D. (1983) *Barrington Moore. Violence, morality and political change*. London: Macmillan

Smith, D. (1984a) 'Morality and method in the work of Barrington Moore', *Theory and Society*, 13: 151–76

Smith, D. (1984b) 'Norbert Elias – established or outsider?', *Sociological Review*, 32 (2): 367–89

Smith, D. (1984c) 'Discovering facts and values: the historical sociology of Barrington Moore', in Skocpol 1984, 313–55

Smith, D. (1988) *The Chicago School. A liberal critique of capitalism*. London: Macmillan

Smith, D. (1990) *Capitalist Democracy on Trial. The transatlantic debate from Tocqueville to the present*. London: Routledge

Smith, D. (1991) *The Rise of Historical Sociology*. Cambridge: Polity Press

Smith, D. (1992) 'Modernity, postmodernity and the new Middle Ages', *Sociological Review*, 40 (4): 754–71

Smith, D. (1996) 'Should Foucault be our guide? Comparing Foucault, Elias and Arendt as potential guides for social science history', *European Social Science History Conference*, May 1996, Noordwijkerhout, Netherlands

Smith, D. (1997) Eurofutures. *Five scenarios for the next millennium*. London: Capstone

Smith, D. (1998a) 'Anthony Giddens and the liberal tradition', *British Journal of Sociology*, 49 (4): 661–9

Smith, D. (1998b) 'Zygmunt Bauman: How to be a successful outsider', *Theory, Culture and Society*, 15 (1): 39–45

Smith, D. (1999a) '*The Civilizing Process* and *The History of Sexuality*: Comparing Norbert Elias and Michel Foucault', *Theory and Society*, 28 (1): 79–100

Smith, D. (1999b) *Zygmunt Bauman. Prophet of Postmodernity*. Cambridge: Polity Press

Smith, D. (1999c) 'Making Europe. Processes of Europe-formation since 1945' in Smith and Wright 1999b

Smith, D. (forthcoming, a) 'Organizations and Humiliation. Looking Beyond Elias', *Organization* (forthcoming)

Smith, D. (forthcoming, b) 'The prisoner and the fisherman. A comparison between Norbert Elias and Michel Foucault' in Triebel et al. forthcoming

Smith, B. and Woodruff Smith, D. (1995) *The Cambridge Companion to Husserl*. Cambridge: Cambridge University Press

Smith, D. and Wright, S. (1999a) 'The turn towards democracy' in Smith and Wright 1999b

Smith, D. and Wright, S. (1999b) *Whose Europe? The turn towards democracy*. Oxford: Blackwell

Spierenberg, P. (1984) *The Spectacle of Suffering. Executions and the evolution of repression*. Cambridge: Cambridge University Press

Spybey, T. (1996) *Globalization and World Society*. Cambridge: Polity Press

Swaan, A. de (1993) 'The politics of agrophobia. On changes in emotional and relational management', *Theory, Culture and Society*, 10 (2): 337–58

Swaan, A. de (1988) *In Care of the State. Healthcare, education and welfare in Europe and the USA in the modern era*. New York: Polity Press

Szakolczai, A. (1996) 'Durkheim, Weber and Parsons and the founding experiences of sociology', *EUI Working Paper SPS No 96/11*, Florence: European University Institute

Szakolczai, A. (1998) *Max Weber and Michel Foucault. Parallel life-works*. London: Routledge

Tainter, J. (1988) *The Collapse of Complex Societies*. Cambridge: Cambridge University Press

Taylor, G. (1995) 'Shame, integrity and self-respect' in Dillon 1995, 157–78

Tester, K. (1992) *Civil Society*. London: Routledge

Tester, K. (1995) *The Inhuman Condition*. London: Routledge

Tenbruck, F. (1987) 'Max Weber and Edward Meyer' in Mommsen and Osterhammel (1987), 234–65

Therborn, G. (1995) *European Modernity and Beyond. The trajectory of European societies 1945–2000*. London: Sage

Thomas, W.I. and Znaniecki, F. (1927) *The Polish Peasant in Europe and America*, 2 volumes. New York: Knopf; originally published 1918–19

Thompson, J. (1998) *Decline in History. The European experience*. Cambridge: Polity Press

Thompson, K. (1982) *Emile Durkheim*. London: Tavistock

Tibi, B. (1995) 'Culture and knowledge. The politics of Islamisation of knowledge as a postmodern project? The fundamentalist claim to de-westernisation', *Theory, Culture and Society*, 12 (1): 1–24

Triebel, A., Kuzmics, H. and Blomert, R. (eds) forthcoming *Zivilisationtheorie in der Balanz*. Leske and Budrich

Tocqueville, A. de (1968) *Democracy in America*, 2 volumes, translated by George Lawrence, edited by J.-P. Mayer and A.P. Kerr with an introduction by J.-P. Mayer. New York: Collins; originally published 1835–40

Turner, S.P. and Factor, R.A. (1994) *Max Weber. The lawyer as social thinker*. London: Routledge

Urry, J. (1995) *Consuming Places*. London: Routledge

Ury, W. (1999) *Getting to Peace. Transforming Conflict at Home, at Work, and in the World*. New York: Viking

Varcoe, I. and Kilminster, R. (1996b) 'Addendum: Culture and power in the writings of Zygmunt Bauman' in Kilminster and Varcoe 1996, 215–47

Villa, D.R. (1996) *Arendt and Heidegger. The Fate of the Political*. Princeton, NJ: Princeton University Press

Wagner, P. (1994) *A Sociology of Modernity. Liberty and discipline*. London: Routledge

Werbner, P. and Modood, T. (eds) (1997) *Debating Cultural Hybridity*. London: Zed Books

Wertheimer, J. (1987) *Unwelcome Strangers. East European Jews in Imperial Germany*. Oxford: Oxford University Press

Whitley, R. (ed.) (1974) *Social Processes of Scientific Development*. London: Routledge

Wievorka, M. et al. (1995) 'L'oeuvre de Norbert Elias, son contenu, sa réception' (round table discussion with M. Wievorka, A. Burguière, R. Chartier, A. Farge and G. Vigarello), *Cahiers internationaux de Sociologie*, 99: 213–35

Wiggershaus, R. (1994) *The Frankfurt School. Its history, theories and political significance*. Cambridge: Polity Press

Wirth, L. (1948) 'Consensus and mass commuication', *American Sociological Review*, 13 (1): 1–15

Wirth, L. (1957) 'Urbanism as a way of life' in Hatt and Reiss 1957, 46–63; originally published in 1938

Wirth, L. (1964a) *On Cities and Social Life, Selected papers*, edited by Albert J. Reiss, Jr. Chicago: University of Chicago Press

Wirth, L. (1964b) 'Preface to Ideology and Utopia' in Wirth 1964b, 125–45; originally published in 1936

Wirth, L. (1964c) 'Ideas and ideals as sources of power in the modern world' in Wirth 1964a, 146–56

Wolf, E.R. (1977) 'Encounter with Norbert Elias' in Gleichman et al. 1977, 28–35

Wouters, C. (1977) 'Informalization and the civilizing process', in Gleichmann, Goudsblom and Korte 1977, 437–53

Wouters, C. (1986) 'Formalization and informalization: changing tension balances in civilizing processes', *Theory, Culture and Society*, 3 (2): 1–18

Wouters, C. (1987) 'Developments in behavioural codes between the sexes: formalization and informalization in the Netherlands 1930–85', *Theory, Culture and Society*, 4 (2–3): 405–20

Wouters, C. (1992) 'On status competition and emotion management. The study of emotions as a new field', *Theory, Culture and Society*, 9 (2): 229–2

Wright, S. (1999) 'A community that can communicate? The linguistic factor in European Integration' in Smith and Wright 1999b

Young, R. (1995) *Colonial Desire. Hybridity in theory, culture and race*. London: Routledge

Young-Bruehl, E. (1982) *For Love of the World*. New Haven: Yale University Press

Zweig, S. (1943) *The World of Yesterday. An autobiography*.

INDEX